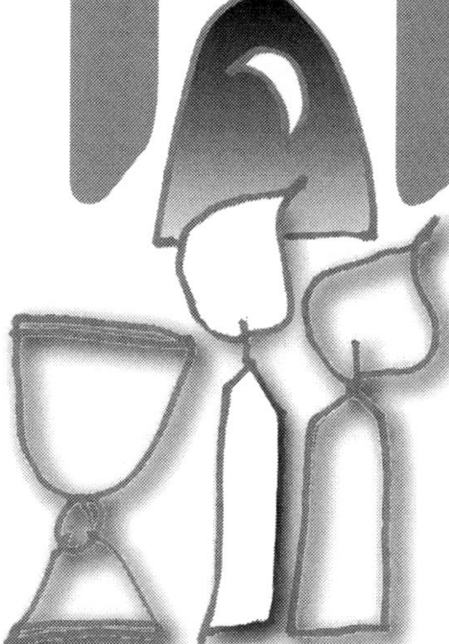

Explorations in Talmud

Tractate ***Shabbat***

שַׁבָּת

MYSHIUR

TALMUD LEARNING INITIATIVE

Printed in the United States

The Rohr Jewish Learning Institute
822 Eastern Parkway, Brooklyn, NY 11213

(888) YOUR-JLI/718-221-6900
www.myJLI.com

ב"ה

The **Rohr Jewish Learning Institute**
gratefully acknowledges
the pioneering support of

George and Pamela Rohr

SINCE ITS INCEPTION
the **Rohr JLI** has been
a beneficiary of the vision, generosity,
care and concern
of the **Rohr family**

In the merit of
the tens of thousands of hours of Torah study
by **JLI** students worldwide,
may they be blessed with health,
Yiddishe Nachas from all their loved ones,
and extraordinary success
in all their endeavors

RABBI TZVI YOSEF KOTLARSKY WAS A POLISH-BORN *CHASID* who escaped war-torn Europe via Japan and China to ultimately participate in the building of the Chabad-Lubavitch school systems in Montreal and Brooklyn, and served as chief administrator of the United Lubavitch Yeshiva for decades.

The Kotlarsky home was noted for its scholarship and devotion to G-d. Rabbi Kotlarsky gave freely of himself, patiently and modestly aiding all who turned to him for assistance.

Rabbi Tzvi Yosef (*Hirschel*) Kotlarsky passed away a week after his 91st birthday. He is survived by his children, Rabbi Moshe Kotlarsky, Rabbi Mendel Kotlarksy, Chumie Hershkop, Esti Wilshansky, Suri Perlman, Freidel Hershkowitz, and Chani Shemtov; and many grandchildren and great-grandchildren.

Many of his descendants serve as Chabad-Lubavitch emissaries around the world.

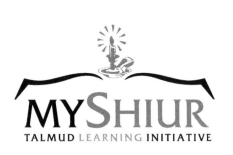

MYSHIUR
TALMUD LEARNING INITIATIVE

JLI
JEWISH LEARNING INSTITUTE

לזכרון
הרב החסיד התמים
ר' צבי יוסף ע"ה
בן הקדושים ר' יעקב דוד שו"ב ומרת דבורה נחמה ע"ה הי"ד
קאטלארסקי
נפטר י"א כסלו ה'תשס"ט
תנצב"ה

THIS COURSE IS LOVINGLY DEDICATED
TO THE ME MORY OF

RABBI TZVI YOSEF KOTLARSKY

WHO ESCAPED THE ASHES OF THE HOLOCAUST,
REBUILT A FAMILY ON THE FOUNDATIONS OF TORAH AND *CHASIDUT,*
AND DEDICATED HIS LIFE
TO THE EDUCATION OF FUTURE GENERATIONS

MAY OUR STUDY OF TORAH BE A TRIBUTE TO HIS LEGACY
AND AN EVERLASTING MONUMENT TO HIS NAME

DEDICATED BY
GEORGE AND PAMELA ROHR AND FAMILY
ON THE OCCASION OF HIS *YAHRTZEIT*
KISLEV 11, 5770

Dear Student

IT IS MY GREAT HONOR AND PLEASURE to present you with **MyShiur** series' newest course, *Explorations in Talmud: Tractate Shabbat.*

For this course, we decided to focus on a practical aspect of Jewish observance and trace its development from its biblical source to its functional implementation in today's modern society. This format presents the Talmud as it was originally intended: a collection of Jewish practices with their reasoning and applications. Of the many categories within Jewish observance, we found the topic of Shabbat to be most appropriate for this course.

Shabbat is one of the most basic and essential aspects of life as a Jew. The laws of Shabbat are both diverse and complex, yet it is impossible to be an observant Jew without confronting them on a weekly basis. To master all of the laws of Shabbat is a great and important feat that is beyond the scope of this course. However, as part of a course in Talmud, the ten lessons that you will encounter in this book provide much of the background information and reasoning behind the laws of Shabbat.

The advent of technology has given birth to new questions and situations in which ancient laws must be applied to modern circumstances that are radically different from those during the Roman Empire (the time-period when the Talmud was compiled). For example, in the Talmud, there are no explicit discussions about opening a refrigerator door or cooking in a microwave on Shabbat. As such, how do we know what to do in these and other similar instances? A thorough analysis of the reasoning that governs the laws of Shabbat offers insight into how the eternity of Torah reaches into the twenty-first century and beyond. When we understand the logic presented in the Talmud, we can apply the same principles to any situation or circumstance. This is the function of Talmud study, to synchronize our minds with the wisdom of He who gave us the Torah, so that we may develop an appreciation and understanding of what we do and why we do it.

In this exciting course, we will trace the biblical origins of the thirty-nine *melachot* and discover the building blocks that comprise *melachah*. We will also find parallels for these *melachot* in our own lives and missions in this world. The intention of this course is to lay the groundwork for the thirty-nine *melachot* of Shabbat, learn the logic behind many of the common ones and discover how they apply to our Shabbat observance today.

I sincerely hope that you will enjoy this course as much as I enjoyed writing it.

I would like to take this opportunity to thank the following individuals for their assistance in the production of this course, without whom this project would not be possible:

Rabbi Moshe Kotlarsky, principal patron of **JLI** and **Mr. George Rohr**, whose generosity and continuous support has allowed **JLI** to bring Jewish heritage to tens of thousands of Jews across the globe.

Rabbi Efraim Mintz, director of **JLI** and the entire staff at **JLI** Central, with special mention of **Rabbi Mendel Sirota** and **Mrs. Mussi Keselman** whose constant effort and tireless devotion are responsible for making **JLI** the tremendous success that it is today.

Rabbi Shmuel Kaplan, chairman and founder of the **MyShiur** initiative, who first conceived of the idea and direction of this course.

The editorial board: **Rabbi Dovid Mochkin, Rabbi Mendy Cohen, Rabbi Moshe Lieberman, Rabbi Shmuel Klatzkin, Rabbi Meir Kaplan,** and **Rabbi Levi Kaplan** for their time and effort in reviewing the material and for their helpful suggestions and advice that helped improve the course material and make it more suitable for a broad audience.

Rabbi Eli Cohen for carefully and meticulously reviewing and proofreading the text.

Rabbi Mendy Halberstam, director of marketing, for consistently availing himself to us and designing a face and voice for our courses.

Rabbi Cheski Edelman for developing the thoughtful and effective PowerPoint presentations for this and all of our courses.

Nachman Levine for designing this aesthetically beautiful book, which makes this learning experience even more pleasurable and **Spotlight Design** for designing the cover.

Rabbi Dr. Shmuel Klatzkin for a careful and professional review of the content, language and sources of the course and for providing his expert linguistic and scholarly advice throughout.

Rabbi Levi Kaplan, director of **MyShiur,** for overseeing the entire project from its inception and for his motivational encouragement and invaluable input and experience that guided every step in the production of this course.

My wife, **Leah**, for her constant companionship, guidance, wisdom and unconditional support and assistance throughout the project.

May their devotion stand them in good stead and may G-d bless all of their endeavors, protect them and their families, grant all of their wishes and see to it that they experience only revealed goodness always and forever.

May G-d protect everyone who studies His holy Torah and bless them with all of their hearts' desires and may we merit to see the rebuilding of the Holy Temple in Jerusalem with the coming of our righteous *Mashiach,* who will teach us innovative Torah insights, may it happen speedily in our days.

Rabbi Zalman Abraham

Table of Contents

Lesson 1

Shabbat

Introduction

What possible connection could there be between the way that the Jewish people in the desert were commanded to build a *Mishkan* and the intricately detailed rules and regulations of Shabbat observance?

TEXT 1A: Exodus 23:12

For six days you shall perform your work — שֵׁשֶׁת יָמִים תַּעֲשֶׂה מַעֲשֶׂיךָ
and on the seventh day you shall rest — וּבַיּוֹם הַשְּׁבִיעִי תִּשְׁבֹּת

TEXT 1B: Exodus 20:9

Do not perform any *melachah* — לֹא תַעֲשֶׂה כָל מְלָאכָה

Discussion Question

If you were to be entrusted with the task of interpreting this verse, —how would you define work or labor?

Part I

The Mishnah: Thirty-Nine *Avot Melachot*

Keys to the Talmud

Chavruta

The word *chavruta* is Aramaic for a friend (*chaver* in Hebrew); it refers to a study partner. Learning with a *chavruta* is one of the hallmarks of Talmud study. What is the value of learning with a partner?

1. Two minds applied to a problem are usually better than one.

2. The need to articulate one's thoughts to another brings greater clarity than when one studies alone.

In addition, the questions and challenges posed by a *chavruta* help point out and clarify misconceptions; each person keeps the other in check.

TEXT 2: **Mishnah, *Shabbat* 7:2**

The primary labors are forty minus one:	אֲבוֹת מְלָאכוֹת אַרְבָּעִים חָסֵר אַחַת
sowing, plowing, reaping	הַזּוֹרֵעַ וְהַחוֹרֵשׁ וְהַקּוֹצֵר
binding sheaves, threshing , winnowing	וְהַמְעַמֵּר הַדָּשׁ וְהַזּוֹרֶה
selecting, grinding, sifting	הַבּוֹרֵר הַטּוֹחֵן וְהַמְרַקֵּד
kneading, baking	וְהַלָּשׁ וְהָאוֹפֶה
shearing wool	הַגּוֹזֵז אֶת הַצֶּמֶר
bleaching it, combing it, dying it	הַמְלַבְּנוֹ וְהַמְנַפְּצוֹ וְהַצּוֹבְעוֹ
spinning, stretching [the threads]	וְהַטּוֹוֶה וְהַמֵּיסֵךְ
making two loops	וְהָעוֹשֶׂה שְׁנֵי בָּתֵּי נִירִין
weaving two threads	וְהָאוֹרֵג שְׁנֵי חוּטִין
separating two threads	וְהַפּוֹצֵעַ שְׁנֵי חוּטִין
tying a knot, untying a knot	הַקּוֹשֵׁר וְהַמַּתִּיר

sewing two stitches	וְהַתּוֹפֵר שְׁתֵּי תְּפִירוֹת
tearing in order to sew two stitches	הַקּוֹרֵעַ עַל מְנָת לִתְפֹּר שְׁתֵּי תְּפִירוֹת
capturing a deer, slaughtering it, skinning it	הַצָּד צְבִי הַשּׁוֹחֲטוֹ וְהַמַּפְשִׁיטוֹ
salting it, curing its hide	הַמּוֹלְחוֹ וְהַמְעַבֵּד אֶת עוֹרוֹ
scraping it [of hair], cutting it up	וְהַמּוֹחֲקוֹ וְהַמְחַתְּכוֹ
writing two letters	הַכּוֹתֵב שְׁתֵּי אוֹתִיּוֹת
erasing in order to write two letters	וְהַמּוֹחֵק עַל מְנָת לִכְתֹּב שְׁתֵּי אוֹתִיּוֹת
building, demolishing	הַבּוֹנֶה וְהַסּוֹתֵר
extinguishing, kindling,	הַמְכַבֶּה וְהַמַּבְעִיר
striking with a hammer,	הַמַּכֶּה בְּפַטִּישׁ
carrying from one domain to another;	הַמּוֹצִיא מֵרְשׁוּת לִרְשׁוּת
these are the primary labors, forty minus one.	הֲרֵי אֵלּוּ אֲבוֹת מְלָאכוֹת אַרְבָּעִים חָסֵר אַחַת

TEXT 3A: **Exodus 35:2-5, 10**

And Moses gathered all the congregation of the people of Israel,	**וַיַּקְהֵל מֹשֶׁה אֶת כָּל עֲדַת בְּנֵי יִשְׂרָאֵל**
and said to them,	**וַיֹּאמֶר אֲלֵהֶם**
These are the words which G-d has commanded, that you should do them.	**אֵלֶּה הַדְּבָרִים אֲשֶׁר צִוָּה ה׳ לַעֲשֹׂת אֹתָם**
Six days shall work be done,	**שֵׁשֶׁת יָמִים תֵּעָשֶׂה מְלָאכָה**
but on the seventh day there shall be to you a holy day,	**וּבַיּוֹם הַשְּׁבִיעִי יִהְיֶה לָכֶם קֹדֶשׁ**
a Sabbath of rest to the Lord;	**שַׁבַּת שַׁבָּתוֹן לַה׳**
whoever does work in it shall be put to death.	**כָּל הָעֹשֶׂה בוֹ מְלָאכָה יוּמָת**
And Moses spoke to all the congregation of the people of Israel, saying,	**וַיֹּאמֶר מֹשֶׁה אֶל כָּל עֲדַת בְּנֵי יִשְׂרָאֵל לֵאמֹר**

Take from among you	**קְחוּ מֵאִתְּכֶם**
an offering to the Lord;	**תְּרוּמָה לַה'**
whoever is of a willing heart,	**כֹּל נְדִיב לִבּוֹ**
let him bring it, an offering of the Lord;	**יְבִיאֶהָ אֵת תְּרוּמַת ה'**
gold, and silver, and bronze . . .	**זָהָב וָכֶסֶף וּנְחֹשֶׁת . . .**
And every wise-hearted among you shall come	**וְכָל חֲכַם לֵב בָּכֶם יָבֹאוּ**
and make all that the Lord has commanded;	**וְיַעֲשׂוּ אֵת כָּל אֲשֶׁר צִוָּה ה'**

TEXT 3B: Rashi, *ad loc.*

For six days:	שֵׁשֶׁת יָמִים
[The Torah] prefaced the warning	הִקְדִּים לָהֶם
[to observe] the Shabbat to the instruction	אַזְהָרַת שַׁבָּת
to perform the work of the *Mishkan*,	לְצִוּוּי מְלֶאכֶת הַמִּשְׁכָּן
to say that it does not override Shabbat [observance].	לוֹמַר שֶׁאֵינָהּ דּוֹחָה אֶת הַשַּׁבָּת

Rabbi Shlomo Yitzchaki (1040–1105). Better known by the acronym *Rashi;* rabbi and famed author of the first comprehensive commentaries on the Talmud and Bible. Born in Troyes, Champagne, Rashi studied in the famed yeshivot of Mainz and Worms. His commentaries, which focus on the simple understanding of the text, are considered fundamental to Torah study. Since their initial printings, they have appeared in virtually every edition of the Talmud and Bible. Amongst Rashi's descendants, were many of the famed Tosafists of France.

The Works Involved in The Construction of the *Mishkan*

Growing Plants for Dyes

TEXT 4A: **Exodus 25:4**

blue, purple, and scarlet	וּתְכֵלֶת וְאַרְגָּמָן
threads (wool)	וְתוֹלַעַת שָׁנִי

Weaving Tapestries

TEXT 4B: **Exodus 35:25**

And all the women that were wise-hearted	וְכָל אִשָּׁה חַכְמַת לֵב
spun with their hands,	בְּיָדֶיהָ טָווּ
and brought that which they had spun,	וַיָּבִיאוּ מַטְוֶה
the blue, the purple wool,	אֶת הַתְּכֵלֶת וְאֶת הָאַרְגָּמָן
the scarlet, and the fine linen	אֶת תּוֹלַעַת הַשָּׁנִי וְאֶת הַשֵּׁשׁ

Preparing Hide Coverings

TEXT 4C: **Exodus 26:14**

And you shall make a covering for the tent	וְעָשִׂיתָ מִכְסֶה לָאֹהֶל
of ram-skins dyed red	עֹרֹת אֵילִם מְאָדָּמִים
and a covering of *Tachash*-skins above	וּמִכְסֵה עֹרֹת תְּחָשִׁים מִלְמָעְלָה

Marking Adjacent Boards

TEXT 4D: **Mishnah, *Shabbat* 12:3**

They would write on the boards of the *Mishkan*	הָיוּ כּוֹתְבִין עַל קַרְשֵׁי הַמִּשְׁכָּן
to know which [board] is its counterpart	לֵידַע אֵיזוֹ בֶּן זוּגוֹ

Constructing and Disassembling the *Mishkan*

TEXT 4E: **Exodus 40:18**

And Moses erected the *Mishkan*,	וַיָּקֶם מֹשֶׁה אֶת הַמִּשְׁכָּן
and laid its sockets,	וַיִּתֵּן אֶת אֲדָנָיו
and set up its boards,	וַיָּשֶׂם אֶת קְרָשָׁיו
and placed [into them] its bars,	וַיִּתֵּן אֶת בְּרִיחָיו
and erected its pillars.	וַיָּקֶם אֶת עַמּוּדָיו

Heating and Cooling to Shape Metals

TEXT 4F: **Exodus 38:27**

And the hundred talents of silver	וַיְהִי מְאַת כִּכַּר הַכֶּסֶף
were for **casting the sockets** of the sanctuary, and the sockets of the veil:	לָצֶקֶת אֵת אַדְנֵי הַקֹּדֶשׁ וְאֵת אַדְנֵי הַפָּרֹכֶת
a hundred sockets for the hundred talents, a talent for a socket.	מְאַת אֲדָנִים לִמְאַת הַכִּכָּר כִּכָּר לָאָדֶן

Completing Gold Plating on the Boards

TEXT 4G: **Exodus 36:34**

And he overlaid the boards with gold	וְאֶת הַקְּרָשִׁים צִפָּה זָהָב

Carrying Donated Materials to the Builders

TEXT 4H: **Exodus 36:3**

And they received from Moses	וַיִּקְחוּ מִלִּפְנֵי מֹשֶׁה
all the donations, which the children of Israel had brought	אֵת כָּל הַתְּרוּמָה אֲשֶׁר הֵבִיאוּ בְּנֵי יִשְׂרָאֵל
for the work of the service of the sanctuary, with which to make it.	לִמְלֶאכֶת עֲבֹדַת הַקֹּדֶשׁ לַעֲשֹׂת אֹתָהּ
And they brought more gifts to him every morning.	וְהֵם הֵבִיאוּ אֵלָיו עוֹד נְדָבָה בַּבֹּקֶר בַּבֹּקֶר

Learning **Activity**

The verses in texts 4a-4h above describe ten general categories of work. Match each of the following specific *melachot* with their role in the construction of the *Mishkan*. Mark down A to indicate that the *melachah* was for growing plants for dyes; B for weaving tapestries; C for preparing hide coverings; D for marking adjacent boards; E for constructing and disassembling the *Mishkan*; F for heating and cooling to shape metals; G for completing gold plating on the boards; and H for carrying donated materials to the builders.

	Sowing		Plowing		Reaping
	Binding Sheaves		Threshing		Winnowing
	Selecting		Grinding		Sifting
	Kneading		Baking (cooking)		Shearing Wool
	Bleaching		Combing		Dyeing
	Spinning		Stretching the Threads		Making Loops
	Weaving Threads		Separating the Threads		Tying a Knot
	Untying a Knot		Sewing		Tearing
	Trapping		Slaughtering		Skinning
	Salting		Tanning		Scraping
	Cutting		Writing		Erasing
	Building		Breaking Down		Extinguishing a Fire
	Kindling a Fire		Striking the Final Hammer Blow		Carrying

TEXT 5: **Talmud, *Shabbat* 74b**

Kneading and baking	וְהַלָּשׁ וְהָאוֹפֶה
Rav Papa said:	אָמַר רַב פַּפָּא
Our Tana left aside	שָׁבַק תַּנָּא דִידַן
the cooking of herbs	בִּישׁוּל סַמְמָנִין
that was done in the *Mishkan*	דַּהֲוָה בְּמִשְׁכָּן
and mentioned baking [that was not. Why]?	וְנָקַט אוֹפֶה
Our Tana chose the order of making bread	תַּנָּא דִידַן סִידּוּרָא דְפַת נָקַט

Keys to the Talmud

***Tana* and *Amora* (Pl. *Tanaim* and *Amoraim*)**

***Tana* refers to a sage from the time of the Mishnah, circa 100 BCE-200 CE, whereas *amorah* refers to a sage of the Gemara (c. 200-500 CE). *Tana* is an Aramaic word that means one who teaches, for the sages of the Mishnah taught us the oral law. *Amora* means "one who says" or articulates, because the sages of the Gemara articulated and clarified ambiguities in the teachings of the *tanaim*.**

Part II

Avot and *Toladot*

TEXT 6: Talmud, *Bava Kama* 2a

Primary labors—	אָבוֹת
this implies that there are subcategories	מִכְּלַל דְאִיכָּא תּוֹלְדוֹת
and their subcategories are similar [in law] to them	תּוֹלְדוֹתֵיהֶן כַּיוֹצֵא בָּהֶן
. . . It makes no difference whether one transgresses a parent *melachah,* for which he brings a sin offering,	. . . לֹא שְׁנָא אָב חַטָּאת
or whether a child *melachah*, for which he must also bring a sin offering	וְלֹא שְׁנָא תּוֹלְדָה חַטָּאת

Understanding the Relationship Between *Avot* and *Toladot*

Learning Activity

Here are some examples of *toladot* that we derive from *avot* because of their similarity in style or in purpose. Fill in the missing blanks to get a feel for how this works. You can pair up with a neighbor and share your thoughts and suggestions. Make use of the Mishnah to identify appropriate *avot* where necessary:

Av	*Toladah*	Similarity
Grinding	Cutting vegetables into tiny pieces for cooking	**Style:** dividing one piece into many small pieces
	Mixing cement	**Style:** joining small pieces by mixing them in liquid and transforming them into a dough-like substance
Shearing (wool)	Plucking a feather from a bird	**Style:**
Dyeing	Preparing dye	**Style:**
	Sticking papers or hides together	**Purpose**: joining two separate things together.
Kindling a fire	Heating metal	**Style:** transforming an object into something that can burn
Plowing	Pulling out weeds	**Purpose**:
	Watering plants	**Purpose**: making plants grow

Learning Exercise (in pairs)

Explain the connection between the *toladah* and its seemingly different *av* by adding P if it is similar in purpose or S if it is similar in style, and in one or two words explaining the similarity.

Av	*Toladah*	P/S?	What is the similarity?
Building	Making cheese		
Sifting	Filtering out sediment from wine		
Bleaching	Squeezing water from a garment		
Slaughtering	Removing a fish from water		
Threshing	Milking an animal		
Baking	Melting down metals		
Harvesting	Removing moss from a moist surface		

Avot and *Toladot*: What is the difference?

TEXT 7: Talmud, *Shabbat* 96b

Why is one called "a primary labor" (*av*)	אַמַאי קָרֵי לָה הַאי אָב
and why is one called "a derivative labor" (*toladah*)?	וְאַמַאי קָרֵי לָה הַאי תּוֹלָדָה
The practical outcome [of the *melachot* being divided into *avot* and *toladot* is]	נַפְקָא מִינָה
that if one [inadvertently] performs two *avot* (primary labors) together	דְאִי עָבִיד שְׁתֵּי אָבוֹת בַּהֲדֵי הֲדָדֵי
Or two *toladot* (derivatives) [from two different *avot*] together	אִי נַמִי שְׁתֵּי תוֹלָדוֹת בַּהֲדֵי הֲדָדֵי
He is liable to bring two [sin offerings]	מִיחַיֵּיב תַּרְתֵּי
Whereas if he performs one *av* (primary labor) and its own *toladah* (derivative) together	וְאִי עָבִיד אָב וְתוֹלָדָה דִידֵיהּ
he is liable to bring only one sin offering.	לֹא מִיחַיֵּיב אֶלָּא חֲדָא

Part IV

Where Does Creation Fit in?

TEXT 8A: **Genesis 2:3**

And G-d blessed the seventh day	וַיְבָרֶךְ אֱלֹהִים אֶת יוֹם הַשְּׁבִיעִי
and made it holy	וַיְקַדֵּשׁ אֹתוֹ
for on it He rested from all His work	כִּי בוֹ שָׁבַת מִכָּל מְלַאכְתּוֹ
which G-d in creating had made.	אֲשֶׁר בָּרָא אֱלֹהִים לַעֲשׂוֹת

Discussion Question

Why does the Talmud not follow the simple reading of the verse and say that creative activities are prohibited because G-d rested from creation on Shabbat? Why bring in the *Mishkan* at all?

TEXT 8B: ***Midrash Tanchuma, Pekudei* 2**

R. Yaakov son of R. Asi said:	אָמַר רַבִּי יַעֲקֹב בְּרַבִּי אַסִי
Why does the verse state:	לָמָה הוּא אוֹמֵר
G-d, I love the habitation of Your house, and the place where Your glory dwells?	ה' אָהַבְתִּי מְעוֹן בֵּיתֶךָ וּמְקוֹם מִשְׁכַּן כְּבוֹדֶךָ
For it [the *Mishkan*] is equivalent to the creation of the world.	בִּשְׁבִיל שֶׁשָּׁקוּל כְּנֶגֶד בְּרִיאַת עוֹלָם
How is this so? Regarding the first day [of creation] the verse states:	כֵּיצַד בָּרִאשׁוֹן כְּתִיב
In the beginning, G-d created the heavens and the earth.	בְּרֵאשִׁית בָּרָא אֱלֹקִים אֵת הַשָּׁמַיִם וְאֵת הָאָרֶץ
Moreover, the verse states: *Who stretches out the heavens like a curtain.*	וּכְתִיב נוֹטֶה שָׁמַיִם כַּיְרִיעָה
Regarding the *Mishkan* what does the verse state? *And you shall make curtains of goats hair.*	וּבְמִשְׁכָּן מַה כְּתִיב וְעָשִׂיתָ יְרִיעוֹת עִזִּים

On the second day [the verse states]: ***Let there be a firmament*** **and the verse further mentions division,**	בְּשֵׁנִי יְהִי רָקִיעַ וְאוֹמֵר בָּהֶן הַבְדָלָה
as the verse states (ibid.): ***And let it divide*** ***between water and water***	שֶׁנֶּאֱמַר וִיהִי מַבְדִּיל בֵּין מַיִם לָמָיִם
and regarding the ***Mishkan*** **the verse states:** ***And the veil shall divide for you.***	וּבְמִשְׁכָּן כְּתִיב וְהִבְדִּילָה הַפָּרוֹכֶת לָכֶם
On the third day, the verse refers to water, as the verse states: ***Let the waters be gathered.***	בְּשְׁלִישִׁי כְּתִיב מַיִם שֶׁנֶּאֱמַר יִקָּווּ הַמַּיִם
And regarding the ***Mishkan*** **it states:** ***You shall*** ***make a laver of brass, and a base of brass . . .***	וּבְמִשְׁכָּן כְּתִיב וְעָשִׂיתָ כִּיוֹר נְחֹשֶׁת וְכַנּוֹ נְחֹשֶׁת וגו'
and you shall put water into it.	וְנָתַתָּ שָׁמָּה מָיִם
On the fourth day [G-d] created luminaries,	בָּרְבִיעִי בָּרָא מְאוֹרוֹת
as the verse states: ***Let there be lights in the firmament of the heaven***	דִכְתִיב יְהִי מְאוֹרוֹת בִּרְקִיעַ הַשָּׁמַיִם
and regarding the ***Mishkan*** **it states:** ***And you shall make a Menorah of gold.***	וּבְמִשְׁכָּן כְּתִיב וְעָשִׂיתָ מְנוֹרַת זָהָב
On the fifth day [G-d] created birds,	בַּחֲמִישִׁי בָּרָא עוֹפוֹת
as the verse states: ***Let the waters swarm with*** ***swarms of living creatures,*** ***and let fowl fly***	שֶׁנֶּאֱמַר יִשְׁרְצוּ הַמַּיִם שֶׁרֶץ נֶפֶשׁ חַיָּה וְעוֹף יְעוֹפֵף
and regarding the ***Mishkan:*** ***And the cherubim shall*** ***spread out their wings on high.***	וּבְמִשְׁכָּן וְהָיוּ הַכְּרוּבִים פּוֹרְשֵׂי כְנָפַיִם לְמַעְלָה
On the sixth day man was created,	בַּשִּׁשִּׁי נִבְרָא אָדָם
as the verse states: ***And G-d created man in His image—*** **He formed him with glory.**	שֶׁנֶּאֱמַר וַיִּבְרָא אֱלֹהִים אֶת הָאָדָם בְּצַלְמוֹ בִּכְבוֹד יוֹצְרוֹ
And regarding the ***Mishkan,*** **the verse states:** ***Man***	וּבְמִשְׁכָּן כְּתִיב אָדָם
referring to the high priest that was appointed to serve before G-d.	שֶׁהוּא כֹּהֵן גָּדוֹל שֶׁנִּמְשַׁח לַעֲבוֹד וּלְשַׁמֵּשׁ לִפְנֵי ה'

On the seventh day:	בַּשְּׁבִיעִי
And the heaven and the earth were finished	וַיְכוּלוּ הַשָּׁמַיִם וְהָאָרֶץ
and regarding the *Mishkan* the verse states:	וּבְמִשְׁכָּן כְּתִיב
Thus was finished all the work.	וַתֵּכֶל כָּל עֲבוֹדַת
Regarding creation of the world	בִּבְרִיאַת הָעוֹלָם כְּתִיב
the verse states: *And G-d blessed*	וַיְבָרֶךְ אֱלֹהִים
and regarding the *Mishkan* the verse states:	וּבְמִשְׁכָּן כְּתִיב
And Moses blessed them.	וַיְבָרֶךְ אוֹתָם מֹשֶׁה
Regarding creation of the world	בִּבְרִיאַת הָעוֹלָם כְּתִיב
the verse states: *And God finished*	וַיְכַל אֱלֹהִים
and regarding the *Mishkan*	וּבְמִשְׁכָּן כְּתִיב
the verse states: *And it came to pass on the day*	וַיְהִי בְּיוֹם כַּלּוֹת
[that Moses] concluded.	
Regarding creation of the world	בִּבְרִיאַת הָעוֹלָם כְּתִיב
the verse states: *and made it holy*	וַיְקַדֵּשׁ אוֹתוֹ
and regarding the *Mishkan* the verse states:	וּבְמִשְׁכָּן כְּתִיב
and anointed it and sanctified it.	וַיִּמְשַׁח אוֹתוֹ וַיְקַדֵּשׁ אוֹתוֹ
Any why is the *Mishkan*	וְלָמָּה הַמִּשְׁכָּן
equivalent to heaven and earth?	שָׁקוּל כְּנֶגֶד שָׁמַיִם וָאָרֶץ
Just as heaven and earth are testimony to Israel	אֶלָּא מַה שָּׁמַיִם וָאָרֶץ הֵם עֵדִים עַל יִשְׂרָאֵל
as the verse states: *I call heaven and earth*	דִּכְתִיב הַעִידֹתִי בָּכֶם הַיּוֹם
to witness against you this day	אֶת הַשָּׁמַיִם וְאֶת הָאָרֶץ
similarly the *Mishkan* is testimony to Israel	אַף מִשְׁכָּן עֵדוּת לְיִשְׂרָאֵל
as the verse states:	שֶׁנֶּאֱמַר
These are the accounts of the Mishkan,	אֵלֶּה פְקוּדֵי הַמִּשְׁכָּן
the Mishkan of the testimony.	מִשְׁכַּן הָעֵדֻת

Key Points

1. Shabbat is reminiscent of G-d's resting from creation on the seventh day. Therefore, on *Shabbat* we refrain from performing *melachah*—creative and constructive activities.

2. Thirty-nine primary activities are biblically prohibited on *Shabbat.* These are called *avot melachot.*

3. These activities are derived from activities needed for the construction of the *Mishkan.*

4. *Avot melachot* include activities required in the preparation of food, clothing and shelter—the primary necessities of man.

4. *Toladot* are equally prohibited activities that are similar to *avot* in style or purpose..

5. The activities used to construct the *Mishkan* resemble the acts of creation on the six days during which G-d created the world.

Terms to Retain

Labor/work	מְלָאכָה/מְלָאכוֹת
Primary (lit.: parent)	אָבוֹת/אָב
Secondary (lit.: offspring)	תּוֹלָדָה/תּוֹלָדוֹת
Sage of the Mishnah	תַּנָא
Sage of the Talmud	אֲמוֹרָא

Lesson 2

Introduction

"Forty minus one" is an odd way of counting to thirty-nine! What is the story behind numberered lists in the Talmud?

In this lesson, we will follow the Talmud on a scholarly journey to discover the source for the number thirty-nine as being the number of *melachot* forbidden on Shabbat, and will discover the deeper meaning behind the *mishnah's* deliberate use of this odd expression. We will study disputes between the sages of the Talmud and between various medieval commentators concerning the fundamentals of how the *melachot* of Shabbat are derived from the descriptions of the work in the Tabernacle. We will witness how the different approaches of the commentaries echo a dispute between the Talmudic sages of the Galilee and of Babylonia, and the versions of the Talmud each produced.

Computations in the Talmud

TEXT 1: **Jerusalem Talmud, *Shekalim* Ch. 5 Law 1**

Rabbi Abahu said:	אָמַר רַבִּי אַבָּהוּ
The verse states (I Chronicles 2:55): "*And the families of* sofrim (scribes) *that dwelt at Jabez*"	כְּתִיב מִשְׁפְּחוֹת סוֹפְרִים יֹשְׁבֵי יַעְבֵּץ
What does the verse want to teach by saying *sofrim*?	מַה תַּלְמוּד לוֹמַר סוֹפְרִים
Is it not because they made Torah into counted items?	אֶלָּא שֶׁעָשׂוּ אֶת הַתּוֹרָה סְפוּרוֹת סְפוּרוֹת
Five people should not separate *terumah*,	חֲמִשָּׁה לֹא יִתְרוֹמוּ
Five [types of grain] are obligated in *challah* . . .	חֲמִשָּׁה דְבָרִים חַיָּיבִין בְּחַלָּה . . .
Thirty-six [cases that make one liable for] excisions are mentioned in the Torah.	שְׁלֹשִׁים וָשֵׁשׁ כְּרֵיתוֹת בַּתּוֹרָה
Thirteen laws [of ritual purity] govern the carcass of a bird of kosher species.	שְׁלֹשָׁה עָשָׂר דָבָר בְּנִבְלַת הָעוֹף הַטָּהוֹר
There are four primary forms of damages.	אַרְבַּע אָבוֹת נְזִיקִין
The primary *melachot* are forty minus one.	אָבוֹת מְלָאכוֹת אַרְבָּעִים חָסֵר אַחַת

further explore the relationship between the laws of Shabbat and the construction of the Tabernacle.

Part I

The Number Thirty Nine

TEXT 2: Talmud, *Shabbat* 49b

Again they sat and asked each other	הָדוּר יָתְבֵי וְקָמִיבַּעְיָא לְהוּ
regarding that which we learned in a *mishnah* [that]	הָא דִתְנַן
the primary *melachot* are forty minus one—	אָבוֹת מְלָאכוֹת אַרְבָּעִים חָסֵר אַחַת
to what do they correspond?	כְּנֶגֶד מִי ?
Rabbi Chanina bar Chama said to them:	אָמַר לְהוּ רַבִּי חֲנִינָא בַּר חָמָא
They correspond to the labors of the Tabernacle.	כְּנֶגֶד עֲבוֹדוֹת הַמִּשְׁכָּן
Rabbi Yonatan the son of Rabbi Elazar said to them:	אָמַר לְהוּ רַבִּי יוֹנָתָן בְּרַבִּי אֶלְעָזָר
Thus said Rabbi Shimon	כָּךְ אָמַר רַבִּי שִׁמְעוֹן
the son of Rabbi Yosei ben Lakonya:	בְּרַבִּי יוֹסֵי בֶּן לָקוֹנְיָא
They correspond to	כְּנֶגֶד
the mentions of "work," "his work" and "work of"	מְלָאכָה מְלַאכְתּוֹ וּמְלֶאכֶת
in the Torah,	שֶׁבַּתּוֹרָה
forty minus one.	אַרְבָּעִים חָסֵר אַחַת

Keys to the Talmud

Ditnan

The word *ditnan* means "We learned in a *mishnah*" and appears in the Talmud whenever a *mishnah* is being quoted.

Class Exercise

Together with a partner examine the Talmud's question and try to come up with variant ways it can be understood. Write them down.

אָבוֹת מְלָאכוֹת אַרְבָּעִים חָסֵר אַחַת כְּנֶגֶד מִי ?

Keys to the Talmud

When Rashi or Tosafot comment, they are normally trying to dispel an incorrect and possibly misleading interpretation.

TEXT 3: **Tosafot, *arbaim avot melachot***

Forty primary *melachot* minus one—	אַרְבָּעִים אָבוֹת מְלָאכוֹת חָסֵר אַחַת
to what do they correspond?	כְּנֶגֶד מִי
Since there are many *melachot* that share similarities	דְהַרְבֵּה מְלָאכוֹת יֵשׁ דְדַמְיָין לְהַדָדֵי
we should have counted all of them as one.	וְהַוָה לָן לְמִחְשְׁבִינְהוּ כּוּלָן כְּאַחַת

Tosafot (١٠th١٣-th centuries). A collection French and German Talmudic commentaries in the form of critical and explanatory glosses; written during the twelfth and thirteenth centuries. Among the most famous authors of Tosafot are Rabbi Yaakov Tam, Rabbi Shimshon ben Avraham of Sens, and Rabbi Shmuel ben Meir. Printed in almost all editions of the Talmud, these commentaries are fundamental to basic Talmudic study.

As the Talmud inquires in chapter *Kelal Gadol*:	כִּדְפָרִיך בְּפֶרֶק כְּלַל גָדוֹל (לקמן עג:)
"Are not winnowing, selecting, and sifting all the same activity?"	הַיְינוּ זוֹרֶה הַיְינוּ בּוֹרֵר הַיְינוּ מְרַקֵד
And on account of the small distinction between them	וּמִשׁוּם חִילוּק מוּעָט שֶׁבֵּינֵיהֶם
we would not have divided them	לאֹ הַוָה מְחַלְקִינָן לְהוּ
were it not for first establishing	אִי לַאו דְקִים לְהוּ
that the thirty-nine *melachot* corresponded to something.	דְל"ט מְלָאכוֹת הֵן כְּנֶגֶד שׁוּם דָבָר
This is why the sages inquire: "To what do they correspond?"	לְכַך בָּעֵי כְּנֶגֶד מִי

Shabbat and the Tabernacle: What is the Connection?

TEXT 4: **Rashi, Shabbat 49b, *Keneged Avodot HaMishkan***

They correspond to the labors of the Tabernacle:	כְּנֶגֶד עֲבוֹדוֹת הַמִּשְׁכָּן
Those that are enumerated there	אוֹתָן הַמְנוּיוֹת שָׁם
in chapter *Kelal Gadol*	בְּפֶרֶק כְּלַל גָּדוֹל
were necessary for the Tabernacle,	הָיוּ צְרִיכִין לַמִּשְׁכָּן
and the Torah portion discussing Shabbat	וּפַרְשַׁת שַׁבָּת
is adjacent to the portion —of the labors of the Tabernacle	נִסְמְכָה לְפַרְשַׁת מְלֶאכֶת הַמִּשְׁכָּן
to learn from it.	לִלְמוֹד הֵימֶנָּה.

Rabbi Shlomo Yitzchaki (١١٠٥–١٠٤٠). Better known by the acronym *Rashi;* rabbi and famed author of the first comprehensive commentaries on the Talmud and Bible. Born in Troyes, Champagne, Rashi studied in the famed yeshivot of Mainz and Worms. His commentaries, which focus on the simple understanding of the text, are considered fundamental to Torah study. Since their initial printings, they have appeared in virtually every edition of the Talmud and Bible. Amongst Rashi's descendants, were many of the famed Tosafists of France.

Counting Mentions of *Melachah*: From Where Does Rabbi Yonatan know this?

TEXT 5: ***Shabbat* 49b, Rashi, *ShebaTorah***

Appearing in the Torah.	שֶׁבַּתּוֹרָה
That are written throughout the entire Torah.	שֶׁכְּתוּבִים בְּכָל הַתּוֹרָה
And this is what the verse [intends] to say:	וְהָכִי קָאָמַר קְרָא
Do not perform all labor—	(שמות כ) לֹא תַעֲשֶׂה כָל מְלָאכָה
corresponding to the number of all [appearances of the word] *melachah* in the Torah.	כְּמִנְיַן כָּל מְלָאכָה שֶׁבַּתּוֹרָה.

TEXT 6: **Tosafot, *Keneged Kol Melachah ShebaTorah***

Corresponding to all mentions of "work" in the Torah	כְּנֶגֶד כָּל מְלָאכָה שֶׁבַּתּוֹרָה
It appears at first glance	לִכְאוֹרָה נִרְאֶה
That [Rabbi Yonatan] derives *melachah* from the Tabernacle as well—	דְיָלִיף נַמִי מִמִּשְׁכָּן
—since for this reason the Torah juxtaposed	שֶׁהֲרֵי לְכָךְ נִסְמְכָה
the portion of Shabbat to the portion of the Tabernacle.	פַּרְשַׁת שַׁבָּת לְפַרְשַׁת מִשְׁכָּן
Moreover, if we do not learn from the Tabernacle	וְעוֹד דְאִי לֹא יָלִיף מִמִּשְׁכָּן
how would we know	אִם כֵּן הֵיכִי יָדְעִינָן
According to [Rabbi Yonatan]	לְדִידֵיה
which are *avot* [primary] *melachot*	הֵי נִינְהוּ אָבוֹת מְלָאכוֹת
and which are *toladot* [secondary ones]?	וְהֵי תּוֹלְדוֹת

It is not reasonable to say	דְאֵין סְבָרָא לוֹמַר
that they chose the important labors of their own accord	שֶׁמִדַעְתָּם בֵּירְרוּ מְלָאכוֹת הַחֲשׁוּבוֹת
and made them *avot* (primary labors).	וַעֲשָׂאוּם אָבוֹת
Furthermore	וְעוֹד
it was clearly taught later in the chapter *HaZorek*:	דִבְהֶדְיָא תְּנַן לְקַמָּן בְּהַזּוֹרֵק
"One who passes [an object] is liable as this was part of the work of the Levites (even though it is not counted as one of the thirty-nine)."	"הַמּוֹשִׁיט חַיָּיב שֶׁכַּךְ הָיְתָה עֲבוֹדַת הַלְוִיִּם"
However, since there are *melachot* (labors) that are similar to one another	אֶלָּא לְפִי שֶׁיֵּשׁ מְלָאכוֹת דוֹמוֹת זוֹ לְזוֹ
and we consider both of them to be *avot* [primary] such as sifting and selecting,	וְאָנוּ עוֹשִׂין שְׁתֵּיהֶן אָבוֹת כְּגוֹן מְרַקֵּד וּבוֹרֵר
for this reason, the sages separated them to complete the number of mentions of the word *melachah* in the Torah	לְכַךְ חִלְּקוּם חֲכָמִים לְהַשְׁלִים מִנְיָן מְלָאכוֹת שֶׁבַּתּוֹרָה
since there are slight differences between them.	הוֹאִיל וַחֲלוּקוֹת קְצָת זוֹ מִזּוֹ
It cannot be said that they [Rabbi Chanina and Rabbi Yonatan] do not argue	וְאִי אֶפְשָׁר לוֹמַר כֵּן דְלָא פְּלִיג
from what the Talmud says shortly	מִדְקָאָמַר בְּסָמוּךְ
[that] "it has been taught in accordance with the opinion that they correspond to the labors of the Tabernacle."	תַּנְיָא כְּמַאן דְאָמַר כְּנֶגֶד עֲבוֹדוֹת הַמִּשְׁכָּן
This implies that they argue.	מַשְׁמַע דִפְלִיגֵי
Moreover, according to the opinion that does not uphold the interpretation of [counting the mentions of] "work of" and "work,"	וְעוֹד לְמַאן דְלֵית לֵיהּ דְרָשָׁא דִמְלֶאכֶת וּמְלָאכָה
how does he know to include winnowing and selecting as two?	מְנָא לֵיהּ דְחָשִׁיב זוֹרֶה וּבוֹרֵר בִּשְׁתַּיִם
Furthermore, later the Talmud implies	וְעוֹד לְקַמָּן מַשְׁמַע

that for the reason that they correspond to the labors of the Tabernacle alone	דְּמִטַּעַם דִּכְנֶגֶד עֲבוֹדוֹת הַמִּשְׁכָּן גְּרֵידָא
they should be included as two.	אִית לָן לְאַחְשׁוֹבִינְהוּ בְּתַרְתֵּי
For Abaye and Rava state in the Chapter *Kelal Gadol*	דְּקָאָמַר אַבַּיֵי וְרָבָא בְּפֶרֶק כְּלָל גָּדוֹל (עג:)
everything [i.e., all labors] that was performed in the Tabernacle	כָּל מִילְּתָא דַּהֲוָאִי בְּמִשְׁכָּן
even though there are others that are similar to them, was nevertheless included.	אַף עַל גַּב דְּאִיכָּא דְּדַמְיָא לַהּ חָשִׁיב לַהּ

Table 1

Comparing Tosafot's Initial and Final Approaches

		Initial Approach No dispute	Final Approach Two different opinions
Rabbi Chanina bar Chama	Tabernacle	Source for ***types*** of *melachot*	Source for ***number*** of *melachot* as well as the types
Rabbi Yonatan ben Rabbi Elazar	39 mentions of work	Source for ***number*** of *melachot*	Source for ***number*** of *melachot* (but does **not** derive the types of *melachah* from the Tabernacle)

Part II

"Forty Minus One"—Which One?

TEXT 7: Talmud, *Shabbat* 49b, continued

Rav Yosef inquired:	בָּעֵי רַב יוֹסֵף
Is "and he entered the house to do his work" (Bereishit 39)	וַיָּבֹא הַבַּיְתָה לַעֲשׂוֹת מְלַאכְתּוֹ
included in the count, or not?	מִמִּנְיָנָא הוּא, אוֹ לֹא?
Abaye said to him: Let us bring a Torah scroll and count.	אָמַר לֵיהּ אַבַּיֵי וְלֵיתֵי סֵפֶר תּוֹרָה וְלִימְנֵי
Did not Rabbah bar bar Chanah[once] say:	מִי לֹא אָמַר רַבָּה בַּר בַּר חַנָּה אָמַר רַבִּי יוֹחָנָן
They did not move from there,	לֹא זָזוּ מִשָּׁם
until they brought a Torah scroll and counted them?	עַד שֶׁהֵבִיאוּ סֵפֶר תּוֹרָה וּמְנָאוּם.

TEXT 7B: Continuation of Talmud, *Shabbat* 49b

[Rav Yosef] answered him: The reason I am in doubt	אָמַר לֵיהּ כִּי קָא מְסַפְּקָא לִי
is because it is written	מִשּׁוּם דִכְתִיב
"and the work was enough."	וְהַמְּלָאכָה הָיְתָה דַיָּם
Is [that verse] to be included in the count	מִמִּנְיָנָא הוּא
And this [would] accord with the one who says	וְהָא כְּמַאן דְאָמַר
[that it was] to "perform his needs," that he entered?	לַעֲשׂוֹת צְרָכָיו נִכְנַס,
Or perhaps	אוֹ דִילְמָא
"and he entered the house to do his work"	וַיָּבֹא הַבַּיְתָה לַעֲשׂוֹת מְלַאכְתּוֹ
is included in the count	מִמִּנְיָנָא הוּא,
and this verse "and the work was enough"	וְהַאי וְהַמְּלָאכָה הָיְתָה דַיָּם
means to say:	הָכִי קָאָמַר
That the task was completed [and therefore is not from the count]?	דִשְׁלִים לֵיהּ עֲבִידְתָא
Let it stand.	תֵּיקוּ.

Euphemisms

TEXT 8: **Talmud, *Sotah* 36b**

And [Yosef] came to the house to do his work.	וַיָּבֹא הַבַּיְתָה לַעֲשׂוֹת מְלַאכְתּוֹ
Rav and Shmuel [dispute the meaning of this verse]	רַב וּשְׁמוּאֵל
One says: He actually came to do his work	חַד אָמַר לַעֲשׂוֹת מְלַאכְתּוֹ מַמָּשׁ
and the other says: He came to do what he needed to do.	וְחַד אָמַר לַעֲשׂוֹת צְרָכָיו נִכְנַס

What is Rav Yosef's Unresolved Question?

TEXT 9: ***Shabbat* 49a, Rashi, *Mishum Dichtiv***

Because it is also written "and the work was enough".	מִשּׁוּם דִּכְתִיב וְהַמְּלָאכָה הָיְתָה דַיָּם
If we count both instances, there would be forty	וְאִי מָנֵינַן לְתַרְוַיְיהוּ הֲווּ אַרְבָּעִים
and since the *mishnah* taught "the primary *melachot* are forty minus one"	וּמִדִּתְנַן אָבוֹת מְלָאכוֹת אַרְבָּעִים חָסֵר אַחַת
there is one that is not in the count.	אִיכָּא חַד דְּלָא מִמִּנְיָנָא
Of each of these two [mentions] it may possible to say that they do not refer to *melachah*	וּבְהָנֵי תְּרֵי דְּאִיכָּא לְמֵימַר דְּלָא מְלָאכָה נִינְהוּ
but I (Rav Yosef) do not know which one to exclude.	וְלָא יָדַעְנָא הֵי מִינַּיְיהוּ נָפִיק
And this is what he (Rav Yosef) is asking:	וְהָכִי קָא מִיבַּעְיָא לֵיהּ
Is *"and the work was enough"* included in the count	וְהַמְּלָאכָה הָיְתָה דַיָּם מִמִּנְיָנָא הִיא
and it refers to actual *work*, and this is what it intends to say:	וּמְלָאכָה מַמָּשׁ קָאָמַר וְהָכִי קָאָמַר
the work that they did, they did sufficiently,	הַמְּלָאכָה שֶׁהָיוּ עוֹשִׂין הָיוּ עוֹשִׂין דַּי
not more or less than necessary.	לֹא פָּחוֹת מִן הַצּוֹרֶךְ וְלֹא יוֹתֵר מִן הַצּוֹרֶךְ
For example: in beating down the plates of metal to plate the boards [of the Tabernacle]	כְּגוֹן רִידּוּדֵי טַסִּין לְצִיפּוּי הַקְּרָשִׁים
they would beat them down sufficiently;	לְדַי הָיוּ מְרַדְּדִין אוֹתָם
and similarly with spinning threads for the coverings.	וְכֵן בִּטּוּוּי שֶׁל יְרִיעוֹת

And [accordingly,	וְהַאי
the verse] "do to his work" is excluded,	לַעֲשׂוֹת מְלַאכְתּוֹ הוּא דְּמַפִּיק
supporting the opinion in Tractate *Sotah*	וּמְסַיֵּיעַ לְמַאן דְּאָמַר בְּמַסֶּכֶת סוֹטָה
that he entered to perform his needs —to lie with her,	לַעֲשׂוֹת צְרָכָיו נִכְנַס —לִשְׁכַּב עִמָּהּ,
but the image of his father appeared to him	אֶלָּא שֶׁנִּרְאֲתָה לוֹ דְּמוּת דְּיוֹקְנוֹ שֶׁל אָבִיו
and said to him:	וְאָמַר לוֹ
Your brothers are destined to be inscribed upon the stones of the [high priest's breastplate on the] *ephod*.	עֲתִידִין אַחֶיךָ לִיכָּתֵב עַל אַבְנֵי אֵפוֹד
Do you wish that your name be erased from among them?	רְצוֹנְךָ שֶׁיִּמָּחֶה שִׁמְךָ מִבֵּינֵיהֶם כו׳
Alternatively,	אוֹ דִּילְמָא
this [verse] "to do his work" refers to actual work	הַאי לַעֲשׂוֹת מְלַאכְתּוֹ—מְלָאכָה מַמָּשׁ הוּא
and this supports the other opinion.	וּמְסַיֵּיעַ לַהּ לְאִידָךְ

TEXT 10: Rashi, *Shabbat* 49b, *VeHai VeHaMelachah*

And this verse, "*and the work was enough*"	וְהַאי וְהַמְּלָאכָה הָיְתָה דַיָּם
does not refer to work,	לַאו מְלָאכָה הִיא
but rather, as scripture implies, it refers to bringing donations	אֶלָּא כִּדְמַשְׁמַע קְרָא בַּהֲבָאַת נְדָבָה
in accordance with the interpretation that they had [already] completed their work,	וּכְמַאן דְּאָמַר שְׁלִימָא לֵיהּ עֲבִידְתָּא
i.e., the work of bringing.	מְלֶאכֶת הַהֲבָאָה
Since they required no more	שֶׁלֹּא הָיוּ צְרִיכִין עוֹד
and anything incumbent upon a person	וְכָל מִידִי דְּרָמֵי עֲלֵיהּ דְּאִינָשׁ
is called work,	קָרֵי לֵיהּ עֲבִידְתָּא
as we say in Tractate *Sota* (33a),	כִּדְאַמְרִינַן בְּמַסֶּכֶת סוֹטָה (לג, א)
"The work which the enemy said it would dispatch against the sanctuary has been eliminated."	בְּטֵילַת עֲבִידְתָּא דְּאָמַר סָנְאָה לְאַיְיתוּיֵא לְהֵיכְלָא
This [word "work"] merely refers to a destroying army.	וְאֵינוֹ אֶלָּא צָבָא מִלְחָמָה לְהַחֲרִיב.

Keys to the Talmud

Teiku

As at the conclusion of our Talmud text, the Talmud uses the word *teiku* when the sages have not been successful in resolving a question. The word *teiku* means "let it stand," similar to the Hebrew *takum*, "get up" or "stand up." In Talmudic terminology it has also been understood as an abbreviation for "*Tishbi Yetaretz Kushyot UVa'ayot*"—"[Elijah] the Tishbite will answer questions and inquiries." According to tradition, when the prophet Elijah will return with the coming of Mashiach, he will answer all of the questions in Torah and Jewish Law that were left unanswered throughout the generations.

TEXT 11: *Penei Yehoshua, Af Al Gav*

Even though	אַף עַל גַּב
the truth of the matter is	דִּלְקוּשְׁטָא דְּמִילְתָא
that scripture mentions forty,	אַרְבָּעִים הוּא דִּכְתִיבָא
Nevertheless the sages had a tradition	אֲפִילוּ הָכִי קִים לְהוּ לְרַבָּנָן
that one is omitted	דְּבָצִיר חַד
and it is not counted	וְלֹא הֲוֵי מִמְּנְיָנָא
and it is	וְהַיְינוּ
either: *"and he entered the house to do his work"*	אוֹ וַיָּבֹא הַבַּיְתָה לַעֲשׂוֹת מְלַאכְתּוֹ
or *"and the work was enough."*	אוֹ וְהַמְּלָאכָה הָיְתָה דַיָּם

Rabbi Yaakov Yehoshua Falk (١٧٥٤–١٦٨٠). Also known as the *Penei Yehoshua* after the title of his illustrious work. In its deep investigation of Talmudic analysis, logic, judgment, and reasoning, he succeeds in uncovering great depth to the Talmud and its early commentators. He served as rabbi in many cities in Europe including Frankfurt, Lvov, and Berlin. One of his students was Rabbi DovBer of Mezeritch, the successor of the Bal Shem Tov.

Keys to the Talmud

Chazarah–Review

One of the important aspects of learning Torah is to review what you have learned. This serves two purposes: 1) not forgetting what you have learned; and 2) making sure you correctly understand what you learned the first time. Even though what we have just learned is still fresh in our memories, the following exercise will help us make sure that we understood the previous Rashis and will help us retain what we have understood.

Learning Activity

Both verses could refer to *melachah* as literal work or as a figure of speech. Rav Yosef was therefore unsure which one is meant literally and which one is a figure of speech. Using Rashi's explanation, explain what the word *melachah* means in the context of each verse if it is meant literally and if it is meant as a figure of speech.

Phrase	As literal work	As a figure of speech
*And he entered the house to do his **work***		
*And the **work** was enough*		

Part III

The Third and Fourth Sources

TEXT 12A: **Talmud, *Shabbat* 70a**

And Moses gathered the entire congregation of Israel,	וַיַּקְהֵל מֹשֶׁה אֶת כָּל עֲדַת בְּנֵי יִשְׂרָאֵל
These are the words . . .	אֵלֶּה הַדְּבָרִים וגו'
For six day you shall do work . . . (Exodus 35:1-2)	שֵׁשֶׁת יָמִים תֵּעָשֶׂה מְלָאכָה.
Words, the words,	דְּבָרִים הַדְּבָרִים
these are the words—	אֵלֶּה הַדְּבָרִים
this corresponds to the thirty-nine *melachot*	אֵלּוּ שְׁלֹשִׁים וְתֵשַׁע מְלָאכוֹת
that were said to Moses at Sinai	שֶׁנֶּאֶמְרוּ לְמֹשֶׁה בְּסִינַי

Keys to the Talmud

Halachah leMoshe miSinai

Literally, "a law attributed to Moses from Sinai." At Sinai, Moses received the Written Law, the Torah, along with the interpretation of this law. Tradition preserved the oral interpretation of the law together with the method through which each is derived from the Torah. Several laws are of biblical mandate but there is no recorded reference to them in the Torah. These were also part of the body of law that Moses received at Sinai. Moses passed them down to the sages of his times who in turn passed them from generation to generation in an unbroken chain of tradition.

Keys to the Talmud

DeOraita* and *DeRabanan

In this lesson we have seen both, how a law can be derived from a specific verse in the Torah, and how a law can be part of the oral tradition without a supporting verse. Such laws are deemed biblical (*de'oraita*—"of the Torah"). These are distinct from the enactments of the sages (*derabanan*—"of the sages"). Though it is true that the rabbis are empowered by the Torah to enact rules as "fences" to guard the Torah and for other purposes, the resulting laws are not considered biblical in origin. In our case, all thirty-nine *melachot* are prohibited by the Torah, although they are not stated explicitly in the Torah.

TEXT 12B: *Shabbat* 70a, Rashi, *Devarim*

Words	—דְּבָרִים
implies two,	מַשְׁמַע תְּרֵי
the adds an additional one	ה׳ לְרַבּוֹת חַד
equaling three,	הֲרֵי שְׁלֹשָׁה
אלה is of the numerical value of thirty-six.	אֵלֶּה בְּגִמַטְרִיָּא שְׁלֹשִׁים וְשֵׁשׁ
All together they are thirty-nine.	הֲרֵי שְׁלֹשִׁים וְתֵשַׁע

דברים in plural = 2

Extra "ה" of הדברים= 1

Subtotal = 3

Add the numerical value of אלה (see below) 36 for a grant total of 39

To calculate the value of the word אלה ("these"), Rashi uses a method called *gematria*.

Keys to the Talmud

Gematria

***Gematria* is a word of Greek origin and possibly derived from *gramma,* meaning "letter" or related to the Greek word from which "geometry" is derived. It is a method of attributing numerical values to letters and by extension to words, and phrases. We primarily use *gematria* for non-literal, non-legal exegesis of the Torah.**

TEXT 13: Mishnah, *Avot* 3:18

Rabbi Eliezer ben Chisma said:	רַבִּי אֱלִיעֶזֶר בֶּן חִסְמָא אוֹמֵר
Calculation of the equinoxes and *gematria* are side dishes to wisdom.	תְּקוּפוֹת וְגִמַטְרִיָּאוֹת פַּרְפְּרָאוֹת לְחָכְמָה

Learning Exercise (1 min.)

Using the following *gematria* table, tally the *gematria* value of the word אלה.

1=א	2=ב	3=ג	4=ד	5=ה	6=ו	7=ז	8=ח	9=ט
10=י	20=כ	30=ל	40=מ	50=נ	60=ס	70=ע	80=פ	90=צ
100=ק	200=ר	300=ש	400=ת					

א = —

ל = —

ה = —

Total = ____________

Key Points

1. Quantifying mitzvot was an important part of ancient learning. This is why our *mishnah* mentions the number of *melachot*.

2. According to the Babylonian Talmud, there are four sources for the number of the thirty-nine *melachot*:

1. The number of activities performed in the Tabernacle;
2. The number of mentions of the word *melachah* in the Torah;
3. The numerical value calculated from the verse these are the words; and
4. from tradition—*halachah leMoshe miSinai*

3. The *mishnah's* expression "forty minus one" alludes to the forty possible mentions of the word *melachah* and the standing dilemma of which one to subtract.

Terms to Retain

For it was taught in a *mishnah*	דִּתְנַן
For it was taught in a *baraita*	דְּתַנְיָא
superfluous	יִתּוּר
The numerical value of Hebrew letters	גְּמַטְרִיָּא
A law Moses received at Sinai	הֲלָכָה לְמֹשֶׁה מִסִּינַי
Of the Torah	דְּאוֹרַיְיתָא
Of the Rabbis	דְּרַבָּנַן

Appendix

deletion(s)	**חֲסֵיר(וֹת)**
addition(s)	**יְתֵיר(וֹת)**

When Was the Count?

TEXT A: Talmud, *Kidushin* 30a

For this reason, the early Sages were called *sofrim* (scribes)	לְפִיכָךְ נִקְרְאוּ רִאשׁוֹנִים סוֹפְרִים
for they counted all the letters of the Torah.	שֶׁהָיוּ סוֹפְרִים כָּל הָאוֹתִיּוֹת שֶׁבַּתּוֹרָה
They used to say:	שֶׁהָיוּ אוֹמְרִים
the letter *vav* of the word *gachon* (Leviticus 11:42) represents the half-way point of the letters of the Torah scroll.	וָא"ו דְגָחוֹן חֶצְיָין שֶׁל אוֹתִיּוֹת שֶׁל סֵפֶר תּוֹרָה
. . . Rav Yosef inquired:	. . . בָּעֵי רַב יוֹסֵף
"The *vav* of the word *gachon*— is it part of this [first] side or part of this [latter] side [of the Torah's letters]?"	וָא"ו דְגָחוֹן מֵהַאי גִיסָא אוֹ מֵהַאי גִיסָא
They said to him: "Let us bring a Torah scroll and count [its letters]!"	אָמַר לֵיהּ נֵיתֵי סֵפֶר תּוֹרָה וְאִימְנִינְהוּ
Did not Rabbah bar bar Channah say:	מִי לֹא אָמַר רַבָּה בַּר בַּר חָנָה
"They did not move from there until they brought a Torah scroll and counted them?"	לֹא זָזוּ מִשָּׁם עַד שֶׁהֵבִיאוּ סֵפֶר תּוֹרָה וּמְנָאוּם
[Rav Yosef] replied to them: "They were versed in the knowledge of deletions and additions.	אָמַר לֵיהּ אִינְהוּ בְּקִיאִי בַּחֲסֵירוֹת וִיתֵרוֹת
We are not versed [and cannot make this calculation]."	אֲנַן לֹא בְּקִיאִינָן

Keys to the Talmud

Chaseirot* and *Yeteirot

In Hebrew, vowels do not appear as letters, but in the form of *nekudot*—diacritical marks that do not appear in texts until centuries after the completion of the Talmud. However, there are certain letters that even in the oldest texts sometimes act as vowels. One example is the *vav* that in addition to making the "v" sound, can also make the "o" and "oo" sounds when it acts as a vowel. These vowels ("o" and "oo") can appear in the form of a *vav* or only as a diacritical mark, without a *vav* present. The same word is spelled sometimes with a *vav* and sometimes without it and it is pronounced the same in each case.

When the Torah uses the extra *vav,* it is called *yateir* (plural: *yeteirot*), or an addition, since it could have been spelled without the *vav* just as well. When the Torah spells it without a *vav*, it is called *chaseir* (plural: *cheseirot*) or a deletion, since the *vav* is deleted. Example: In the first portion of the *Shema* (Deuteronomy 6:9), *mezuzot* is spelled מזזות without a second *vav,* an example of *chaseir*. In the second portion of the *Shema* (Deuteronomy 11:20), the same word *mezuzot* is spelled מזוזות with a second *vav*, an example of *yateir*.

TEXT B: Rashi, *Lo Zazu MiSham*

They did not move from there.	לֹא זָזוּ מִשָּׁם
I do not know where [i.e., regarding what matter] [the statement of Rabbah bar bar Channah] was taught.	לֹא יָדַעְנָא הֵיכָא אִיתְּמַר

Advanced Learning Challenge

However,	וּמִיהוּ
it is possible that it was taught regarding the letter *vav* of *gachon*	אֶפְשָׁר לְעִנְיַן וָי"ו דְגָחוֹן אִתְּמַר
since they question [Rav Yosef] using this [statement] in Tractate *Kidushin* as well	מִדְּפָרְכִינָן לָהּ נַמִי בְּקִדּוּשִׁין
in the case of the *vav* of the word *gachon*.	גַּבֵּי וָי"ו דְגָחוֹן
[Rav Yosef] answered that	וּמְתַרְצִינָן

they were experts	אִינְהוּ הֲווּ
in the deletions and additions [to accurately tally the letters of the Torah].	בְּקִיאֵי בְּחַסֵרוֹת וִיתֵרוֹת
Deduce from here	שְׁמַע מִינָּה
that [the statement of Rabbah bar bar Channah] was taught regarding letters	לְעִנְיַן אוֹתִיּוֹת אִיתְּמַר
whereas here,	וְהָכָא
it cannot be learned this way.	לֵיכָּא לְשַׁנּוּיֵי הָכִי

Lesson 3

Introduction

How is carrying an object from one domain to another considered to be a constructive activity? In this lesson, we will examine the way in which the *avot melachot* were performed in the *Mishkan*. We will follow a dispute between medieval commentaries and see how the various positions in that dispute reflect a divergence between the Jerusalem Talmud and the Babylonian Talmud. We will explore the *melachah* of carrying an object, thereby transferring it from one domain to another, and discover its uniqueness and centrality to Shabbat. Along the way, we will learn about such things as imaginary walls and see how innovations --unexpected, counterintuitive laws—are viewed by the Talmud.

Part I

The *Mishkan* Comparison

Keys to the Talmud

Ditnan* vs. *Detanya

The word *ditnan* means "we learned in a Mishnah" and appears in the Talmud whenever a Mishnah is being quoted. *Detanya*, on the other hand, refers to something taught in a *baraita* or *tosefta,* (teachings from mishnaic authors that were never incorporated into the formal compilation of the Mishnah).

Keys to the Talmud

Baraita

A *baraita* is a selection of statements from the authors of the Mishnah that frequently appear in the Talmud but that were not incorporated into the formal compilation of the Mishnah. In the study halls of Israel and Babylonia, the sages of the Mishnah discussed and debated the oral tradition. The content of these discussions was extracted, preserved and compiled by Rabbi Yehudah the Prince to become the Mishnah.

TEXT 1: Talmud, *Shabbat*, 49b

There is a *baraita* in accordance with the opinion of the one who said that they correspond to the labors of the *Mishkan*.	תַּנְיָא כְּמַאן דְּאָמַר כְּנֶגֶד עֲבוֹדוֹת הַמִּשְׁכָּן
For it was taught [in a *baraita*]:	דְּתַנְיָא
Liability is incurred only for forms of *melachah*	עַל מְלָאכָה אֵין חַיָּיבִין אֶלָּא
that had a counterpart in the *Mishkan*.	שֶׁכַּיּוֹצֵא בָּהּ הָיְתָה בַּמִּשְׁכָּן
They sowed, hence you should not sow;	הֵם זָרְעוּ וְאַתֶּם לֹא תִּזְרְעוּ
they reaped, hence you should not reap.	הֵם קָצְרוּ וְאַתֶּם לֹא תִּקְצְרוּ

Discussion Questions

Rashi states that the *av melachah* of baking was derived from the labor of cooking herbs in the *Mishkan*'s dye-making process. Why do we not derive baking directly from the baking of the showbread or of the bread offerings that accompanied the sacrifices?

TEXT 2: Rashi, *Shabbat* 49b *Heim*

They	הֵם
planted and harvested herbs	זָרְעוּ וְקָצְרוּ סַמָּנִין
to dye the blue yarn and the ram skin [coverings].	לִצְבּוֹעַ תְּכֵלֶת וְעוֹרוֹת אֵילִים
They also ground and kneaded herbs to make dyes	וְטָחֲנוּ וְלָשׁוּ נַמִּי סַמָּנִין לִצְבּוֹעַ
and the baking that is stated in the Mishnah among the primary [*avot*] *melachot*	וְאוֹפֶה דְקָתָנֵי בְּמַתְנִיתִין בְּאָבוֹת מְלָאכוֹת
[refers to] the cooking of herbs	הוּא בִּישּׁוּל סַמָּנִין
but [is counted as baking] because it follows the order of making bread.	אֶלָּא דְנָקַט סִידּוּרָה דְפַּת
This is what the [Talmud] explains in chapter *Kelal Gadol*.	וְהָכִי מְפָרֵשׁ בְּפֶּרֶק כְּלָל גָּדוֹל (שבת עד,ב)

Rabbi Shlomo Yitzchaki (1040–1105). Better known by the acronym *Rashi;* rabbi and famed author of the first comprehensive commentaries on the Talmud and Bible. Born in Troyes, Champagne, Rashi studied in the famed yeshivot of Mainz and Worms. His commentaries, which focus on the simple understanding of the text, are considered fundamental to Torah study. Since their initial printings, they have appeared in virtually every edition of the Talmud and Bible. Amongst Rashi's descendants, were many of the famed Tosafists of France.

TEXT 3: *Eglei Tal*, Introduction, 2

Does it mean that it was only after they were instructed about the work of the *Mishkan*	אִם לְאַחַר שֶׁנִּצְטַוּוּ עַל מְלֶאכֶת הַמִּשְׁכָּן
that they planted and harvested?	זָרְעוּ וְקָצְרוּ וכו'
Or perhaps they were already available from before [the instruction]	אוֹ דִילְמָא דְמִכְּבַר הָיָה מָצוּי בְּיָדָם
but nevertheless,	אֶלָּא דְמִכָּל מָקוֹם
since these things require plowing and planting, etc.,	דְמֵאַחַר שֶׁדְּבָרִים אֵלוּ בָּאִים עַל יְדֵי חֲרִישָׁה וּזְרִיעָה וכו'
they are considered as if they were performed in the [construction of the] *Mishkan*?	חָשִׁיב דְּבָרִים אֵלוּ הָיָה בְּמִשְׁכָּן.

Rabbi Avraham Borenstein of Sochatchov (1839–1910). Chassidic Rebbe and Talmudist. Rabbi Borenstein authored the *Avnei Nezer*, a compilation of his responsa literature, and *Eglei Tal*, an explanation of the thirty-nine forbidden actions of Shabbat. He was the son-in-law of the Rebbe of Kotzk, with whom he studied almost daily for seven years. Many of his teaching are cited by his son and successor, Rabbi Shmuel Borenstein in the work *Shem MeShmuel*, a Biblical commentary.

Part II

For the Building of the *Mishkan* or for its Service?

Discussion Questions

Rashi states that the *av melachah* of baking was derived from the labor of cooking herbs in the *Mishkan*'s dye-making process. Why do we not derive baking directly from the baking of the showbread or of the bread offerings that accompanied the sacrifices?

TEXT 4A: **Talmud, *Shabbat* 75a**

[The Mishnah stated:] Slaughtering it . . .	וְהַשּׁוֹחֲטוֹ
One who slaughters—why is he liable?	שׁוֹחֵט מִשּׁוּם מַאי חַיָּיב
Rav says: Because of dyeing	רַב אָמַר מִשּׁוּם צוֹבֵעַ
and Shmuel says:	וּשְׁמוּאֵל אָמַר
Because of taking a life.	מִשּׁוּם נְטִילַת נְשָׁמָה

TEXT 4B: **Rashi, *Ad Loc.***

One who slaughters—why is he liable?	שׁוֹחֵט מִשּׁוּם מַאי מִיחַיֵּיב
Where was there slaughtering in the work of the *Mishkan*	שְׁחִיטָה בִּמְלֶאכֶת הַמִּשְׁכָּן הֵיכָא
and what was its purpose?	וּמַאי עֲבִידְתָּה
If it was for the red dyed ram's hides,	אִי מֵעוֹרוֹת אֵילִים מְאָדָּמִים
why would they require [kosher] slaughtering?	שְׁחִיטָה לָמָּה לִי בְּהוּ
Strangulation would also suffice.	בַּחֲנִיקָה נַמִּי סַגִּי

Dissenting View

TEXT 5: **Responsum from Rav Hai Gaon**

In response to your question concerning the *avot melachot*	וְשֶׁשְּׁאַלְתֶּם מַהוּ אָבוֹת מְלָאכוֹת
that we learn from the work of the *Mishkan*	דְגַמְרִינָן מִמַּעֲשֶׂה מִשְׁכָּן
[regarding which the Talmud] states, “they sowed and you do not sow” —	וְאָמַר הֵם זָרְעוּ וְאַתֶּם לֹא תִזְרְעוּ
where did they sow and harvest in the *Mishkan*?	זְרִיעָה וּקְצִירָה הֵיאָךְ הֲוָאִי בְּמִשְׁכָּן
Answer: In the daily perpetual offering.	תְּשׁוּבָה. הֲלֹא יֵשׁ בְּקָרְבָּן תָּמִיד כָּל יוֹם
There was one tenth of an *eifah* of fine flour	עֲשִׂירִית הָאֵיפָה סֹלֶת
and pancakes in Aaron's daily offering	וּבְקָרְבָּן אַהֲרֹן חֲבִיתִּים שֶׁבְּכָל יוֹם
and a basket of *matzot* in the inaugural offerings.	וּבְמִילוּאִים סַל הַמַּצוֹת
One cannot say that they relied	וְאִי אֶפְשָׁר שֶׁיְּהֵא סְמוּכִין
on getting flour from elsewhere.	כִּי תֵצֵא לָהֶם סֹלֶת מִמָּקוֹם אַחֵר
Rather, they planted.	אֶלָּא זָרְעוּ
We also find a similar reference in the Talmud of the West [the Jerusalem Talmud]:	וְאַף כְּלָשׁוֹן הַזֶּה כְּתַלְמוּד מַעֲרָבָא
We deduce the *avot melachot* from the *Mishkan*.	אָבוֹת מְלָאכוֹת מִמִּשְׁכָּן לָמַדְנוּ
What plowing was there in the *Mishkan*?	וּמַה חֲרִישָׁה הָיְתָה בְּמִשְׁכָּן
They would plow to plant spices	שֶׁהָיוּ חוֹרְשִׁין לִיטַע סַמְמָנִין
and these spices were used for the incense.	וְסַמְמָנִין אֵלוּ הֵם שֶׁל קְטוֹרֶת
This included plowing, planting and harvesting.	וְיֵשׁ בְּזֹאת חֲרִישָׁה וּזְרִיעָה וּקְצִירָה.

Rav Hai Gaon (939–1038). Rabbi, author and poet; head of Rabbinical court and Gaon. Born to a distinguished family which included amongst its ancestors Exilarchs and heads of Yeshivah; Rav Hai succeeded his aged father Rav Sherira, as Gaon of Pumpedita (in modern-day Iraq). As head of the rabbinical court and later as head of the Yeshivah Rav Hai was seen as the leader of world Jewry which is evident in his correspondence with Jewish communities worldwide, some of which is still extant. He authored works on Jewish law, Talmud, the Hebrew language, poetry and Tanach; most of which has not been preserved. With his passing at the ripe age of 99, the epoch of Gaonim came to a close.

Table 1

	Rashi	Rav Hai Gaon
Mishkan Comparison	Construction	Construction and Temple Service
Planting, Harvesting . . .	For herbs to dye curtains	To bake bread for sacrifices
Reason for Order of Making Bread	Perhaps for order and simplicity	Because baking bread is the *av*

Discussion Question

How does Rav Hai understand the Talmud's query about the *av* of slaughtering, if we derive the laws of Shabbat from Temple services as well?

Keys to the Talmud

Leshitato

***Leshitato,* (literally: following his opinion) is a term often used in Talmudic study to point out how a Torah scholar (in both Talmudic and modern times) follows the same logic or line of thinking in several instances. Sometimes, it points out how two disputes between scholars originate from the same fundamental difference in understanding.**

TEXT 6A: *Shabbat* 92a, *Mishnah*

If one carries out [an item]	הַמּוֹצִיא
whether with the right or hand left hand,	בֵּין בִּימִינוֹ בֵּין בִּשְׂמֹאלוֹ
inside his lap or over his shoulder,	בְּתוֹךְ חֵיקוֹ אוֹ עַל כְּתֵיפָיו
he is liable	חַיָּיב
for it is like the carrying of the family of Kehat.	שֶׁכֵּן מַשָּׂא בְּנֵי קְהָת

TEXT 6B: **Rashi, *Shabbat* 92b**

For it is like the carrying of the family of Kehat:	שֶׁכֵּן מַשָּׂא בְּנֵי קְהָת
[As described in the verse,] "They shall carry upon their shoulders;" (*Bamidbar* 7)	בַּכָּתֵף יִשָּׂאוּ (במדבר ז)
[whereas carrying] in the right hand, left hand, and lap	וְיָמִין וּשְׂמֹאל וְחֵיק
are the regular ways [of carrying].	אוֹרַח אַרְעָא
I have found In the name of Rabbi Yitzchak bar Yehudah	וּבְשֵׁם רַבֵּינוּ יִצְחָק בַּר יְהוּדָה מָצָאתִי
Who said in the name of Rav Hai [Gaon]	שֶׁאָמַר בְּשֵׁם רַב הָאי
that the Jerusalem Talmud states explicitly:	שֶׁמְּפוֹרָשׁ בְּהַתַּלְמוּד יְרוּשַׁלְמִי
"And Elazar son of Aaron the priest was charged with [carrying]	וּפְקוּדַת אֶלְעָזָר בֶּן אַהֲרֹן הַכֹּהֵן
the oil for illumination, the incense of spices	שֶׁמֶן הַמָּאוֹר וּקְטוֹרֶת הַסַּמִּים
the gift [of pancakes brought with the twice-daily] perpetual [offering]	וּמִנְחַת הַתָּמִיד
and the anointing oil" (*Bamidbar* 4)	וְשֶׁמֶן הַמִּשְׁחָה (במדבר ד)
one [oil was carried] in the right hand	[שֶׁמֶן] אֶחָד בְּיָמִין
and the other [oil was carried] in the left hand	[וְשֶׁמֶן] אֶחָד בִּשְׂמֹאל
and the incense in his lap	וְהַקְּטוֹרֶת בְּחֵיקוֹ
and the pancakes on his shoulder."	וְהַחֲבִיתִּין בַּכָּתֵף

Table 2

	Rashi	Rav Hai Gaon
Talmud	Babylonian	From all *Mishkan* activities and services
Derivation from *Mishkan*	Only from construction	For showbread
Planting, Harvesting etc.	For dyes used in dyeing tapestries	Of oils, incense and pancakes used in the *Mishkan* service
Carrying	Of the *Mishkan* itself and its vessels	Could be derived from slaughtering of sacrifices
Slaughtering	Not derived from slaughtering of sacrifices	**Action**

After Construction

TEXT 7: **Talmud, *Berachot* 17a**

[The following was] a common expression from the mouth of Rav:	מְרַגְלָא בְּפוּמֵיה דְרַב
The World to Come is not like this world.	לֹא כְּעוֹלָם הַזֶה הָעוֹלָם הַבָּא
In the World to Come there is no eating or drinking,	הָעוֹלָם הַבָּא אֵין בּוֹ לֹא אֲכִילָה וְלֹא שְׁתִיָה
there is no propagation and no business,	וְלֹא פְּרִיָה וְרִבְיָה וְלֹא מַשָּׂא וּמַתָּן
no jealousy, no hatred and no rivalry.	וְלֹא קִנְאָה וְלֹא שִׂנְאָה וְלֹא תַּחֲרוּת
Rather, the righteous will sit with their crowns on their heads	אֶלָא צַדִיקִים יוֹשְׁבִין וְעַטְרוֹתֵיהֶם בְּרָאשֵׁיהֶם
and delight in the radiance of the Divine Presence.	וְנֶהֱנִים מִזִיו הַשְׁכִינָה
As it is stated (Exodus 24:11): "they gazed at G-d, and they ate and drank."	שֶׁנֶאֱמַר (שמות כ"ד) וַיֶחֱזוּ אֶת הָאֱלֹהִים וַיֹאכְלוּ וַיִשְׁתּוּ

Part III

Domains and Transfer

TEXT 8: **Continuation of Talmud, *Shabbat* 49a**

They lifted up the boards from the ground to the wagon;	הֵם הֶעֱלוּ אֶת הַקְרָשִׁים מִקַרְקַע לָעֲגָלָה
hence you should not carry from a public to a private domain.	וְאַתֶּם לֹא תַּכְנִיסוּ מֵרְשׁוּת הָרַבִּים לִרְשׁוּת הַיָחִיד
They lowered the boards from the wagon to the ground;	הֵם הוֹרִידוּ אֶת הַקְרָשִׁים מֵעֲגָלָה לַקַרְקַע
hence you should not carry out	וְאַתֶּם לֹא תוֹצִיאוּ
from a private to a public domain.	מֵרְשׁוּת הַיָחִיד לִרְשׁוּת הָרַבִּים
They transported [boards, etc.,] from wagon to wagon;	הֵם הוֹצִיאוּ מֵעֲגָלָה לָעֲגָלָה
hence you should not carry	וְאַתֶּם לֹא תוֹצִיאוּ
from one private domain to another.	מֵרְשׁוּת הַיָחִיד לִרְשׁוּת הַיָחִיד

The Four Domains

TEXT 9: **Talmud, *Shabbat* 6a**

The Rabbis taught in a *baraita*:	תָּנוּ רַבָּנָן
There are four domains with regard to the Shabbat:	אַרְבַּע רְשׁוּיוֹת לְשַׁבָּת
a private domain, a public domain,	רְשׁוּת הַיָּחִיד וּרְשׁוּת הָרַבִּים
a *karmelit* and an exempt area.	וְכַרְמְלִית וּמָקוֹם פָּטוּר

Part IV

TEXT 10: **Rashi, *Shabbat* 49b, "*Karka*" and "*Agalah*"**

The ground [of the desert]	קַרְקַע
Was a public domain.	רְשׁוּת הָרַבִּים
The wagon	עֲגָלָה
was a private domain	רְשׁוּת הַיָּחִיד
since it was [at least] ten [handbreadths] tall	שֶׁגְּבוֹהָה עֲשָׂרָה
and [at least] four cubits wide.	וּרְחָבָה אַרְבָּעָה

Fig. #1

The Levites passing *Mishkan* boards onto the wagons and from wagon to wagon.

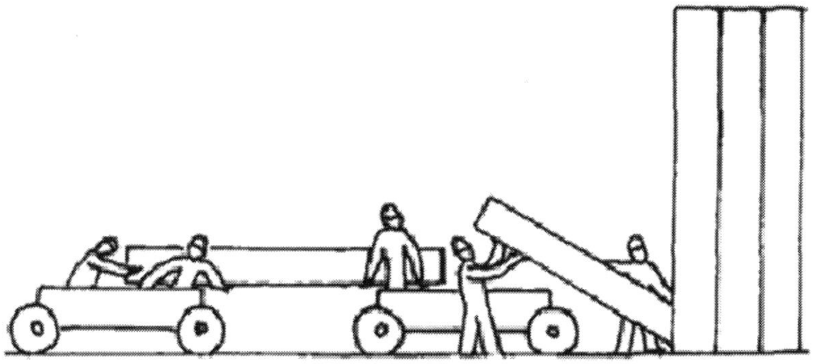

Keys to the Talmud

Gud Achit Mechitzta* and *Gud Asik Mechitzta

One of the laws passed down from Sinai, *halachah leMoshe miSinai*, is the law of imaginary walls. In certain instances, when a wall or barrier does not meet the required height or does not descend all the way to the ground, we apply the principles of *gud achit*–extend the wall downwards or *gud asik*– extend the wall upwards. When the proper conditions are met, Jewish law considers the wall to be raised to the required height or lowered to the ground even though it does not physically extend there.

TEXT 11A: **Talmud, *Shabbat* 101a, *Baraita***

Rabbi Yosei the son of Rabbi Yehudah says:	רַבִּי יוֹסֵי בְּרַבִּי יְהוּדָה אוֹמֵר
If one stuck a pole in the [ground of the] public domain	נָעַץ קָנֶה בִּרְשׁוּת הָרַבִּים
and on top of it was a basket [four cubits wide]	וּבְרֹאשׁוֹ טְרַסְקָל
and one threw [an object from the public domain] and it landed on its top,	וְזָרַק וְנָח עַל גַּבָּיו
he is liable.	חַיָּיב
This proves	אַלְמָא
that we say: Extend the walls downward.	אַמְרִינָן גּוּד אָחִית מְחִיצָתָא

Fig #2 **The Case of Rabbi Yosei the son of Rabbi Yehudah**

Height=**10**
Area=**4x4** handbreadths

TEXT 11B: **Tosafot, *Shabbat* 49b, *Heim He'elu Kerashim***

They lifted boards etc.	הֵם הֶעֱלוּ קְרָשִׁים כו'
Even the sages,	אֲפִילוּ רַבָּנָן
who disagree with Rabbi Yosei the son of Rabbi Yehudah	דִּפְלִיגִי אֲרַבִּי יוֹסֵי בְּרַבִּי יְהוּדָה
in the case of one who stuck a pole [into the ground] of the public domain	גַּבֵּי נָעַץ קָנֶה בִּרְשׁוּת הָרַבִּים
on top of which was a basket,	וּבְרֹאשׁוֹ טְרַסְקָל
and they don't uphold the principle of "extend [the wall] downwards"—	וְלֵית לְהוּ גּוּד אָחֵית
will [nevertheless] admit with regard to the wagon	מוֹדוּ בַּעֲגָלָה
that it is considered a private domain,	שֶׁהִיא רְשׁוּת הַיָּחִיד
since the wagon itself has a height of ten	כֵּיוָן דְעֲגָלָה גוּפָהּ יֵשׁ אוֹרֶךְ בִּזְקִיפָה עֲשָׂרָה
and a width of [at least] four,	וְרוֹחַב אַרְבָּעָה
even though beneath it was a public domain.	אַף עַל פִּי שֶׁתַּחְתֶּיהָ רְשׁוּת הָרַבִּים
And in Chapter *Kol Gagot* I elaborated further.	וּבְרֵישׁ כָּל גַּגּוֹת הֶאֱרַכְתִּי יוֹתֵר

Tosafot (10th-13th centuries). A collection French and German Talmudic commentaries in the form of critical and explanatory glosses; written during the twelfth and thirteenth centuries. Among the most famous authors of Tosafot are Rabbi Yaakov Tam, Rabbi Shimshon ben Avraham of Sens, and Rabbi Shmuel ben Meir. Printed in almost all editions of the Talmud, these commentaries are fundamental to basic Talmudic study.

Fig. #3 The Levites Wagons with a Height of Ten Handbreadths (including their load)

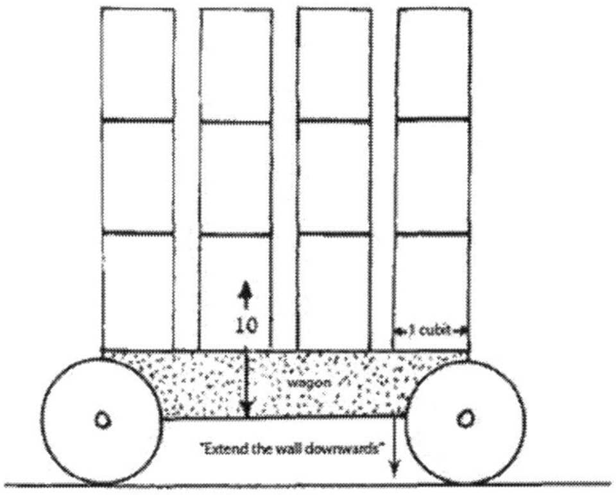

Part V

Discussion Question

In the previous lesson, we learned that *melachot* are constructive labors performed in the preparation of food, clothing, and shelter. How is transferring considered to be a constructive labor? Seemingly, its only effect is to transfer an object from one place to another, but the object itself is not changed. What creative accomplishment is contained in the act of transferring from one domain to another?

Transferring: The Least Constructive, Yet Most Essential *Melachah*

Transferring: A Weak *Melachah*

TEXT 12A: **Tosafot, *Shabbat* 2a, *Yetziot***

Rabbeinu Tam interprets	מְפָרֵשׁ רַבֵּינוּ תָּם
[the reason why the tractate] opens with [the laws of] carrying-out . . .	דְּפָתַח בִּיְצִיאוֹת . . .
since it is an inferior *melachah,*	מִשּׁוּם דִּמְלָאכָה גְּרוּעָה הִיא
as I will explain.	כְּמוֹ שֶׁאֲפָרֵשׁ

First Explanation

TEXT 12B: **Tosafot, *Shabbat* 2a, *Pashat***

Transferring is an inferior *melachah,*	הוֹצָאָה מְלָאכָה גְּרוּעָה הִיא
for what difference does it make whether one carries out from a private domain to a public domain	דְּמַה לִי מוֹצִיא מֵרְשׁוּת הַיָּחִיד לִרְשׁוּת הָרַבִּים
or one carries out from a private domain to [another] private domain?	מַה לִי מוֹצִיא מֵרְשׁוּת הַיָּחִיד לִרְשׁוּת הַיָּחִיד

Second Explanation

TEXT 13: **Ramban, *Shabbat* 2a, *Ve'lka***

It is novel and astonishing	חִידּוּשׁ הוּא
that in a private domain	שֶׁבִּרְשׁוּת הַיָּחִיד

one is permitted to carry a heavy load	מוּתָּר לִישָּׂא מַשָּׂא גָּדוֹל
yet if one carries out into the public domain [an item the size] of a fig, one is liable.	וְאִם הוֹצִיא לִרְשׁוּת הָרַבִּים כִּגְרוֹגֶרֶת חַיָּיב
This is not the case with regards to other *avot melachot*	מַה שֶּׁאֵין כֵּן בִּשְׁאָר אָבוֹת מְלָאכוֹת
whose [prohibitions] are not [dependent upon the] division of domains	שֶׁאֵינָן חֲלוּקוֹת בִּרְשׁוּיוֹת
but are prohibited in their own right.	אֶלָּא אִיסּוּרָן מֵחֲמַת עַצְמָן

Rabbi Moshe ben Nachman (1194–1270). Also known as Nachmanides or by the acronym *Ramban*; Considered the foremost authority on Jewish law of his time. Nachmanides authored a popular biblical commentary which includes kabbalistic insights. Born in Spain, he served as leader of Iberian Jewry. He was summoned by King James of Aragon, to a public disputation with Pablo Cristiani, a Jewish apostate, in 1263. Resulting persecution led to his eventual expulsion from Spain. Settling in Israel, Nachmanides helped reestablish communal life in Jerusalem.

Third Explanation

TEXT 14: *Or Zarua,* Vol 2 section 82

And one who carries out	וְהַמּוֹצִיא
Later in Chapter *HaZoreik*, [the Talmud] inquires	לְקַמָּן בְּפֶּרֶק הַזּוֹרֵק בָּעֵי
where carrying out is written [in the Torah].	הוֹצָאָה הֵיכָא כְּתִיבָה
It does not attempt to derive it from the *Mishkan*	וְלֹא בָּעֵי לְמֵילְפָה מִמִּשְׁכָּן
even though it was performed in the *Mishkan*	אַף עַל גַּב דְּהַוְיָא בְּמִשְׁכָּן
since it was not a significant labor,	מִשּׁוּם דִּמְלָאכָה שֶׁאֵינָה חֲשׁוּבָה [הִיא]
for what creative labor is accomplished by transferring [an object] from a domain?	דְּמַה מְלָאכָה עָשָׂה שֶׁהוֹצִיאוֹ מֵרְשׁוּת
It was an object and now too it remains an object!	מֵעִיקָּרָא חֵפֶץ וְהַשְׁתָּא נַמִּי חֵפֶץ

Rabbi Yitzchak ben Moshe of Vienna (ca. 1180–1250). Student of the German Tosafists. His fame comes from his halachik work and commentary to the Talmud, *Or Zaruah*. This work was subsequently quoted by many halachic authorities and is influential in Jewish law. His son Rabbi Chaim wrote a compendium of his father's work, which for many generations was the only widely used version of the *Or Zaruah*. In the 19th century, the original work was found and published. Among his students was the *Maharam* of Rothenburg.

Table 3

	Tosafot	Ramban	*Or Zarua*
Weakness of Transferring	**Counterintuitive:** Little difference between one domain and another	**Counterintuitive:** No distinction between heavier and lighter items	Nothing constructive about it

The Need For a Biblical Source

TEXT 15A: **Talmud, *Shabbat* 96b**

Where is carrying-out itself written in the Torah?	הוֹצָאָה גּוּפָהּ הֵיכָא כְּתִיבָא
Rabbi Yochanan said:For scripture states	אָמַר רַבִּי יוֹחָנָן דְּאָמַר קְרָא
"And Moses commanded, and they sounded the proclamation in the camp . . ."	(שמות לו) וַיְצַו מֹשֶׁה וַיַּעֲבִירוּ קוֹל בַּמַּחֲנֶה
Where did Moses reside?	מֹשֶׁה הֵיכָן הֲוָה יָתִיב
In the camp of the Levites	בְּמַחֲנֵה לְוִיָּה
and the camp of the Levites was a public domain	וּמַחֲנֵה לְוִיָּה רְשׁוּת הָרַבִּים הֲוָאי
and [Moses was in effect] saying to the Israelites:	וְקָאָמַר לְהוּ לְיִשְׂרָאֵל
Do not take out and bring [materials for the construction of the *Mishkan*]	לֹא תַפִּיקוּ וְתֵיתוּ
from your private domain to the public domain.	מֵרְשׁוּת הַיָּחִיד דִּידְכוּ לִרְשׁוּת הָרַבִּים

TEXT 15B: **Exodus 16: 29**

See that G-d has given you the Shabbat;	**רְאוּ כִּי ה' נָתַן לָכֶם הַשַּׁבָּת**
therefore He will give you on the sixth day	**עַל כֵּן הוּא נֹתֵן לָכֶם בַּיּוֹם הַשִּׁשִּׁי**
bread for two days;	**לֶחֶם יוֹמָיִם**
every man should reside in his place,	**שְׁבוּ אִישׁ תַּחְתָּיו**

let no man go out of his place on the seventh day	אַל יֵצֵא אִישׁ מִמְּקֹמוֹ בַּיּוֹם הַשְּׁבִיעִי

TEXT 15C: Jeremiah 17:22

Do not take out a load from your houses on the Shabbat day	וְלֹא תוֹצִיאוּ מַשָּׂא מִבָּתֵּיכֶם בְּיוֹם הַשַּׁבָּת

Transferring: A Central *Melachah*

E Pluribus Unum

TEXT 16: *Tanya*, Chapter 33

This is the meaning of the verse, "Let Israel rejoice in its Maker(s),"	וְזֶהוּ שֶׁכָּתוּב יִשְׂמַח יִשְׂרָאֵל בְּעוֹשָׂיו
meaning: Whoever is of the seed of Israel	פֵּירוּשׁ שֶׁכָּל מִי שֶׁהוּא מִזֶּרַע יִשְׂרָאֵל
ought to rejoice in the joy of G-d,	יֵשׁ לוֹ לִשְׂמוֹחַ בְּשִׂמְחַת ה'
who is happy and joyous with His abode amongst the creatures of the lower spheres,	אֲשֶׁר שָׂשׂ וְשָׂמֵחַ בְּדִירָתוֹ בְּתַחְתּוֹנִים
who are on the level of the actual physical [world of] *Asiyah*.	שֶׁהֵם בְּחִינַת עֲשִׂיָּה גַּשְׁמִיִּת מַמָּשׁ
For this reason, the plural form "makers" is used,	וְזֶהוּ שֶׁכָּתוּב בְּעוֹשָׂיו לָשׁוֹן רַבִּים
for it refers to our physical world that is filled with *kelipot* and *sitra achra*	שֶׁהוּא עוֹלָם הַזֶּה הַגַּשְׁמִי הַמָּלֵא קְלִיפּוֹת וְסִטְרָא אַחֲרָא
which is called a public domain, [i.e. a domain of multiplicity,] and "mountains of separation."	שֶׁנִּקְרָא רְשׁוּת הָרַבִּים וְטוּרֵי דִפְרוּדָא

[G-d's joy in the fusion of this plurality is aroused] when they are transformed into light and they become a private domain [i.e., a unified realm] for G-d's unity	וְאִתְהַפְּכָן לִנְהוֹרָא וְנַעֲשִׂים רְשׁוּת הַיָּחִיד לְיִחוּדוֹ יִתְבָּרֵךְ
through this faith [in G-d's unity].	בֶּאֱמוּנָה זוֹ

Rabbi Shne'ur Zalman of Liadi (1745–1812). Known as "the Alter Rebbe" and "the Rav"; Born in Liozna, Belarus; buried in Hadiach, Ukraine; Chassidic Rebbe and founder of the Chabad movement; among the principle students of the Magid of Mezeritch. His numerous works include the *Tanya,* an early classic of Chassidism; *Torah Or and Likutei Torah*, and *Shulchan Aruch HaRav,* a rewritten code of Jewish law. He was succeeded by his son, Rabbi Dovber of Lubavitch.

TEXT 17: **Exodus 16:23**

Tomorrow is a rest day, a holy Shabbat for G-d.	**שַׁבָּתוֹן שַׁבַּת קֹדֶשׁ לַה' מָחָר**

Moshit—Passing

TEXT 18: **Talmud, *Shabbat* 49b**

They transferred from wagon to wagon	הֵם הוֹצִיאוּ מֵעֲגָלָה לַעֲגָלָה
and you likewise should not transfer from one private domain to another.	וְאַתֶּם לֹא תוֹצִיאוּ מֵרְשׁוּת הַיָּחִיד לִרְשׁוּת הַיָּחִיד
From one private domain to another. What is he doing?	מֵרְשׁוּת הַיָּחִיד לִרְשׁוּת הַיָּחִיד מַאי קָא עָבִיד
Abaye and Rava both say—	אַבַּיֵי וְרָבָא דְאַמְרֵי תַּרְוַיְיהוּ
others say it was Rav Adda bar Ahavah—	וְאִיתֵּימָא רַב אַדָּא בַּר אַהֲבָה
[The *baraita* speaks of transfer] from one private domain to another private domain by way of the public domain.	מֵרְשׁוּת הַיָּחִיד לִרְשׁוּת הַיָּחִיד דֶּרֶךְ רְשׁוּת הָרַבִּים

TEXT 19: **Rashi, *ad loc.***

By way of the public domain	דֶּרֶךְ רְשׁוּת הָרַבִּים
for the airspace between the wagons is a public domain.	דַּאֲוִיר שֶׁבֵּין הָעֲגָלוֹת רְשׁוּת הָרַבִּים

TEXT 20: **Mishnah, 11:2**

[If there are] two balconies, one opposite the other, in a public domain,	שְׁתֵּי גְזוּזְטְרָאוֹת זוֹ כְּנֶגֶד זוֹ בִּרְשׁוּת הָרַבִּים
one who hands over or throws an object from one to the other	הַמּוֹשִׁיט וְהַזּוֹרֵק מִזּוֹ לָזוֹ
is exempt.	פָּטוּר
If both [balconies] were on one side,	הָיוּ שְׁתֵּיהֶן בִּדְיוֹטָא אַחַת
one who passes is liable,	הַמּוֹשִׁיט חַיָּב
[whereas] one who throws is exempt,	וְהַזּוֹרֵק פָּטוּר
for this was the manner of the work of the Levites [when loading the *Mishkan* boards onto the wagons for transport from one encampment to another].	שֶׁכַּךְ הָיְתָה עֲבוֹדַת הַלְוִיִּם
There would be two wagons, one after the other in the public domain,	שְׁתֵּי עֲגָלוֹת זוֹ אַחַר זוֹ בִּרְשׁוּת הָרַבִּים
and they would pass the boards from this [wagon] to the other,	מוֹשִׁיטִין הַקְּרָשִׁים מִזּוֹ לָזוֹ
but they would not throw them.	אֲבָל לֹא זוֹרְקִין

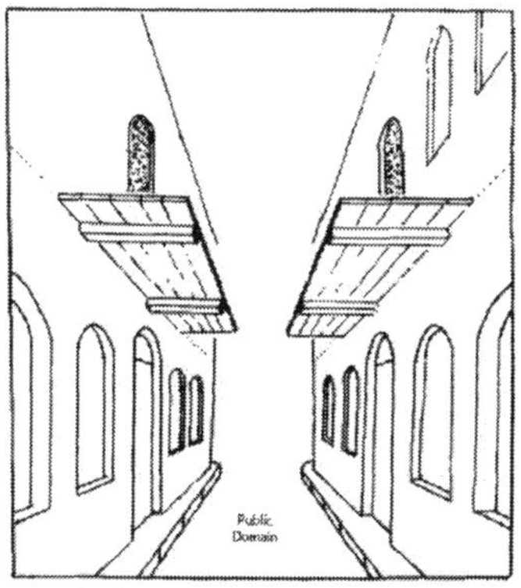

Two balconies one opposite the other on two sides of the public domain

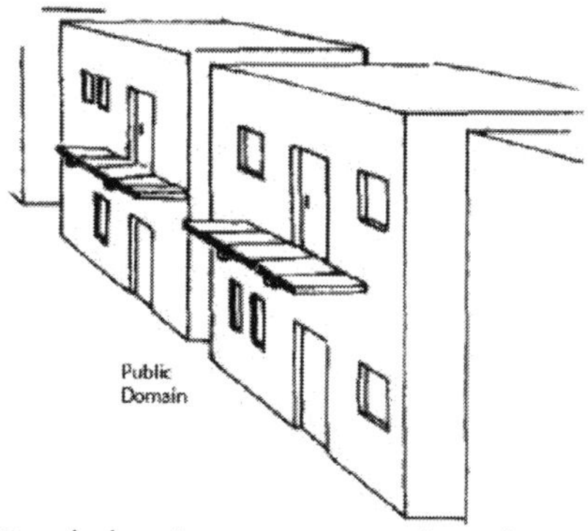

Two balconies one next to the other on one side of the public domain

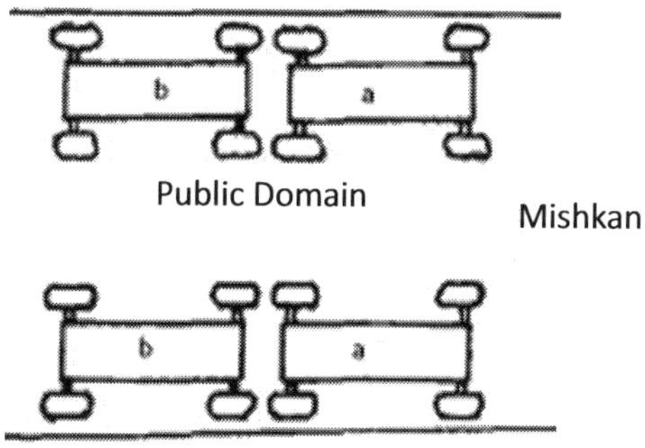

Formation of the Levites wagons

TEXT 21: **Ramban, *Shabbat* 2a, *Velka***

Carrying out is an innovation . . .	. . . הוֹצָאָה חִידוּשׁ הוּא
Because it is innovative,	הוֹאִיל וְחִידוּשׁ הוּא
nothing more can be derived from it,	אֵין לְךָ בָּהּ
beyond the actual innovation.	אֶלָּא חִדּוּשָׁהּ בִּלְבָד

Key Points

1. The Talmud quotes a *baraita* to support the view of Rabbi Chanina that we derive the number of thirty-nine *melachot* from the *Mishkan* and not from the mentions of the word *melachah* in the Torah.

2. Rashi and Rav Hai Gaon dispute whether the *melachot* are derived solely from the construction of the *Mishkan* or also from its service.

3. The *melachot* represent man's efforts in preparing food, clothing, and shelter. When Mashiach comes, when this world has been fully transformed into a dwelling for G-d, there will be no need for such pursuits.

4. The *baraita* cites three *melachot* of transferring, indicating both a superiority and a weakness of this *melachah* in comparison to other *melachot*.

5. There is more Talmudic material on transferring than any on other *melachah*.

6. The Talmud seeks a unique source for it (something it does not do for other *melachot*).

7. There are multiple unique biblical sources for the *melachah* of transferring.

8. That transferring is a *melachah* is counterintuitive because it is determined not by a quality of the item itself (e.g., weight) as in the definition of other *melachot*, but by the boundary lines of domains, things entirely external to the object.

9. It is not a constructive *melachah*.

10. Transferring represents carrying in the products of our efforts from the public domain of the working world in which we labor to construct a Tabernacle for G-d into the private domain that is the domain of G-d's unity, i.e. making the Tabernacle (other *melachot*) a dwelling for G-d's unity.

11. An innovation cannot be extended to other instances so long as it remains an innovation.

Terms to Retain

A teaching of the sages of the Mishnah that was not included in the Mishnah	בְּרַיְיתָא
Following his opinion	לְשִׁיטָתוֹ
Carrying out	הוֹצָאָה
Uprooting	עֲקִירָה
Placing down	הֲנָחָה
Change of domain	שִׁינּוּי רְשׁוּת
Public domain	רְשׁוּת הָרַבִּים
Private domain	רְשׁוּת הַיָּחִיד
Public domain by Rabbinic sanction	כַּרְמְלִית
Non-prohibited domain	מָקוֹם פְּטוּר

Appendix

Chart: The Four Domains

Domain	Definition	Common Examples	Law	Status
Reshut HaRabim/ Public Domain	Public thoroughfare at least **16** cubits wide	A highway or a main artery in a large city	May not transfer to another domain (except *makom petur*) or more than **4** cubits within public domain	Scriptural
Reshut HaYachid/ Private Domain	Private area of at least 4x4 cubits, walled by partitions of at least ten hand-breadths height	A home or enclosed plot of land	May not transfer to another domain (except *makom petur*)	Scriptural
Makom Petur/ Exempt Area	Area less than **4x4** cubits or private area without walls of **10** handbreadths	Top of a tall fire hydrant, telephone booth, or electric wiring box	Permitted to transfer from or to public or private domain	Not restricted
Karmelit/ Rabbinic Public Domain	Area similar to public domain but lacking certain essential criteria	Side streets, narrow alleyways or public parks	Same as public domain by rabbinic mandate	Rabbinic

Lesson 4

Shabbat

Introduction

Melechet Machshevet

This course is comprised of two parts taken from two different chapters in Tractate *Shabbat* that each explain the *mishnah* that outlines the thirty-nine *avot melachot.* In the first part (lessons one to three), we learned that the activities involved in the construction of the Tabernacle define what is considered *melachah*, an activity prohibited on Shabbat. There we saw how the laws of Shabbat are derived from the activities involved in the construction of the Tabernacle.

In Section Two of this course, we will look at the Tabernacle paradigm to determine not so much **what** is considered *melachah*, but **how** *melachah* is performed. In this short introduction, we will focus on *melechet machshevet*, the term that best defines what a *melachah* is.

Introduction

Melechet Machshevet

TEXT 1A: **Exodus 35:33**

To perform all *melechet machshavet*. לַעֲשׂוֹת בְּכָל מְלֶאכֶת מַחֲשָׁבֶת

Keys to the Talmud

Shoresh

Perhaps the most important key to *lashon hakodesh*, biblical Hebrew, is knowledge of roots (*shorashim*), the sequences of (usually) three letters that convey a root meaning to all words in which they appear.

Examples of words and their roots:

ספרים (books), סיפור (story), לספור (to count), ספרות (literature) share the root of ס.פ.ר s.p.r. —counting, telling.

מכתב (letter), כתיבה (writing), כתובה (marriage document) share the root of כ.ת.ב *k.t.b.*—writing.

חשבון (account), מחשבה (thought), חישוב (calculation) share the root of ח.ש.ב *ch.sh.v.*—thinking or calculating.

לפתוח (to open), פתיחה (opening), פתחון (opener), פותח (open) from the root פ.ת.ח *f.t.ch.*—opening, and so on.

Learning Activity

Write/Pair/Share

Which of the following words, all built from the root *chet-shin-bet*, contain the correct context for the root as it appears in our key word, *machshevet*—מחשבת?

מַחֲשָׁבָה	*Machshavah*	Thought	
חוֹשֵׁב	*Chosheiv*	Skillful	
חָשׁוּב	*Chashuv*	Important	

TEXT 1B: Talmud, *Chagigah* 10a

Mishnah: The laws of Shabbat	הִלְכוֹת שַׁבָּת
are like mountains suspended by a hair	הֲרֵי הֵם כַּהֲרָרִים הַתְּלוּיִן בְּשַׂעֲרָה
for there are few scriptural references	שֶׁהֵן מִקְרָא מוּעָט
yet numerous laws.	וַהֲלָכוֹת מְרוּבּוֹת..
Talmud: What is the meaning of *like mountains suspended by a hair*?	גמרא מַאי כַּהֲרָרִין הַתְּלוּיִן בְּשַׂעֲרָה
The Torah forbade *melechet machshevet*	מְלֶאכֶת מַחֲשֶׁבֶת אָסְרָה תּוֹרָה
while *melechet machshevet* is not written.	וּמְלֶאכֶת מַחְשֶׁבֶת לֹא כְּתִיבָא

TEXT 1C: Rashi, *Chagigah 10a, Melechet Machshevet*

Melechet machshevet:	מְלֶאכֶת מַחֲשֶׁבֶת—
. . . this is only a slight hint.	. . . זֶהוּ רֶמֶז מוּעָט
Since *melechet machshevet* is not stated regarding Shabbat	דְּאִילּוּ מְלֶאכֶת מַחֲשֶׁבֶת בְּשַׁבָּת לֹא כְּתִיבָא
but is stated regarding the Tabernacle,	אֶלָּא בְּמִשְׁכָּן הוּא דִּכְתִיב

and since in *Parshat Vayakhel*, [the Torah] juxtaposed	וּלְפִי שֶׁסָּמַךְ בְּפָרָשַׁת וַיַּקְהֵל
the portion of Shabbat to the portion of the Tabernacle,	פָּרָשַׁת שַׁבָּת לְפָרָשַׁת מִשְׁכָּן
we learn [to apply] *melechet machshevet* to Shabbat.	אָנוּ לְמֵדִין מְלֶאכֶת מַחְשֶׁבֶת לְשַׁבָּת

Rabbi Shlomo Yitzchaki (1040–1105). Better known by the acronym *Rashi;* rabbi and famed author of the first comprehensive commentaries on the Talmud and Bible. Born in Troyes, Champagne, Rashi studied in the famed yeshivot of Mainz and Worms. His commentaries, which focus on the simple understanding of the text, are considered fundamental to Torah study. Since their initial printings, they have appeared in virtually every edition of the Talmud and Bible. Amongst Rashi's descendants, were many of the famed Tosafists of France.

Applications of *Melechet Machshevet*

TEXT 2A: **Exodus 31:4**

To devise skillful works, to work in gold, in silver, and in copper	**לַחְשֹׁב מַחֲשָׁבֹת לַעֲשׂוֹת בַּזָּהָב וּבַכֶּסֶף וּבַנְּחֹשֶׁת**

TEXT 2B: **Talmud, *Bava Kama* 2a**

That which was considered important in the Tabernacle	הַךְ דַּהֲוָה בְּמִשְׁכָּן חֲשִׁיבָא
is called an *av.*	קָרֵי לֵיהּ אָב

Check List

❑	פְּסִיק רֵישָׁא	*pesik reisha*	inevitable consequence
❑	דָבָר שֶׁאֵינוֹ מִתְכַּוֵין	*davar she'eino mitkaven*	unintended consequence
❑	מְלָאכָה שֶׁאֵינָה צְרִיכָה לְגוּפָה	*melachah she'einah tzerichah legufah*	inadvertent *melachah*
❑	מִתְעַסֵק	*mitasek*	substitute purpose
❑	כַּוָנָה לִמְלָאכָה	*kavanah limelachah*	intent to be *melachah*
❑	שִׁינוּי	*shinui*	unusual or backhanded manner
❑	גְרָמָא	*gerama*	indirect act of *melachah*
❑	מְקַלְקֵל	*mekalkel*	destructive act
❑	אֵינוֹ מִתְקַיֵים	*eino mitkayem*	temporary effect
❑	חֲצִי שִׁיעוּר	*chatzi shi'ur*	incomplete measure
❑	חֲצִי מְלָאכָה	*chatzi melachah*	incomplete *melachah*

Part I

Binyan Av: Setting a Precedent

Introduction

TEXT 3A: Talmud, *Shabbat* 73b

Plowing	וְהַחוֹרֵשׁ
It was taught in a *baraita*:	תַּנָא
plowing, digging, and furrowing	הַחוֹרֵשׁ וְהַחוֹפֵר וְהַחוֹרֵץ
are all one *melachah*.	כּוּלָן מְלָאכָה אַחַת הֵן

1+1+1=1?

TEXT 3B: Maimonides, Laws of Shabbat 7:2

One who plows, digs, or makes a furrow	אֶחָד הַחוֹרֵשׁ אוֹ הַחוֹפֵר אוֹ הָעוֹשֶׂה חָרִיץ
[has preformed] an *av melachah*,	הֲרֵי זֶה אָב מְלָאכָה
since each one of them plows the land,	שֶׁכָּל אַחַת וְאַחַת מֵהֶן חֲפִירָה בְּקַרְקַע
and they are all one.	וְעִנְיָן אֶחָד הוּא

Rabbi Moshe ben Maimon (1135–1204). Better known as Maimonides or by the acronym, the *Rambam*. Born in Cardoba, Spain. After the conquest of Cardoba by the Almohads, who sought to forcibly convert the Jews to Islam, he fled and eventually settled in Cairo. There he became the leader of the Jewish community and served as court physician to the vizier of Egypt. His rulings on Jewish law are considered integral to the formation of Halachic consensus. He is most noted for authoring the *Mishneh Torah*, an encyclopedic arrangement of Jewish law. His philosophical work, *Guide to the Perplexed,* is also well-known.

TEXT 4: *Shabbat* 73b, Rashi, *Melachah Achat*

Are all one melachah	מְלָאכָה אַחַת הֵן
He is only liable for one,	אֵינוֹ חַיָּיב אֶלָּא אַחַת
since they are all to soften the soil.	דְכוּלְהוּ לְרִפּוּיֵי אַרְעָא עֲבִידִי

Discussion Question

How does Rashi's explanation of how all three activities are one compare with Maimonides' explanation? What is the underlying difference between Rashi's and Maimonides' understanding of how to determine what is an *av* and what is a *toladah*?

Keys to the Talmud

Binyan Av

Binyan Av, **(somewhat literally, building of a general principle) is a rule in biblical hermeneutics in which the Torah establishes a precedent that we apply to similar instances in which the Torah does not explicitly mention the rule.**

TEXT 5: **Talmud, *Sanhedrin* 30a**

Once it has been stated "a witness shall not stand,"	מִמַּשְׁמַע שֶׁנֶּאֱמַר לֹא יָקוּם עֵד
do I not know that it is one?	אֵינִי יוֹדֵעַ שֶׁהוּא אֶחָד
Why must it state "one"?	מַה תַּלְמוּד לוֹמַר אֶחָד
This builds a general principle:	זֶה בָּנָה אָב
any place where the term "witness" is stated	כָּל מָקוֹם שֶׁנֶּאֱמַר עֵד
it denotes two	הֲרֵי כָּאן שְׁנַיִם
unless the verse specifies one.	עַד שֶׁיְּפָרֵט לְךָ הַכָּתוּב אֶחָד

Table 1

	Rashi	Maimonides
Av	Plowing	Plowing, digging a hole, and making a furrow
Toladah	Digging a hole, and making a furrow	
Definition of *Avot*	An **actual activity** from among **39** specific activities	**39 principles** derived from activities performed in the construction of the Tabernacle

Part II

Purpose

TEXT 6A: Talmud, *Shabbat* 73b

Rav Sheishet said:	אָמַר רַב שֵׁשֶׁת
If someone had a small mound [of earth]	הָיְתָה לוֹ גַּבְשׁוּשִׁית
and removed it:	וְנָטְלָהּ
in the house, he is liable on account of building;	בְּבַיִת חַיָּיב מִשּׁוּם בּוֹנֶה
in the field, he is liable on account of plowing.	בַּשָּׂדֶה חַיָּיב מִשּׁוּם חוֹרֵשׁ

TEXT 6B: *Shabbat* 73b, Rashi, *Bayit*

[In the] house:	—בַּיִת
—building is applicable	שַׁיָּיךְ בִּנְיָן
since he intends to level the floor.	שֶׁמִּתְכַּוֵּין לְהַשְׁווֹת קַרְקָעִיתוֹ

TEXT 6C: Shabbat 73b, Rashi, *Mishum Choreish*

On account of plowing	מִשּׁוּם חוֹרֵשׁ
since it softens the earth.	דִּמְרַפֵּי אַרְעָא

TEXT 7A: Talmud, *Shabbat* 73b, continued

Rava Said:	אָמַר רָבָא
If one had a hole and filled it:	הָיְתָה לוֹ גּוּמָא וְטָמְמָהּ
if in the house,	בְּבַיִת
he is liable on account of building;	חַיָּיב מִשּׁוּם בּוֹנֶה
if in the field,	בַּשָּׂדֶה
he is liable on account of plowing.	מִשּׁוּם חוֹרֵשׁ

TEXT 7B: **Shabbat 73b, *Rashi, guma***

If one had a hole and filled it —with dirt,	גּוּמָא וְטָמְמָה בֶּעָפָר—
this is considered plowing	הַיְינוּ חוֹרֵשׁ
since the dirt that he used for filling	שֶׁהֶעָפָר שֶׁמִּילְאָהּ בּוֹ
is soft and good for planting	הָוֵי רָפוּי וְטוֹב לִזְרִיעָה
and he leveled the ground	וְהִשְׁוָה לַקַּרְקַע
to be planted along with [the rest of] the field.	לִהְיוֹת נִזְרַע עִם הַשָּׂדֶה

Part III

Mekalkel: Destructive Activity

TEXT 8A: **Talmud, Shabbat 73b, continued**

Rabbi Abba said:	אָמַר רַבִּי אַבָּא
One who digs a hole on Shabbat	הַחוֹפֵר גּוּמָא בְּשַׁבָּת
only requiring its earth	וְאֵינוֹ צָרִיךְ אֶלָּא לַעֲפָרָהּ
is exempt	פָּטוּר עָלֶיהָ
even according to Rabbi Yehudah who said	וַאֲפִילוּ לְרַבִּי יְהוּדָה דְּאָמַר
that one who performs a *melachah* whose end is not needed	מְלָאכָה שֶׁאֵינָהּ צְרִיכָה לְגוּפָהּ
is [nevertheless] liable for it.	חַיָּיב עָלֶיהָ
This ruling applies when [the person] rectifies something.	הָנֵי מִילֵּי מְתַקֵּן
In this instance, however, he is destroying.	הַאי מְקַלְקֵל הוּא

TEXT 8B: **Rashi, *Shabbat* 73b, *Ela***

Only requiring its earth —to cover excrement.	אֶלָא לַעֲפָרָה לְכַסּוֹת צוֹאָה

TEXT 8C: **Rashi, *Shabbat* 73b, *Patur***

He is exempt [from liability] for the act …	פָּטוּר עָלֶיהָ
This does not constitute building [when it is performed] in a house	וְאֵין כַּאן מִשׁוּם בִּנְיַן בְּבַיִת
Since it is destructive	דְקִלְקוּל הוּא
and it is of no use for planting either.	וּלִזְרִיעָה נַמִי לֹא חַזְיָא
However, if he needed it	אֲבָל אִם הָיָה צָרִיךְ לָהּ
he is liable on account of building	חַיָּיב מִשּׁוּם בּוֹנֶה
According to the view of Rabbi Yehudah	לְרַב יְהוּדָה
in Chapter *HaMatznia* (*Shabbat* 93b)	בְּפֶרֶק הַמַצְנִיעַ (שבת צג, ב)
regarding one who carries out a dead corpse in a bed.	גַּבֵּי מוֹצִיא אֶת הַמֵת בְּמִטָה

TEXT 8D: ***Shabbat* 73b, Rashi, *Metakein***

Rectifies	מְתַקֵן
as in carrying out a dead corpse for burial	כְּמוֹ מוֹצִיא אֶת הַמֵת לְקוֹבְרוֹ
he does not desire the carrying out itself	אֵינוֹ צָרִיךְ לְגוּפָהּ דְהוֹצָאָה
nor [does he require] the corpse	וְלֹא לַמֵת
but [his intent is]to empty his home	אֶלָא לְפַנוֹת בֵּיתוֹ
while [an example of] carrying out that is needed [is]:	וְהוֹצָאָה הַצְרִיכָה לְגוּפָהּ
[when,] for example, he needs a certain item in a different location.	כְּגוֹן שֶׁהוּא צָרִיךְ לְחֵפֶץ זֶה בְּמָקוֹם אַחֵר

Keys to the Talmud

***Melachah She'einah Tezrichah LeGufah*—Substitute Purpose**

Optional Section

TEXT 8F: ***Shabbat* 73b, Rashi, *Mekalkel Hu***

He is ruining:	מְקַלְקֵל הוּא
his house.	—אֶת בֵּיתוֹ

TEXT 9: **Talmud, *Shabbat* 105b**

All acts of destruction are exempt.	כָּל הַמְקַלְקְלִין—פְּטוּרִין

Keys to the Talmud

***Mekalkel*—An Act of Destruction**

The *melachot* performed in the Tabernacle had a constructive purpose. Therefore, a *melachah* performed as a completely destructive act, *mekalkel* is not similar to its counterpart in the Tabernacle in this definitive respect. It is therefore not scripturally prohibited as *melachah*, even when it is identical to the labor in the Tabernacle in every other respect.

TEXT 10: ***Sanhedrin* 84b Rashi, *Kol HaMekalkelin***

All acts of destruction are exempt [from punishment for] the violation of Shabbat	כָּל הַמְקַלְקְלִין פְּטוּרִין בְּחִלּוּל שַׁבָּת
since the Torah states *melechet machshevet.*	דִּמְלֶאכֶת מַחֲשֶׁבֶת כְּתִיב

Keys to the Talmud

Patur

In Shabbat terminology, when the Talmud (or commentary) uses the term *patur*—exempt—in reference to *melachah*, it is exempting the deed from biblical penalty but the deed remains restricted by rabbinic mandate. Only when the Talmud uses the term *mutar,* permissible, is one allowed in principle to go ahead and perform that activity on Shabbat.

Table 2

חַיָּב	**Intentional violation** with witnesses and warning	Death by Stoning
חַיָּב	**Unintentional violation**	Sin offering
פטוּר (אֲבָל אָסוּר)	**Exempt** (but prohibited)	Scripturally permissible but prohibited by rabbinic mandate
מוּתָּר	**Permissible**	Permissible even by rabbinic law

The Sages' Responsibility to Create a Buffer Zone to Protect Biblical Law

TEXT 11A: Talmud, *Yevamot* 21a

And you shall guard my charge (Leviticus 18:30)	וּשְׁמַרְתֶּם אֶת מִשְׁמַרְתִּי
Make a guarding for my charge.	עֲשׂוּ מִשְׁמֶרֶת לְמִשְׁמַרְתִּי

TEXT 11B: Mishnah, *Avot* 1:1

Moses received the Torah from Sinai and handed it [to Joshua]...	מֹשֶׁה קִבֵּל תּוֹרָה מִסִּינַי וּמְסָרָהּ . . .
[and through the chain of tradition] to the members of the Great Assembly.	לְאַנְשֵׁי כְּנֶסֶת הַגְּדוֹלָה
They said: "...Create a fence around the Torah."	הֵם אָמְרוּ . . . וַעֲשׂוּ סְיָיג לַתּוֹרָה

Discussion Question

David Friedman lost his temper one Shabbat and smashed a plate and broke a window. Should his act be considered a *melachah*? If David's actions were entirely destructive, his act should not be considered a *melachah* but rather the exempt act of demolition—*mekalkel*. Perhaps, however, since his destructive activity gave expression to his anger, it serves some constructive purpose and should nonetheless be considered a *melachah*.

Constructive Destruction

Keys to the Talmud

The Role of Maimonides in Talmudic Exegesis

Maimonides wrote the first codification of Talmudic law. Although his predecessors (including the Ge'onim, Rav Alfasi (Rif), and others) clarified their positions on many issues in Jewish law, in his work *Mishneh Torah,* Maimonides authored the first genuine codification of Jewish law, and still the only one covering all its subject areas. Maimonides sets down the conclusions of Talmudic debate without confusing the reader with all the complex discussion that often leads up to the final ruling. In addition, Maimonides was the first to restructure the entire Talmudic law into a new, clear and rationally ordered system of categories. Maimonides' code broke new ground, and all subsequent codes, such as the *Tur* and the *Shulchan Aruch*, rely on it heavily.

Maimonides wrote the fourteen-volume *Mishneh Torah* in a style that begins every topic by first clearly defining the subject matter and subsequently enumerating its laws. It is therefore the custom of Talmudic scholars to scrutinize Maimonides' definition and description to gain insight into Maimonides' understanding of the Talmud's text and logic.

TEXT 12: **Maimonides, Laws of Shabbat 12:1**

One who ignites a fire of any size is liable	הַמַּבְעִיר כָּל שֶׁהוּא חַיָּב
when he needs the ashes.	וְהוּא שֶׁיְּהֵא צָרִיךְ לְאֵפֶר
If, however, he ignites a fire in a destructive manner, he is exempt,	אֲבָל אִם הִבְעִיר דֶּרֶךְ הַשְׁחָתָה פָּטוּר
since he is destroying (*mekalkel*).	מִפְּנֵי שֶׁהוּא מְקַלְקֵל

One who ignites a pile of grain belonging to another	וְהַמַּבְעִיר גְּדִישׁוֹ שֶׁל חֲבֵירוֹ
or torches his dwelling is liable	אוֹ הַשּׂוֹרֵף דִּירָתוֹ חַיָּיב
even though he destroys	אַף עַל פִּי שֶׁהוּא מַשְׁחִית
because his intent is to take revenge from his enemy.	מִפְּנֵי שֶׁכַּוָּונָתוֹ לְהִנָּקֵם מִשּׂוֹנְאוֹ
And, indeed, he becomes calmed and his anger is settled,	וַהֲרֵי נִתְקָרְרָה דַּעְתּוֹ וְשָׁכְכָה חֲמָתוֹ
just as one who rends [his clothing] over a deceased relative or out of anger, who is liable	וְנַעֲשָׂה כְּקוֹרֵעַ עַל מֵתוֹ שֶׁהוּא חַיָּיב אוֹ בַּחֲמָתוֹ
and as one who wounds another during a fight,	וּכְחוֹבֵל בַּחֲבֵירוֹ בִּשְׁעַת מְרִיבָה
since, in all these instances, they fulfill the intent of his evil inclination.	שֶׁכָּל אֵלּוּ מְתַקְּנִים הֵן אֵצֶל יִצְרָן הָרַע
Similarly, one who ignites a candle or firewood	וְכֵן הַמַּדְלִיק אֶת הַנֵּר אוֹ אֶת הָעֵצִים
to provide warmth or light is liable.	בֵּין לְהִתְחַמֵּם בֵּין לְהָאִיר הֲרֵי זֶה חַיָּיב
Heating metal to refine it in water	הַמְחַמֵּם אֶת הַבַּרְזֶל כְּדֵי לְצָרְפוֹ בַּמַּיִם
is considered a *toladah* [subcategory] of kindling for which one is liable.	הֲרֵי זֶה תּוֹלֶדֶת מַבְעִיר וְחַיָּיב

Optional Section

Introduction to Studying the Rogatchover Gaon's Works

Keys to the Talmud

***Chakirah*—Talmudic investigation**

***Chakirah* means "an investigation." It is used in Talmudic study halls to describe a method of Talmudic inquiry that involves examining two or more possible explanations for a given Talmudic concept or dilemma. The power of this approach is that it allows the student to weigh the various alternative approaches against each other and personally arrive at a definitive understanding of what the conclusion is and why it must be understood that way. It can be described as a logical experiment that allows the student to experience the logical process himself. It also works as a process of elimination, as it involves ruling out other possible approaches to understanding the Talmud's logic until the last remaining possibility is affirmed as conclusive.**

Action or Outcome?

OPTIONAL TEXT 13: Rogatchover Gaon, *Dvinsk Responsa* Vol. 2 Responsum 35

The definition of kindling involves great dispute and requires much contemplation.	גֶדֶר הַבְעָרָה יֵשׁ בָּזֶה מַחְלוֹקֶת גְדוֹלָה וְעִיוּן רַב
Is the *melachah* the existence of fire,	אִם הַמְלָאכָה הוּא מְצִיאוּת הָאֵשׁ
and conversely, removing a fire,	וּלְהֵפֶך סִילוּק הָאֵשׁ
or is it the consumption caused by fire,	אוֹ מַה שֶׁעַל יְדֵי זֶה כָּלָה מַה שֶׁדוֹלֵק
and conversely, what remains, that which was not burnt?	וּלְהֵיפֶך מַה שֶׁנִשְׁאָר מַה שֶׁלֹא דָלַק
I have greatly elaborated upon this subject.	וְהֶאֱרַכְתִּי בָּזֶה הַרְבֵּה
The opinion of our great master Maimonides is	וְשִׁיטַת רַבֵּנוּ הַגָדוֹל הרמב"ם ז"ל הוּא
that the cause of liability is the act itself	שֶׁהַחַיָיב הוּא עֶצֶם הַדָבָר
and there is much evidence to support this.	וּרְאָיוֹת הַרְבֵּה
We have established that	דְקַיְימָא לָן

even one who kindles or extinguishes a fire of the least size is also liable.	מַבְעִיר וּמְכַבֶּה כָּל שֶׁהוּא גַּם כֵּן חַיָּיב
Similarly one who carries out a fire of any size is liable.	וְכֵן בְּמוֹצִיא אֵשׁ חַיָּיב בְּכָל שֶׁהוּא
If the liability were because of the substance that was burned,	וְאִם הֲוָה מִשּׁוּם דָּבָר הַנִּדְלָק
Each thing according to its type would require a minimum size	הֲוָה צָרִיךְ שִׁיעוּר כָּל אֶחָד כְּפִי מַה שֶּׁהוּא
[Kindling is thus different from] cooking, for which liability is only established from the substance that is cooked	אֲבָל בִּישֵּׁל דְּחַיָּיב רַק מִשּׁוּם דָּבָר הַנִּתְבַּשֵּׁל
for which there is a minimum required size, the size of a fig.	צָרִיךְ שִׁיעוּר כִּגְרֹגֶרוֹת

Rabbi Yosef Rosen (1858–1936). Also known as the "Rogatchover *Gaon*"; one of the prominent Talmudic scholars of the early 20th century. Born in Rogachev, Belarus, to a Chassidic family, his unusual capabilities were noticed at a young age. At thirteen he was brought to Slutsk to study with Rabbi Yosef Ber Soloveichik. For a full year he remained there studying primarily with the rabbi's son, the legendary Rabbi Chaim Soloveitchik. Later, he studied with Rabbi Moshe Yehoshua Leib Diskin. He was the Rabbi of the Chasidic community in Dvinsk, Latvia. His works, titled *Tzafnat Pa'neach*, are famed for both their depth and difficulty.

Key Points

1. *Melechet machshevet* defines the *melachah* that is prohibited on Shabbat as acts of intent, skill, or significance.

2. The thirty-nine *avot melachot* are,

- *according to Rashi,* thirty-nine specific activities that act as paradigms from which toladot are derived; whereas
- *according to Maimonides,* thirty-nine principles. Any activity that includes that principle is an *av,* activities that are similar to the principle are considered *toladot*

3. The purpose of the act defines the category it belongs to: in your home, digging is building, whereas in the field, digging is plowing.

4. Destructive acts are not *melachah.*

5. Destroying something to give expression to anger or grief can be considered constructive.

6. Maimonides rules, that the *melachah* of kindling is the act of kindling itself not the process of burning that produces charcoal.

7. Kindling to produce a byproduct best defines the *melachah* of kindling since *melachah* means an activity that has a constructive output.

Terms to Remember

Thought/Intent/Calculation	מַחֲשָׁבָה
Skill/Dexterity/Coordination	חוֹשֵׁב
Significant/Valuable/Prominent	חָשׁוּב
Liable	חַיָּיב
Exempt (but not permissible)	פָּטוּר
Prohibited (but not necessarily liable)	אָסוּר
Permissible	מוּתָּר
Precedent	בִּנְיַן אָב
Destroying	מְקַלְקֵל
Substitute purpose (an act not performed for its own sake)	מְלָאכָה שֶׁאֵינָה צְרִיכָה לְגוּפָא
Talmudic investigation	חַקִירָה

Lesson 5

Introduction

In the previous lesson, we covered the concepts of *melechet machshevet* and *mekalkel* and established an accurate definition of the *av melachah* of kindling a fire.

In this lesson, we will explore an aspect of *melechet machshevet* that relates to the skill and dexterity involved in a prohibited act. We will see that, in some instances, a particular method and manner is required for the act to be considered a *melachah*. We will learn about irregularities and how they shape the concept of *melachah*, and we will examine various possible sources for the *melachah* of milking.

Part I

Methods of Harvest

TEXT 1A: **Talmud, *Shabbat* 73b**

Reaping:	וְהַקּוֹצֵר
It was taught [in a *baraita*]:	תַּנָא
Reaping, cutting, and harvesting	הַקּוֹצֵר הַבּוֹצֵר וְהַגּוֹדֵר
collecting and plucking	וְהַמַּסִּיק וְהָאוֹרֶה
are all considered one *melachah*.	כּוּלָן מְלָאכָה אַחַת

TEXT 1B: **Rashi, *Shabbat* 73b, *Goder***

***Goder*:**	גּוֹדֵר
means harvesting dates.	בִּתְמָרִים
***UMoseik*:**	וּמוֹסֵק
means harvesting olives.	בְּזֵיתִים
***Oreh*:**	אוֹרֶה
means harvesting figs.	בִּתְאֵנִים

Rabbi Shlomo Yitzchaki (1040–1105). Better known by the acronym *Rashi;* rabbi and famed author of the first comprehensive commentaries on the Talmud and Bible. Born in Troyes, Champagne, Rashi studied in the famed yeshivot of Mainz and Worms. His commentaries, which focus on the simple understanding of the text, are considered fundamental to Torah study. Since their initial printings, they have appeared in virtually every edition of the Talmud and Bible. Amongst Rashi's descendants, were many of the famed Tosafists of France.

Discussion Questions

What newfound understanding does the Talmud convey by telling us that reaping, cutting, harvesting, collecting, and plucking are all one *melachah*? In what ways do these forms of harvest essentially differ from each other? In what ways are they similar? Is the harvest of other crops so different from reaping grain that it might not have been included in the *melachah* of reaping?

Style and Purpose

The Talmud in the Codes

TEXT 2A: **Maimonides, Laws of Shabbat 7:4**

The same is true of one who reaps grain or legumes	אֶחָד הַקּוֹצֵר תְּבוּאָה אוֹ קִטְנִית
or cuts grapes or harvests dates	אוֹ הַבּוֹצֵר עֲנָבִים אוֹ הַגּוֹדֵר תְּמָרִים
or collects olives or plucks figs —	אוֹ הַמּוֹסֵק זֵיתִים אוֹ הָאוֹרֶה תְּאֵנִים
these are all one *av melachah*	כָּל אֵלּוּ אָב מְלָאכָה אַחַת הֵן
since each one of them is intended to uproot something from its source of growth.	שֶׁכָּל אַחַת מֵהֶן לַעֲקוֹר דָּבָר מִגִּידּוּלָיו מִתְכַּוֵּון

Rabbi Moshe ben Maimon (1135–1204). Better known as Maimonides or by the acronym, the Rambam. Born in Cardoba, Spain. After the conquest of Cardoba by the Almohads, who sought to forcibly convert the Jews to Islam, he fled and eventually settled in Cairo. There he became the leader of the Jewish community and served as court physician to the vizier of Egypt. His rulings on Jewish law are considered integral to the formation of Halachic consensus. He is most noted for authoring the *Mishneh Torah*, an encyclopedic arrangement of Jewish law. His philosophical work, *Guide to the Perplexed*, is also well-known.

TEXT 2B: ***Beit HaBechirah LeHaMeiri, Shabbat 73a, HaKotzer***

One who reaps	הַקּוֹצֵר
That is the *av* [*melachah*] with regard to [things that grow from] seeds	וְהוּא אָב לִזְרָעִים
And its *toladot* [include:]	וְתוֹלָדוֹת שֶׁלּוֹ
cutting grapes, harvesting dates	בּוֹצֵר בַּעֲנָבִים וְגוֹדֵר בִּתְמָרִים
Collecting olives, plucking figs and the like.	וּמוֹסֵק בְּזֵיתִים וְאוֹרֶה בִּתְאֵנִים וְדוֹמֵיהֶן

Rabbi Menachem HaMeiri (1249–1310). Born in the Provence, France; famous rabbi, Talmudist and authority on Jewish law. His monumental work *Beit HaBechirah* is a digest summarizing the discussions of the Talmud along with the commentaries of the major subsequent rabbis in a lucid style and language. Despite its stature, the work was largely unknown for many generations, and is thus excluded from general consensus of rabbinic law.

Learning Exercise

(Write/Pair/Share)

Identify the primary difference between Maimonides' and Meiri's codification of our *sugya*:

Maimonides	Meiri

Shemitah

TEXT 3: Leviticus 25:4-5

And in the seventh year	וּבַשָּׁנָה הַשְּׁבִיעִת
the land shall have complete rest,	שַׁבַּת שַׁבָּתוֹן יִהְיֶה לָאָרֶץ
a *Shabbat* for G-d—	שַׁבָּת לַה'
your field you shall not sow	שָׂדְךָ לֹא תִזְרָע
and your vineyard you shall not prune.	וְכַרְמְךָ לֹא תִזְמֹר
The after-growth of your harvest you shall not reap	אֵת סְפִיחַ קְצִירְךָ לֹא תִקְצוֹר
and the grapes you set aside for yourself you shall not cut;	וְאֶת עִנְּבֵי נְזִירֶךָ לֹא תִבְצֹר
it shall be a year of rest for the land.	שְׁנַת שַׁבָּתוֹן יִהְיֶה לָאָרֶץ

TEXT 4: Talmud, *Moed Katan* 3a

Cutting grapes is included in [the *melachah* of] reaping.	בְּצִירָה בִּכְלַל קְצִירָה
What law did the Merciful One intend in writing it?	לְמַאי הִלְכְתָא כְּתָבִינְהוּ רַחֲמָנָא
To teach	לְמֵימְרָא
that only for these *toladot* is one liable,	דְאַהַנֵי תּוֹלָדוֹת מִיחַיֵּיב
but for others [*toladot*], one is not liable.	אַאַחְרַנֵייתָא לֹא מִיחַיֵּיב

Table 1

		Maimonides		Meiri
Reaping Grain	Detaching the stalk from the organism's source of nourishment	***Av***		***Av***
Cutting Grapes	Detaching the fruit **only from the branch,** not the organism's ultimate source of nourishment	***Shabbat***	**Av: *Melechet Machshevet*** —For Shabbat— similarity of purpose overrides style differences	***Toladah***
		Sabbatical Year	***Toladah***	***Toladah***

Part II

Perspectives and Differences: The Flowerpot

Discussion Question

What better defines the *av melachah* of reaping:

—severing a growing thing from its place of attachment

or

—removing a growing thing from its life source?

Keys to the Talmud

***Nafka Mina*—"What emerges from it?"**

The term *nafka mina* is closely associated with a *chakirah.* When a Talmudic argument asks for the *nafka mina* between two opinions, it is trying to identify the practical difference in outcome that would occur from following out each of the differing views. By bringing what is often an abstract logical debate down to real-world outcomes, this method demonstrates sharply the differences between the two perspectives in the *chakirah*.

TEXT 5: Talmud, *Shabbat* 81b

If [a perforated flowerpot] was resting on the ground	הָיָה מוּנָּח עַל גַּבֵּי קַרְקַע
and he placed it on top of pegs,	וְהִנִּיחוֹ עַל גַּבֵּי יְתֵדוֹת
he is liable on account of detaching.	מִיחַיֵּיב מִשּׁוּם תּוֹלֵשׁ
If it was resting on top of pegs	הָיָה מוּנָּח עַל גַּבֵּי יְתֵידוֹת
and he placed it on the ground,	וְהִנִּיחוֹ עַל גַּבֵּי קַרְקַע
he is liable on account of planting.	חַיָּיב מִשּׁוּם נוֹטֵעַ

TEXT 6: Rashi, *Chayav Mishum Tolesh*

He is liable on account of detaching—	חַיָּיב מִשּׁוּם תּוֹלֵשׁ
since it no longer benefits from the ground's vapor.	דְּאֵינוֹ נֶהֱנֶה שׁוּב מֵרֵיחַ הַקַּרְקַע
However, it is apparent to me	וְלִי נִרְאֶה
that this not really a true [Torah] liability	דְּהַאי חַיָּיב לָאו דַּוְקָא
but rather is prohibited [rabbincally] since it is similar to detaching.	אֶלָּא אָסוּר מִשּׁוּם דְּדָמֵי לְתוֹלֵשׁ

TEXT 7: **Maimonides, Laws of Shabbat 8:4**

A pile of earth upon which grass has grown—	גַּבְשׁוּשִׁית שֶׁל עָפָר שֶׁעָלוּ בָּהּ עֲשָׂבִים
if he lifted it from the ground and placed it upon pegs	הִגְבִּיהָהּ מֵעַל הָאָרֶץ וְהִנִּיחָהּ עַל גַּבֵּי יְתֵדוֹת
he is liable on account of plucking.	חַיָּב מִשּׁוּם תּוֹלֵשׁ

Table 2

		Rashi	Maimonides
Chakirah	Definition of the *melachah* of reaping	Severing a growing thing from its place of attachment	Removing a growing thing from its life source
Nafka Mina	Lifting a flowerpot off the ground	Not a *melachah* (prohibited only by Rabbinic sanction)	Liable on account of the *melachah* of reaping

Part III

Unconventional Methods: Microwave Cooking

TEXT 8: **Talmud, *Shabbat* 73b**

Rav Pappa said:	אָמַר רַב פָּפָּא
One who throws a lump of dirt at a palm tree	הַאי מַאן דְשָׁדָא פִּיסָא לְדִיקְלָא
and dislodges dates	וְאַתַּר תַּמְרֵי
is liable on two counts,	חַיָּיב שְׁתַּיִם
one on account of detaching	אַחַת מִשּׁוּם תּוֹלֵשׁ

and one on account of extracting.	וְאַחַת מִשּׁוּם מְפָרֵק
Rav Ashi said:	רַב אַשִׁי אָמַר
This is not the ordinary manner of detaching	אֵין דֶּרֶךְ תְּלִישָׁה בְּכַךְ
and this is not the ordinary manner of stripping.	וְאֵין דֶּרֶךְ פְּרִיקָה בְּכַךְ

TEXT 9: **Rashi, *Shabbat* 73b, *DeShada***

Throws a lump of dirt at a palm tree	דְשָׁדָא פִּיסָא לְדִיקְלָא
He threw a clod of earth at a palm tree	זָרַק פִּיסַת רְגָבִים לְדֶקֶל
And severed some dates	וְאַתַּר תַּמְרֵי
He caused the dates to fall.	הֵשִׁיר הַתְּמָרִים

TEXT 10: **Rashi, *Shabbat* 73b, *Ein Derech***

This is not the normal method of detaching and extracting—	אֵין דֶּרֶךְ תְּלִישָׁה וּפְרִיקָה בְּכַךְ –
by means of throwing.	עַל יְדֵי זְרִיקָה
Rather, either it is performed by hand or with a utensil.	אֶלָּא אוֹ בְּיַד אוֹ בִּכְלִי
And this is detaching in a backhanded manner	וְתוֹלֵשׁ כִּלְאַחַר יַד הוּא
[for which] he is exempt.	וּפָטוּר

Keys to the Talmud

Shinui—a deviation—and *kile'achar yad*—backhandedly

One of the criteria of *melechet machshevet* is that the *melacha* must be a *ma'aseh choshev*, an act that is performed in the manner of a craftsman. In the absence of this condition, one is not liable for performing the *melachah*. A *shinui*, i.e., a deviation from the normal method of doing a *melachah*, can be enough to exempt a person from liability.

One instance of a *shinui* is *kil'eachar yad*—in a backhanded manner. Examples of performing a *melachah kil'eachar yad* include writing with one's left hand (for a right-handed person), and grinding with the handle of a knife or spoon. In most instances, rabbinic sanction, acting as a fence to protect the law, prohibits the performance of a *melachah* done with a *shinui* because of its similarity to the biblically prohibited act. Later in this lesson we will discuss the guidelines which determine when a *melachah* performed with a *shinui* is prohibited.

Table 4

Cooking in the sun	Permitted
Moving a perforated flowerpot	Resembles a *melachah*
Writing with the weaker hand	Not *melachah* because of irregular method

Unconventional Cooking

TEXT 11A: **Talmud, *Shabbat* 39a**

Rav Nachman said:	אָמַר רַב נַחְמָן
in the sun—all agree that it is permissible.	בְּחַמָּה דְכוּלֵּיה עָלְמָא לֹא פְּלִיגִי דְשָׁרֵי

Four Types of Cooking

Table 5

Scenario	Ruling
בִּישׁוּל בְּאוֹר Cooking directly on fire	Biblically prohibited
בִּישׁוּל בְּתוֹלְדוֹת הָאוֹר Cooking with derivatives of fire	Biblically prohibited
בִּישׁוּל בְּחַמָּה Cooking directly in the heat of the sun	Permissible
בִּישׁוּל בְּתוֹלְדוֹת הַחַמָּה Cooking on derivatives of the heat of the sun	Prohibited by rabbinic sanction because it appears no different from cooking on derivatives of fire

TEXT 11B: **Rashi, *Shabbat* 39a, *DeShari***

That it is permissible	דְשָׁרֵי
since this is not the normal method of cooking.	דְאֵין דֶרֶךְ בִּישּׁוּלוֹ בְּכַךְ

Flowerpots

TEXT 12: **Talmud, *Shabbat* 108a**

One who plucks [a plant] from a perforated flowerpot is liable	הַתּוֹלֵשׁ מֵעָצִיץ נָקוּב חַיָּיב
[but] from a non-perforated one, is exempt.	וְשֶׁאֵינוֹ נָקוּב פָּטוּר
There it isn't growing normally;	הָתָם לָאו הַיְינוּ רְבִיתֵיה
here it is growing normally.	הָכָא הַיְינוּ רְבִיתֵיה

TEXT 13: **Rashi, *Shabbat* 108a *Lav Hainu Revitei***

***It isn't growing normally*—**	לָאו הַיְינוּ רְבִיתֵיה –
It is not usual to plant there.	דְאֵין דֶרֶךְ זְרִיעָה שָׁם

Left-Handed Inscriptions

TEXT 14: ***Chelkat Mechokek, Shulchan Aruch Even HaEzer* 123:5**

After the fact, a *get* is kosher if written with the left hand	בְּדִיעֲבַד כָּשֵׁר הַגֵּט אִם כָּתַב בִּשְׂמֹאל
even if [the scribe] is not ambidextrous	אַף שֶׁאֵינוֹ שׁוֹלֵט בִּשְׁתֵּי יָדָיו
although with regard to Shabbat	אַף עַל גַּב דִלְעִנְיַן שַׁבָּת
if one wrote with his left hand it is not considered writing . . .	כָּתַב בִּשְׂמֹאלוֹ ל או כָּתַב הִיא . . .
since on Shabbat *melechet machshevet* is required.	דְבְּשַׁבָּת בָּעֵינַן מְלֶאכֶת מַחְשֶׁבֶת

Rabbi Moshe ben Yitzchak Yehudah Leima (ca. 1604–1657). Rabbi, author and famed halachic authority. Circa 1650 he assumed the rabbinate of Vilna where on the rabbinical court he served together with the renowned Rabbi Shabetai HaCohen, author of *Siftei Kohen*. He commenced authoring glosses to the *Even HaEzer* section of the Shulchan Aruch titled *Chelkat Mechokek*, but passed away before the project was complete. The incomplete work was subsequently printed by his son and is seen as an authoritative work of halachah.

Shinui of the Essence vs. *Shinui* in the Method

The Microwave

TEXT 15: *Igerot Moshe, Orach Chaim* vol. 3:52

It is certainly considered a method of *melachah*	וַדַאי שֶׁהוּא דֶרֶךְ מְלָאכָה
since they get so hot that they are able to cook	מֵאַחַר שֶׁהֵם חַמִים טוּבָא שֶׁיְכוֹלִין לְבַשֵׁל
. . . whereas heating in the sun . . . is not commonly used for cooking . . .	דְתוֹלָדוֹת הַחַמָה . . . אֵין הַדֶרֶךְ כָּל כַּךְ לְבַשֵׁל . . .
That being so, with a microwave oven	. . . וְאִם כֵּן בְּהַמְיַיקְר-וֵייו אָווֶעְן
that is as suited for cooking as actual fire,	שֶׁטוֹב לְבַשֵׁל בּוֹ כְּמוֹ בְּאֵשׁ מַמָשׁ
and with those who have such an oven	וְאֵלוּ שֶׁיֵשׁ לָהֶם תַנוּר כָּזֶה
use it more frequently than cooking on a fire,	. . . מִשְׁתַמְשִׁים בּוֹ יוֹתֵר מִבִּשׁוּל דְבְּאֵשׁ
its prohibition can certainly be derived from that of cooking on the fire	וַדַאי יֵשׁ לְמֵילַף מִבִּשׁוּל דְאוּר
that existed in the Tabernacle as a *toladah*—	בַּחֲשִׁיבוּת תוֹלָדָה דְהָיָה בְּמִשְׁכָּן
it is, with respect to all of its laws, just like the *av* of cooking on a fire	שֶׁהוּא לְכָל הַדִינִים כְּהָאָב דְבִשׁוּל עַל יְדֵי הָאוּר
In the scope of its prohibition, and its liability.	. . . לְאִיסוּר וּלְחִיוּב

Rabbi Moshe Feinstein (1895–1986). Rabbi and leading halachik authority of the 20th century. Born near Minsk, Belorussia; became rabbi of Luban in 1921; immigrated to the United States in 1937 and became the dean of Mesivta Tiferes Yerushalayim in New York. Rabbi Feinstein became the leading halachic authority of his epoch and his rulings are always considered. His halachic decisions have been published in a multi-volume collection titled *Igerot Moshe*. He also published works on the Talmud and was known for his fine character traits.

The Spiritual Message of *Shinui*

Optional Section

Identifying the *Melachah* of Milking

TEXT 16: **Rashi, *Shabbat* 73b, *Mefarek***

***Extracting*—**	מְפָרֵק
is a *toladah* of threshing	תּוֹלָדָה דְּדָשׁ
since one strips the grain from its husk,	שֶׁמְּפָרֵק תְּבוּאָה מִשִּׁבֳּלֶיהָ
an expression related to stripping a load from a donkey—	לָשׁוֹן פּוֹרֵק מִן הַחֲמוֹר
décharge[ment] in Old French	דישקארגיי"ר בלעז
(to unload or uproot something from its place	לִפְרוֹק מַשָּׂא לַעֲקוֹר דָּבָר מִמְּקוֹמוֹ
—Rabbeinu Levi).	(—רַבֵּינוּ לֵוִי[ה])
I have also found something similar in the responsa of Rabbeinu Meshulam the Gaon	וְגַם בִּתְשׁוּבַת רַבֵּינוּ מְשׁוּלָּם הַגָּאוֹן מָצָאתִי כֵּן
and this is similar, extracting dates from the clusters.	וְאַף זֶה מְפָרֵק הַתְּמָרִים מִן הַמַּכְבֵּדוֹת

TEXT 17: **Tosafot, *Shabbat* 73b *VeAchat Mishum Mefarek***

***And one on account of extracting*—**	וְאַחַת מִשּׁוּם מְפָרֵק
It does not appear to Rabbeinu Yitzchok to be as Rashi explains,	אֵין נִרְאֶה לר"י כְּמוֹ שֶׁמְּפָרֵשׁ רש"י
that he strips the tree of its load, [i.e.] from the fruit that are on it.	שֶׁמְּפָרֵק הָאִילָן מִמַּשָּׂאוֹ מִן הַפֵּירוֹת שֶׁעָלָיו
Rather, it is as Rabbeinu Shmuel explains,	אֶלָּא כְּמוֹ שֶׁפֵּירֵשׁ רַבֵּינוּ שְׁמוּאֵל
that the dates have an outer husk	שֶׁיֵּשׁ עַל הַתְּמָרִים קְלִיפָּה הָעֶלְיוֹנָה

and when he hits the dates	וּכְשֶׁהוּא מַכֶּה בִּתְמָרִים
he extracts the husk from the dates.	מְפָרֵק אֶת הַקְלִיפָּה מִן הַתְּמָרִים
It is similar to threshing	וַהֲוֵי כְּמוֹ דָשׁ
in that he extracts the grain from the stalk.	שֶׁמְפָרֵק אֶת הַתְּבוּאָה מִן הַשִּׁבּוֹלֶת

Tosafot (10th-13th centuries). A collection French and German Talmudic commentaries in the form of critical and explanatory glosses; written during the twelfth and thirteenth centuries. Among the most famous authors of Tosafot are Rabbi Yaakov Tam, Rabbi Shimshon ben Avraham of Sens, and Rabbi Shmuel ben Meir. Printed in almost all editions of the Talmud, these commentaries are fundamental to basic Talmudic study.

Tosafot: Milking

TEXT 18A: **Tosafot, *Shabbat* 73b, *Mefarek***

***Extracting*—**	מְפָרֵק
Rashi explains that it is a *toladah* of *threshing*.	פֵּירוּשׁ רשׁ״י דַהֲוָה תוֹלָדָה דְדָשׁ
Rabbeinu Tam finds this difficult	וְקָשֶׁה לְרַבֵּינוּ תַּם
since at the end of Chapter *HaMatznia* [the Talmud] says	אָמַר דִבְשִׁילְהֵי הַמַצְנִיעַ (לקמן צה.)
that one who milks is liable on account of extracting	דְחוֹלֵב חַיָּיב מִשּׁוּם מְפָרֵק
but were [extracting] a *toladah* of threshing,	וְאִי הֲוָה תוֹלָדָה דְדָשׁ
[it would contradict] the later statement (75a) regarding one who cracks open a *chilazon*	הָא אָמַר לְקַמָּן גַּבֵּי הַפּוֹצֵעַ חִלָּזוֹן
that according to the Rabbis there, threshing applies only to things grown from the ground.	דִלְרַבָּנָן אֵין דִישָׁה אֶלָּא בְּגִידוּלֵי קַרְקַע

TEXT 18B: **Tosafot, *Shabbat* 73b, *Mefarek***

And you cannot say	וְאֵין לוֹמַר
that only in the case of the *chilazon,* which is a type of fish,	דְדַוְקָא חִלָזוֹן שֶׁהוּא דָג
did the sages exempt him,	פַּטְרֵי רַבָּנָן
since it is not *gedulei karka,*	דְלֹא הָוֵי גִידוּלֵי קַרְקַע
but for milking they hold him liable	אֲבָל בְּחוֹלֵב מְחַיְּיבֵי
since an animal is considered *gedulei karka,*	דִבְהֵמָה חֲשִׁיבָא גִידוּלֵי קַרְקַע
as is evident that the beginning of chapter *BaKol Me'arvin.*	כִּדְמוּכָח בְּרֵישׁ בַּכֹּל מְעָרְבִין (עירובין דף כז,ב)

Gidulei Karka—"Grown from the Ground" or "Nourished from the Ground"?

Since [it must be that the sages' reasoning is that] they derive it (i.e. the prohibition of threshing) from the spices in the Tabernacle	דְהָא עַל כָּרְחָךְ טַעֲמָא דְרַבָּנָן מִשּׁוּם דְיַלְפִינָן לְהוּ מִסַמְמָנִין שֶׁבַּמִשְׁכָּן
then there is no threshing with anything other than plants.	דְאֵין דִישָׁה אֶלָא בְּגִידוּלֵי קַרְקַע
Compared to something that actually grows from the ground,	לְגַבֵּי דָבָר הַגָדֵל מַמָשׁ מִן הַקַרְקַע
an animal is not considered "grown from the ground,"	לֹא חֲשִׁיבָא בְּהֵמָה גִידוּלֵי קַרְקַע
as stated in chapter *HaSocher Et HaPoalim*:	כִּדְאַמְרִינָן בְּהַשׂוֹכֵר אֶת הַפּוֹעֲלִים (ב"מ פט.)
"Just as threshing is unique in that it applies to *gidulei karka*	מַה דַיִשׁ מְיוּחָד שֶׁהוּא גִידוּלֵי קַרְקַע
and [therefore] a worker may eat from it,	וּפוֹעֵל אוֹכֵל בּוֹ
similarly everything etc.	אַף כָּל כוּ'
[This comes] to exclude milking and making cheese, etc."	יָצָא הַחוֹלֵב וְהַמְגַבֵּן כוּ'

TEXT 18C: **Tosafot, *Shabbat* 73b *Mefarek***

And it would be a difficult position to assert	וְדוֹחֵק לוֹמַר
that the *baraita* in *HaMatznia* accords with Rabbi Yehudah who disagrees later on with the sages.	דִּבְרַיְיתָא דְהַמַּצְנִיעַ אַתְיָא כְּרַבִּי יְהוּדָה דִּפְלִיג לְקַמָּן אַדְּרַבָּנָן

TEXT 18D: **Tosafot, *Shabbat* 73b, *Mefarek***

It appears to Rabbeinu Tam	וְנִרְאֶה לְרַבֵּינוּ תָּם
That one who extracts is liable on account of smoothing	דִּמְפָרֵק חַיָּיב מִשּׁוּם מְמַחֵק
for when milking, one scrapes the udder and smooths it.	דִּכְשֶׁחוֹלֵב מְמַחֵק אֶת הַדַּד וּמַחֲלִיקוֹ

TEXT 18E: **Tosafot, *Shabbat* 73b, *Mefarek***

And this (approach of Rabbeinu Tam) is not apparent to Rabbeinu Yitzchak,	וְאֵין נִרְאֶה לְרַבֵּינוּ יִצְחָק
since in chapter *Chavit* (*Shabbat* 144b) we say	דִּבְפֶּרֶק חָבִית (לקמן קמד,ב) אַמְרִינַן
that one may milk directly into a pot of food but not into an empty dish	חוֹלֵב אָדָם לְתוֹךְ הַקְּדֵרָה אֲבָל לֹא לְתוֹךְ הַקְּעָרָה
but according to Rabbeinu Tam, there should be no difference between milking into a pot or a dish.	ולְרַבֵּינוּ תָּם מַה לִּי לְתוֹךְ הַקְּדֵרָה מַה לִּי לְתוֹךְ הַקְּעָרָה
However, according to the interpretation of Rashi, it comes out well	וּלְפֵירוּשׁ הַקּוּנְטְרֵס אָתֵי שַׁפִּיר
since initially when [the milk] was in the udder it was considered food	דְּמֵעִיקָּרָא כְּשֶׁהָיָה בְּדַדִּין חָשִׁיב אוֹכֶל

and when one milks into a pot [it is now] also considered food	וּכְשֶׁחוֹלֵב לְתוֹךְ הַקְּדֵרָה (דְּהַשְׁתָּא) נַמִּי הָוֵי אוֹכֶל
and it is not similar to threshing that causes a change [from inedible to edible].	וְלֹא דָּמֵי לְדָשׁ שֶׁנִּשְׁתַּנָּה

TEXT 18F: **Tosafot, *Shabbat* 73b, *Mefarek***

It appears that according to Rashi's interpretation the law accords with Rabbi Yehudah.	וְנִרְאֶה דִּלְפֵירוּשׁ הַקּוּנְטְרֵס הֲלָכָה כְּרַבִּי יְהוּדָה

From here until the end of Tosafot is not critical and may be skipped to save time.

Since it says in chapter *Af Al Pi* (*Ketubot* 60a):	דְּהָאָמַר בְּפֶרֶק אַף עַל פִּי (כתובות ס.)
Rabbi Marinus said: one who cries out of pain may suckle milk (directly from a cow) on Shabbat.	אָמַר רַבִּי מְרִינוּס גּוֹנֵחַ יוֹנֵק חָלָב בְּשַׁבָּת
What is the reason?	מַאי טַעְמָא
Since it is extracting in an unusual manner	מְפָרֵק כִּלְאַחַר יָד הוּא
and the rabbis did not decree [against it] when someone was in pain.	וּבִמְקוֹם צַעַר לֹא גָזְרוּ רַבָּנָן
And Rav Yosef rules there in accordance with Rabbi Marinus	וּפְסִיק הָתָם רַב יוֹסֵף הִלְכְתָא כְּרַבִּי מְרִינוּס
and it does not appear [plausible] to say that even according to the sages it is a rabbinic prohibition	וְאֵין נִרְאֶה לוֹמַר דְּאַף לְרַבָּנָן אָסוּר מִדְּרַבָּנָן
since it appears like stripping	דְּמֵיחְזֵי כִּמְפָרֵק
and although it is only prohibited by rabbinic mandate	וְאַף עַל גַּב דְּלֹא אַסִירָא אֶלָּא מִדְּרַבָּנָן
it was only permitted	לֹא שָׁרֵי
because there are two [reasons to permit:]	אֶלָּא מִשּׁוּם דְּאִיכָּא תַּרְתֵּי
[because it is performed in] a backhanded manner	כִּלְאַחַר יָד
and it is an instance of pain.	וּבִמְקוֹם צַעַר

Learning Exercise

Write/Pair/Share

List the reasons you have seen in Tosafot to support each position and to reject the other position. Include proofs from Talmudic sources.

Rashi (supported by Rabbeinu Yitzchak)	Rabbeinu Tam
Milking is a *toladah* of **threshing**.	Milking is a *toladah* of **smoothing.** Milking entails scraping and smoothing the udders (hide) of the cow.
Underlying reasoning: We are more focused on the purpose of the work.	**Underlying reasoning:** We look at the method of the forbidden act.
Proposition: Milking is a *toladah* of extracting. Extracting is the same *av* as threshing.	**Objection:** Sages (*Shabbat* 75a): Threshing applies only to *gidulei karka*, things grown from the ground.
Possible resolution: The law follows the opinion of Rabbi Yehudah that threshing applies even to non-*gidulei karka*, things that do not grow from the ground.	**Objection:** It is unlikely that the law would accord with Rabbi Yehudah who maintains that threshing is not limited to *gidulei karka,* and not the sages, for rarely does the minority prevail against a majority.
Proof: *Shabbat* 144b: One may milk directly into a pot of food but not into an empty pot. Rabbeinu Tam's understanding that milking is based on threshing cannot account for this ruling.	
Further Support: Rabbi Marinus' ruling also fits in better according to Rabbi Yehudah than according to the sages, thus suggesting that the Talmud does rule like Rabbi Yehudah and thereby removing Rabbeinu Tam's objection.	

Key Points

1. Although the styles of harvesting differ for each kind of plant, all methods are part of the one *melachah* of harvesting.

2. Maimonides maintains that all types of harvesting are part of the *av melachah*, whereas Meiri maintains that they are *toladot* of the *melachah* of harvesting.

3. The harvesting of grain is directly from its life-source, the ground, whereas other species are harvested not directly from the ground but from a plant or tree.

4. Harvesting is:

Rashi: Harvesting is the act of ***severing*** the produce from its life-source.
Maimonides: Harvesting is the act of ***removing*** a plant from its life-source.
Difference: whether removing a perforated flowerpot from the ground is considered harvesting.

5. A *melachah* that is performed with a *shinui* (not in the ordinary manner) is not considered a *melachah.*

6. There is a difference between a *shinui* in the defining essence of the *melachah* (cooking in the sun) and a *shinui* in the manner in which a *melachah* is performed (writing with weaker hand).

7. In the transformation of this world into an abode for G-d, both the end and the means are important to G-d.

Terms to Retain

A change	שִׁינּוּי
In an irregular, backhanded, manner	כִּלְאַחַר יַד
What emerges from it —the practical difference between two sides of a dispute	נַפְקָא מִינָּא
Reaping, one who reaps	קוֹצֵר
Threshing, one who threshes	דָּשׁ
Extracting, one who extracts	מְפָרֵק
Milking, one who milks	חוֹלֵב
Things that grow from the ground	גִּידּוּלֵי קַרְקַע
Smoothing, one who smooths	מְמַחֵק

Lesson 6

Introduction

One of the primary characteristics of the *melachot* is that they are acts of creation. On Shabbat we refrain from *melachah* to remind us that G-d rested from creation on the seventh day. Generally, *melachot* involve transforming the materials of the world into something newly useful; in this way they are creative acts. Planting grows something new; harvesting transforms vegetation into foodstuff; and cooking changes raw foodstuff into edible, prepared food.

There are several *melachot,* such as transferring, gathering and sorting, that do not seem to have this same creative aspect. Generally, *melachot* bring about a definitive, productive transformation. By contrast, these *melachot* do not involve the transformation of an essential substance from one state to another.

In this lesson, we will learn a *sugya* in the Talmud that focuses on several of these *melachot.* Our primary goal will be to discover, from the Talmudic perspective, what useful and productive change these *melachot* bring about.

Part I

Innovative Gathering

TEXT 1: Talmud, *Shabbat* 73b

Gathering together	וְהַמְעַמֵּר
Rava said:	אָמַר רָבָא
One who gathers salt from the *milchata* (salt evaporation pond)	הַאי מַאן דְּכָנִיף מִילְחָא מִמִּלְחָתָא
is liable on account of gathering.	חַיָּיב מִשּׁוּם מְעַמֵּר
Abaye retorts:	אַבַּיֵי אָמַר
Gathering applies only to items that are grown from the ground.	אֵין עִימּוּר אֶלָּא בְּגִידּוּלֵי קַרְקַע

Keys to the Talmud

Biblical Referencing

From time immemorial, the Written Torah has been the most authoritative source for any Jewish term, concept and phrase in the Hebrew language. In Talmudic study and likewise in any form of Torah study, whenever a doubt arises as to the meaning or origin of a word, term, or concept, we seek a verse in the Torah that will shed light on the matter. In addition, the Torah is accompanied by a wealth of commentary whose various perspectives offer together a well-founded basis for understanding almost any concept found in scriptural verse. Even in the creation of modern Hebrew, scholars use the Written Torah as the primary source and foundation for the formation of new words and terms.

Keys to the Talmud

Targum Yonatan ben Uziel

Yonatan ben Uziel, a disciple of Hillel the Elder, wrote the most authoritative *targum* (translation and interpretation) of the books of the Prophets (*Nevi'im*). In Talmudic times, communities would recite his commentary aloud together with the text of the Prophets in the recital of the *Haftarot*. His *Targum* is to the Prophets what *Targum Onkelos* is to the Torah. There is a place in Amukah in the north of Israel, that by tradition is the resting place of Yonatan ben Uziel. Many people flock to this holy site to pray for a blessing to find a spouse or to have children.

TEXT 2: Talmud, *Megilah* 3a

Rabbi Yirmiyah— some say it was Rabbi Chiya son of Abba—said:	וְאָמַר רַבִּי יִרְמְיָה וְאִיתֵּימָא רַבִּי חִיָּיא בַּר אַבָּא
The translation of the Torah [to Aramaic] was composed by Onkelos the convert	תַּרְגּוּם שֶׁל תּוֹרָה אוּנְקְלוֹס הַגֵּר אֲמָרוֹ
who learned it from Rabbi Eliezer and Rabbi Yehoshua.	מִפִּי רַבִּי אֱלִיעֶזֶר וְרַבִּי יְהוֹשֻׁעַ
The translation of the Prophets [to Aramaic]	תַּרְגּוּם שֶׁל נְבִיאִים
was composed by Yonatan son of Uziel	יוֹנָתָן בֶּן עוּזִּיאֵל אֲמָרוֹ
who learned it from [the prophets] Chagai, Zachariah and Malachi,	מִפִּי חַגַּי זְכַרְיָה וּמַלְאָכִי
and [when Yonatan composed the translation] the Land of Israel shook	וְנִזְדַּעְזְעָה אֶרֶץ יִשְׂרָאֵל
over an area of four hundred *parsangs* by four hundred *parsangs* [the entire area of Israel]	אַרְבַּע מֵאוֹת פַּרְסָה עַל אַרְבַּע מֵאוֹת פַּרְסָה.
and a heavenly voice emanated, saying:	יָצְתָה בַּת קוֹל וְאָמְרָה
Who is this that has revealed My secrets to mortal beings?	מִי הוּא זֶה שֶׁגִּילָּה סְתָרַיי לִבְנֵי אָדָם
Yonatan son of Uziel rose to his feet and said:	עָמַד יוֹנָתָן בֶּן עוּזִּיאֵל עַל רַגְלָיו וְאָמַר
I am the one who revealed Your secrets to mortal beings	אֲנִי הוּא שֶׁגִּלִּיתִי סְתָרֶיךָ לִבְנֵי אָדָם

It is revealed and known before you that I did it not for my own glory	גָלוּי וְיָדוּעַ לְפָנֶיךָ שֶׁלֹּא לִכְבוֹדִי עָשִׂיתִי
and not for the glory of my father's house.	וְלֹא לִכְבוֹד בֵּית אַבָּא
Rather I did it for Your glory,	אֶלָּא לִכְבוֹדְךָ עָשִׂיתִי
that disagreement should not spread amongst Israel.	שֶׁלֹּא יִרְבּוּ מַחֲלוֹקֶת בְּיִשְׂרָאֵל.
He further wished to reveal the translation of Scripture.	וְעוֹד בִּיקֵּשׁ לְגַלּוֹת תַּרְגּוּם שֶׁל כְּתוּבִים,
A heavenly voice emanated and said to him: You have done enough.	יָצְתָה בַּת קוֹל וְאָמְרָה לוֹ דַּיֶּיךָ
Why? Because it contains a reference to the end of days when Mashiach will come.	מַאי טַעֲמָא מִשּׁוּם דְּאִית בֵּיהּ קֵץ מָשִׁיחַ.

Milchata: Salt Evaporation Ponds

Let us now see how Rashi uses these building blocks (the scriptural verse and *Targum Yonatan*) to explain the meaning of the new term found in the Talmud: *milchata*.

TEXT 3: Rashi, *Shabbat* 73b, *DeChanif*

***Who gathers salt from the* milchata—**	דְּכָנִיף מִילְחָא מִמִּלְחָתָא
He collected salt from *misrefot mayim*	שֶׁצָּבַר מֶלַח מִמִּשְׂרְפוֹת מַיִם
which is translated (in *Targum Yonatan* to Joshua 11:8) as furrows of the sea	דְּמִתַּרְגְּמִינַן חֲרִיצֵי יַמָּא (יהושע יא)
that draw water into themselves from the sea,	שֶׁמַּמְשִׁיךְ לְתוֹכוֹ מַיִם מִן הַיָּם
the sun evaporates [the water]	וְהַחַמָּה שׂוֹרְפָתָן
and it becomes salt.	וְהֵן נַעֲשִׂין מֶלַח
That furrow is called [by the Talmud] a *milchata* (salt evaporation pond).	וְאוֹתוֹ חָרִיץ קָרֵי מִילְחָתָא

Rabbi Shlomo Yitzchaki (1040–1105). Better known by the acronym *Rashi;* rabbi and famed author of the first comprehensive commentaries on the Talmud and Bible. Born in Troyes, Champagne, Rashi studied in the famed yeshivot of Mainz and Worms. His commentaries, which focus on the simple understanding of the text, are considered fundamental to Torah study. Since their initial printings, they have appeared in virtually every edition of the Talmud and Bible. Amongst Rashi's descendants, were many of the famed Tosafists of France.

Defining the Act of Gathering

TEXT 4: **Rashi, *Shabbat* 73b, *Mishum***

On account of gathering together	מִשּׁוּם מְעַמֵּר
since it is also like gathering stalks (of grain).	שֶׁאַף הוּא כִּמְאַסֵּף בְּשִׁבָּלִין הוּא

Discussion Questions

This similarity between gathering salt and gathering stalks of grain seems obvious. What possible misunderstanding does Rashi wish to clarify? Why might we not have understood this on our own?

Exceptions to the *Melachah* of Gathering

Keys to the Talmud

Rishonim

The *Rishonim*, literally, "the first ones," were leading rabbis from the eleventh to fifteenth century CE, from the time following the *Geonim* up until the compilation of the *Shulchan Aruch*, the most widely-accepted code of Jewish law. Following the close of the Talmud, c. 500 CE, the leading rabbis, first called *Savura'im* and then later *Geonim,* spent more of their time in standardizing texts and issuing legal rulings than in the elucidation of and commentary on the Talmud. Thus, the *Rishonim* serve as the primary and earliest source of commentary and insight into the Talmud. Some of the more famous *Rishonim* include Rashi, the Tosafists, Maimonides, Raavad, Rif, Rosh, Rabbeinu Yonah, Rashba, Nachmanides, Ran, Ritva, Meiri and Mordechai.

Gidulei Karka

TEXT 5A: **Tosafot Rid, *Shabbat* 73b, *VeHaMe'amer***

If his fruit became scattered in his courtyard or field and he gathered them,	נִתְפַּזְּרוּ לוֹ פֵּירוֹת בַּחֲצֵרוֹ אוֹ בְּשָׂדֶה וְלִיקְטָן
should he be liable on account of gathering?	יִתְחַיֵּיב מִשּׁוּם מְעַמֵּר
The answer:	תְּשׁוּבָה
Gathering only applies at the time of detachment from the ground	אֵין מְעַמֵּר אֶלָּא בִּשְׁעַת תְּלִישָׁתוֹ מִן הַקַּרְקַע
since this is the beginning of its gathering.	שֶׁזֶּה הוּא תְּחִלַּת לִיקּוּטוֹ
But fruit that was already gathered and now became scattered—	אֲבָל פֵּירוֹת שֶׁנִּלְקְטוּ כְּבַר וְעַכְשָׁיו נִתְפַּזְּרוּ
this is not (the *melachah* of) gathering.	אֵין זֶה מְעַמֵּר

Rabbi Yeshayahu ben Mali of Trani (ca. 1180–1260). Italian rabbi and author. As one of the earlier rabbinic authorities on the Italian peninsula he authored works on the Talmud in two formats. One parallels the style of the Tosafot as critical and explanatory glosses; the other, an analysis of the variant opinions and rendering decisions in Talmudic law. Much of the latter work has been preserved by subsequent codifiers who quote him quite frequently.

TEXT 5B: ***Beit HaBechirah, Shabbat* 73b, *VeYesh Sho'alim***

In one's house it is permissible to gather	בְּבֵיתוֹ מוּתָּר לְעַמֵּר
since the manner of gathering is only in the place where he harvested.	שֶׁאֵין דֶּרֶךְ עִמּוּר אֶלָּא בְּמָקוֹם שֶׁקָּצַר שָׁם
. . . This is what they said: "Someone who gathers salt from the salt ditches . . ."	וְהוּא שֶׁאָמְרוּ דְּכָנִיף מִלְחָא מִמִּלְחָתָא . . .

Rabbi Menachem HaMeiri (1249–1310). Born in the Provence, France; famous rabbi, Talmudist and authority on Jewish law. His monumental work *Beit HaBechirah* is a digest summarizing the discussions of the Talmud along with the commentaries of the major subsequent rabbis in a lucid style and language. Despite its stature, the work was largely unknown for many generations, and is thus excluded from general consensus of rabbinic law.

Learning Exercise

As accurately as you can, try define the distinction between Tosefot Rid's and Meiri's exclusions from the *melachah* of gathering?

Write/Pair/Share

Tosefot Rid	Meiri

Gidulei Karka –Grown from the Ground

TEXT 6: ***Peri Megadim, Mishbetzot Zahav, Orach Chaim* 340:5**

Salt from the salt evaporation ponds (see Rashi, *Shabbat* 73b)—	וּמֶלַח מִמִּשְׁרְפוֹת הַמַּיִם עַיֵּין רש"י שבת ע"ג,ב
But [gathering] salt that is coarse like stone and [gathering] stones from the place where they were hewn	הָא מֶלַח גַּס כְּאֶבֶן וַאֲבָנִים מִמָּקוֹם שֶׁנֶּחְצְבוּ

is the actual *melachah* of gathering together and they are considered *gidulei karka* (grown from the ground).

הֲוֵי מְעַמֵר מַמָשׁ וְגִדוּלֵי קַרְקַע הֵם

Rabbi Yosef Teumim (1727–1792). Rabbi and prolific author; most famous for his comprehensive works on parts of the *Shulchan Aruch* titled *Peri Megadim*. He succeeded his father as Rabbi of Livov, Poland, and later served in Frankfurt Oder. He authored many works, mostly on Talmudic and halachic topics, which reveal profundity of wisdom and clarity of thought. His rulings are regarded with high esteem by subsequent authorities.

Discussion Question

What *nif'al*—productive outcome—is accomplished through gathering? Seemingly, there is no actual change in the substance, the only result is that previously it was scattered and now it is gathered. What inherent constructive difference does the act of gathering make?

Keys to the Talmud

Aliba DeHilchata—From a Legal Perspective

The Talmud is mostly not a book of theoretical discussions. The Talmud conveys the deliberations of the Oral Tradition as it determines the rules and the implications of the law that G-d gave to Moses at Sinai. The Talmud's many discussions often revolve around how to understand and apply that law to different circumstances. In essence, the Talmud contains in potential form the beginnings of a code of Jewish law, organizing biblical law into general subject matters. However, the Talmud leaves many of its disputes unresolved. Furthermore, Talmudic discussions are subject to differences of interpretation, resulting in differences of opinion among the *rishonim* and *acharonim* (later commentators) as to what the final decision should be. Thus, later rabbis found it necessary to distill the many disputes and discussions into an actual codification of the law. These codes attempt to represent a sum total of the whole of the legal teachings of Judaism in the topic areas they cover.

TEXT 7: *Shulchan Aruch HaRav*, 340:15

Gathering is one of the *avot melachot*	הַמְעַמֵּר הוּא מֵאָבוֹת מְלָאכוֹת
that was [performed] in the Tabernacle with planted herbs.	שֶׁהָיָה בַּמִּשְׁכָּן בְּסַמָּנִים הַזְּרוּעִים
Gathering applies only when it is gathered in the place of its growth,	וְאֵין עִימּוּר אֶלָּא כְּשֶׁמְּאַסְפוֹ בִּמְקוֹם גִּידּוּלוֹ
in the way that standing grain was harvested, by raking in the stalks in the place where they were grown.	כְּעֵין קָמָה קְצוּרָה שֶׁמְּגַבֵּב הַשִּׁבֳּלִים בִּמְקוֹם גִּידּוּלָן
So too, one who collects fruits and gathers them together	וְכֵן הַמְאַסֵּף פֵּירוֹת וּמְקַבְּצָן יַחַד
in the place where they fell from the tree.	בִּמְקוֹם שֶׁנָּפְלוּ מִן הָאִילָן
However, if they were scattered in a different place, it is permissible to gather them,	אֲבָל אִם נִתְפַּזְּרוּ בְּמָקוֹם אַחֵר מוּתָּר לְקַבְּצָם
as stated in *Siman* 335.	כמ״ש בסי׳ של״ה.
Gathering only applies to *gidulei karka*.	וְאֵין עִימּוּר אֶלָּא בְּגִידּוּלֵי קַרְקַע
However, by rabbinic order	אֲבָל מִדִּבְרֵי סוֹפְרִים
it is prohibited even for non-*gidulei karka*	אָסוּר אַף שֶׁלֹּא בְּגִידּוּלֵי קַרְקַע
to be gathered in the place of their growth—	לְקַבְּצָם בִּמְקוֹם גִּידּוּלָם
for example, to gather salt from saltpans	כְּגוֹן לְקַבֵּץ מֶלַח מִמִּשְׂרְפוֹת הַמַּיִם
that scorch (the seawater) and it becomes salt —	שֶׁשּׂוֹרְפָתָן וְנַעֲשִׂים מֶלַח
and the same applies to anything similar to this.	וְכֵן בְּכָל כַּיּוֹצֵא בָּזֶה
(Some say that	(וְיֵשׁ אוֹמְרִים
one who presses fruit together until they become as one	שֶׁהַמְדַבֵּק פֵּירוֹת עַד שֶׁנַּעֲשׂוּ גוּף אֶחָד
is liable on account of gathering even when not at the location of their growth,	חַיָּיב מִשּׁוּם מְעַמֵּר אֲפִילוּ שֶׁלֹּא בִּמְקוֹם גִּידּוּלָם

for example,) one who gathers figs and presses them together to make a round cake	כְּגוֹן) הַמְקַבֵּץ דְבֵילָה וְעָשָׂה מִמֶּנּוּ עִיגּוּל
or one who pierced figs and threaded a string through them	אוֹ שֶׁנָּקַב תְּאֵנִים וְהִכְנִיס הַחֶבֶל בָּהֶם
until they were gathered and became like one	עַד שֶׁנִּתְקַבְּצוּ וְנַעֲשׂוּ גּוּף אֶחָד
This is a *toladah* of gathering and he is liable;	הֲרֵי זֶה תּוֹלָדַת מְעַמֵּר וְחַיָּיב
the same applies to all similar acts.	וְכֵן כָּל כַּיּוֹצֵא בָּזֶה
(One must be stringent in accordance with this view.)	(וְצָרִיךְ לְהַחְמִיר כְּדִבְרֵיהֶם)

Rabbi Shne'ur Zalman of Liadi (1745–1812). Known as "the Alter Rebbe" and "the Rav"; Born in Liozna, Belarus; buried in Hadiach, Ukraine; Chassidic Rebbe and founder of the Chabad movement; among the principle students of the Magid of Mezeritch. His numerous works include the *Tanya,* an early classic of Chassidism; *Torah Or and Likutei Torah*, and *Shulchan Aruch HaRav,* a rewritten code of Jewish law. He was succeeded by his son, Rabbi Dovber of Lubavitch.

Learning **Exercise**

Write/Pair/Share

How many unique practical examples can you come up with for the *melachah* of gathering?

Part II

Threshing: Between Cotton and Wool

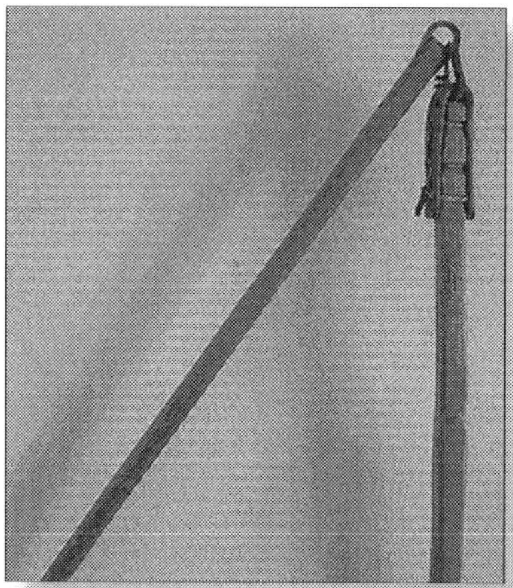

TEXT 8: Talmud, *Shabbat* 74a, continued

Threshing—	וְהַדָּשׁ
It was taught [in a *baraita*]:	תַּנָא
threshing, beating, and striking	הַדָּשׁ וְהַמְנַפֵּץ וְהַמְנַפֵּט
are all one *melachah*.	כּוּלָן מְלָאכָה אַחַת הֵן

TEXT 9: Rashi, *Shabbat* 73b, *HaMenapetz and VeHaMenafet*

Beating:	הַמְנַפֵּץ
—flax from its stalks	פִּשְׁתָּן בְּגִבְעוֹלִין
Striking:	וְהַמְנַפֵּט
cotton with a bow	צֶמֶר גֶּפֶן בְּקֶשֶׁת
as the craftsmen do.	כְּדֶרֶךְ הָאוּמָּנִין
Cotton grows from the ground.	וְצֶמֶר גֶּפֶן גִּידוּלֵי קַרְקַע הוּא

Therefore [the Tana] refers to striking it as a *toladah* of threshing,	לְהָכִי קָרֵי נִיפּוּט דִילֵיה תּוֹלָדָה דְדָשׁ
since he extracts seeds from it	שֶׁמְפָרֵק גַרְעִינִין מִמֶנוּ
and he does not call it a *toladah* of combing wool.	וְלֹא קָרֵי לֵיה תּוֹלָדַת מְנַפֵּץ דְצֶמֶר.

TEXT 10: **Rabbeinu Chananel, *Shabbat* 73b**

Threshing is the extracting of waste that is attached to the food,	הַדָשׁ הוּא הַמְפָרֵק הַפְּסוֹלֶת הַמְחוּבֶּרֶת בְּאוֹכֶל
preparing it for selecting	וּמְכִינָתָן לִבְרֵירָה
or for sifting by winnowing or by using a sieve.	אוֹ כְּבָרָה בִּזְרִיָה אוֹ בְּהַרְקָדָה
Menapetz is beating out dirt from the food.	הַמְנַפֵּץ נוֹפֵץ עַפְרוּרִיוֹת מִן הָאוֹכֶל
Menafet is rubbing the ears [between one's fingers to remove the husks].	וְכֵן הַמְנַפֵּט מוֹלֵל שִׁבָּלִים
Thus, [in contradistinction,] winnowing, selecting and sifting	נִמְצָא זוֹרֶה בּוֹרֵר וּמְרַקֵד
all remove waste that is mixed into food	כּוּלָן מַעֲבִירִין פְּסוֹלֶת הַמְעוּרֶבֶת בְּאוֹכֶל
but is not attached	וְאֵינָה מְחוּבֶּרֶת
such as a shell that needs to be broken off	כְּגוֹן קְלִיפָה שֶׁצְרִיכָה פִּרוּק
or like dirt that requires beating and the like.	אוֹ כְּגוֹן עַפְרוּרִית שֶׁצָרִיךְ נִפּוּץ וכו׳

Rabbeinu Chananel ben Chushiel (ca. 965–1055). His father was a sage in the yeshiva of Sura, but when on a trip to raise funds for brides, was captured. Ransomed by the Jewish community of Kairoun, North Africa, he remained there, established a Yeshivah and to a degree is responsible for the subsequent prevalence of Torah in the occident. One of his students was his son Chananel who continued his father's legacy as spiritual leader of the community. R. Chananel was of the first to write commentaries to entire sections of the Talmud. One of his novelties was to parallel and contrast passages of the Jerusalem Talmud, a neglected study in many circles, with the Babylonian Talmud. He was a wealthy individual and had nine daughters.

Part III

Variations of Separating

TEXT 11: Talmud, *Shabbat* 73b, continued

Winnowing, selecting, grinding, sifting—	הַזּוֹרֶה הַבּוֹרֵר וְהַטּוֹחֵן וְהַמְרַקֵּד
Winnowing is the same as selecting which is the same as sifting.	הַיְינוּ זוֹרֶה הַיְינוּ בּוֹרֵר הַיְינוּ מְרַקֵּד
Abaye and Rava both say:	אַבַּיֵי וְרָבָא דְּאָמְרֵי תַּרְוַיְיהוּ
Anything that was done in the Tabernacle,	כָּל מִילְתָא דַּהֲוָיָא בְּמִשְׁכָּן
although there are [other *melachot*] that are similar to it,	אַף עַל גַּב דְּאִיכָּא דְּדַמְיָא לַהּ
he lists [as a separate *av melachah*].	חָשֵׁיב לַהּ

TEXT 12: Rashi, *Shabbat* 73b, *Hachi Garsinan*

Such is our version (of the Talmud's text)—	הָכִי גַּרְסִינַן
"Winnowing is the same as selecting which is the same as sifting."	הַיְינוּ זוֹרֶה הַיְינוּ בּוֹרֵר הַיְינוּ מְרַקֵּד

Keys to the Talmud

***Girsa'ot*—versions of a text**

***Girsa* comes from the same root as the word *ligros*, to read or study. Before Johannes Gutenberg invented the printing press in 1440, scribes would copy books by hand. Human error was responsible for many mistakes seeping into the writings of antiquity, including into versions of the Talmud. Even after the invention of the printing press, because the plates for printing were set by hand, printing mistakes made their way into books, and some remain until this very day. For this reason, in Talmudic study there is a significant emphasis placed on discovering the correct and original version. At times this entails using logic and a deep appreciation of the subject to choose between different possibilities to find the original version. Rashi, concentrating on the simple meaning of the text, often clarifies what he understands to be the original version from the tradition he received from his teachers and what, according to his understanding of the Talmud, made most sense. Determining the correct *girsa* is of utmost**

importance as a slight change in the wording of the Talmud can have a profound impact on the outcome of how we understand a particular statement.

TEXT 13: **Rashi, *Shabbat* 73b, *Haynu***

***(Haynu)* Is the same as**	הַיְינוּ
is like *hei nihu*—(a more common way of saying) "is the same as"	כְּמוֹ הֵי נִיהוּ
meaning, that the Tana of our *mishnah* separates them into three	כְּלוֹמַר דְּמַפְלִיג לְהוּ תַּנָּא דְּמַתְנִיתִין לִתְלַת
but aren't they all one *melachah*	וַהֲלֹא כּוּלָן מְלָאכָה אַחַת הֵן
of separating food from waste?	דִּמְפָרֵישׁ אוֹכֶל מִן הַפְּסוֹלֶת

Optional Reading

TEXT 14: **Talmud, *Ta'anit* 20b**

Sturdy [buildings] are the same as [buildings] not prone to collapse!	הֵי נִיהוּ בְּרִיאוֹת הֵי נִיהוּ שֶׁאֵינָן רְאוּיוֹת לִיפּוֹל
Dilapidated [buildings] are the same as [buildings] that are prone to collapse!	הֵי נִינְהוּ רְעוּעוֹת הֵי נִיהוּ רְאוּיוֹת לִיפּוֹל

TEXT 15: **Rashi, *Shabbat* 74a, *Af Al Gav***

Even though there are Others	אַף עַל גַּב דְּאִיכָּא אַחֲרִיתִּי
in [the thirty-nine *avot melachot*] that are similar to it	בַּהֲדָה דְּדַמְיָא לַהּ
he considers both to be *avot*	חַשְׁבִינְהוּ לְתַרְוַיְיהוּ כְּאָבוֹת
although they are [really] one [and the same *melachah*].	וְאַף עַל גַּב דְּחָדָא נִינְהוּ

TEXT 16: **Ran, Rif, *Shabbat* 31b *Matnitin***

Winnowing with a winnowing shovel into the wind,	הַזּוֹרֶה בְּרַחַת לְרוּחַ
selecting the waste with one's hands,	הַבּוֹרֵר פְּסוֹלֶת בְּיָדָיו
sifting with a sieve	הַמְרַקֵּד בְּנָפָה
... [the Tana] counts them as *avot*	חָשִׁיב לְתַרְוַייהוּ בְּאָבוֹת...
since their actions are not similar	כֵּיוָן שֶׁאֵין מַעֲשֵׂיהֶן שָׁוִין
and they are not performed at the same time	וְאֵינָן בִּזְמַן אֶחָד
but one after the other:	אֶלָּא זֶה אַחַר זֶה
winnowing is for straw,	זוֹרֶה בְּתֶבֶן
selecting is for pebbles,	בּוֹרֵר בִּצְרוֹרוֹת
sifting is for bran.	מְרַקֵּד בְּסוּבִּין

Rabbi Nissim ben Reuven of Gerona (1320–1380). Known by the acronym *Ran*; Influential Talmudist and authority on Jewish law; Among the last great Spanish Talmudic scholars. Considered the outstanding halachic authority of his generation, queries came to him from throughout the Diaspora. His works include commentaries on the Talmud and on Rabbi Yitzchak Alfasi's code, responsa literature, a commentary on the Bible, and a collection of sermons, *Derashot HaRan*, which elucidates fundamentals of Judaism.

Table 1

Straw	Shovel and Wind	Winnowing	***Zoreh***
Pebbles	Hand	Selecting	***Borer***
Bran	Sieve	Sifting	***Meraked***

Keys to the Talmud

The Jerusalem Talmud

The Jerusalem Talmud, known as Talmud Yerushalmi or the Talmud of the Land of Israel, is the version of the Talmud compiled by the sages of the Land of Israel.

TEXT 17: **Jerusalem Talmud, *Shabbat* Ch. 7 Law 2**

If someone spat, and the wind scattered [his saliva]	רָקַק וְהִפְרִיחָתוֹ הָרוּחַ
he is liable on account of winnowing	חַיָּב מִשּׁוּם זוֹרֶה
and for anything that is assisted by wind	וְכָל דָּבָר שֶׁהוּא מְחוּסָּר לְרוּחַ
he is liable on account of winnowing.	חַיָּב מִשּׁוּם זוֹרֶה

Part IV

A Deeper Dimension
—Productivity in the *Melachot* of Refining Grain

TEXT 18: *Sefer HaMa'amarim Te'erav*, vol. 2, p. 1067

Gathering is the concept of *and you shall gather your grain.*	מְעַמֵּר הוּא עִנְיָן וְאָסַפְתָּ דְגָנֶךָ
This refers to inner selflessness,	שֶׁזֶּהוּ הַבִּיטּוּל פְּנִימִי
that one gathers in the sparks of good	שֶׁמְּאַסֵּף אֶת הַנִּיצוֹץ הַטּוֹב
from separation into unity	מִן הַפִּירוּד אֶל הַיִּחוּד
in order that the animal soul	וְהַיְינוּ שֶׁהַנֶּפֶשׁ הַבְּהֵמִית
will be subservient to G-dliness.	יִהְיֶה בּוֹ הַבִּיטּוּל לֶאֱלֹקוּת
This is the concept of separating off evil and coarseness	וְהוּא עִנְיָן הַפְרָדַת הָרַע וְהַחוּמְרִיּוּת
while dedicating the good within it to G-dliness inspired with love.	וְהַטּוֹב שֶׁבּוֹ יִהְיֶה לֶאֱלֹקוּת בְּהִתְעוֹרְרוּת אַהֲבָה

Rabbi Shalom DovBer Schneersohn (1860–1920). Also known by the acronym "*Rashab.*" Chassidic Rebbe and fifth leader of the Chabad movement.Author of many volumes of Chassidic discourses. He established the Lubavitcher network of *yeshivot*, *Tomchei Temimim*. Born in Lubavitch, he became Rebbe at the age of 22 upon the passing of his father, the *Maharash*. His leadership proved critical during the tumultuous end of the Czarist regime and Russian revolution. During World War One, he fled to Rostov-on-the-Don, Russia, where he is buried.

Key Points

1. In this lesson we cover three *sugyot* or passages of Talmudic discussion on three different subjects. At the end we consider how they can all be integrated and offer a lesson with direct application in our lives as Jews.

***Sugya* 1:** Gathering salt

Rava: Gathering salt is a *toladah* of gathering.
Abaye: Gathering only applies to *gidulei karka* (items that grow in the ground).

Tosafot Rid: *Gidulei karka* defines the kinds of material with which the *melachah* is done—grown produce at the time of their initial gathering following their harvest.
Meiri: *Gidulei karka* defines the location where it is done—gathering from the field and not from salt evaporation ponds.

Abaye: The *melachah* is defined by the achievement (*nif'al*.) Other activities producing the same result are included in a *melachah* even when the method is not the same.
Rava: The *melachah* is defined by the act (*po'el*) (in this case, of gathering) and includes similar activity involving a different location and type of species.

***Sugya* 2:** Beating flax and striking cotton is the same *melachah* as threshing wheat.

Rashi: Same act of threshing with different substances (flax and cotton).
Rabbeinu Chananel: Different methods of achieving the same result.

***Sugya* 3**: Winnowing, selecting, and sifting are the same *melachah* of separating food from waste but are counted as individual *avot* because they represent different activities in the construction of the Tabernacle.

The Jerusalem Talmud isolates the *melachah* of winnowing from the concept of separating. The result has modern application in the case of certain air-pressure sprays.

2. The *melachot* of gathering and separating symbolize our task of gathering the sparks of holiness in the world and separating them from their mundane or evil husks to transform the world into a Tabernacle for G-d.

Terms to Retain

Gathering	מְעַמֵּר
Threshing	דָּשׁ
Winnowing	זוֹרֶה
Selecting/Sorting	בּוֹרֵר
Sifting	מְרַקֵּד
Translation of the Bible that serves as commentary as well	תַּרְגּוּם
Is the same as	הַיְינוּ
First ones—medieval commentaries on the Talmud	רִאשׁוֹנִים
The act itself	פּוֹעֵל
The accomplishment of the act	נִפְעַל

Lesson 7

Introduction

What makes an activity important? When is an activity listed as a unique *av melachah*, even when its function is the same as other *melachot*? Is the significance of an activity lessened because certain people can go without doing it? Can quantity define quality?

In this lesson, we will explore the fundamentals of what makes a *melachah* deserving of the title *av melachah*. We will discuss examples of *melachot* omitted from the Mishnah's list of *avot melachot* and seek to identify the shortcomings that account for their omission.

This train of thought will lead us to a renowned *sugya*, the *sugya* of *chatsi shiur*, half measures. We will have an opportunity to study a topic that is debated in several tractates of the Talmud and affects many mitzvot

Part I

The Same or Similar

TEXT 1: *Shabbat* 74a, Tosafot, *Af Al Gav*

Although there are others that are similar to it, he lists them	אַף עַל גַּב דְּאִיכָּא דְּדַמְיָא לָהּ חָשִׁיב
The reason he does not include lining up and beating	וְהָא דְּלֹא חָשִׁיב שׁוֹבֵט וּמְדַקְדֵּק
is because they are entirely included in stretching and weaving.	לְפִי שֶׁהֵם לְגַמְרֵי בִּכְלַל מֵיסֵךְ וְאוֹרֵג

Tosafot (10th-13th centuries). A collection French and German Talmudic commentaries in the form of critical and explanatory glosses; written during the twelfth and thirteenth centuries. Among the most famous authors of Tosafot are Rabbi Yaakov Tam, Rabbi Shimshon ben Avraham of Sens, and Rabbi Shmuel ben Meir. Printed in almost all editions of the Talmud, these commentaries are fundamental to basic Talmudic study.

Keys to the Talmud

***VeHa DeLo*—The reason why it [he] does not**

The words *veha delo* generally signify a hidden question that the Talmud (or in this case Tosafot) seeks to answer or a rejected option that it wishes to clarify.

Weaving

Weaving is the process of producing fabric in which two distinct sets of threads, called the warp

Lining up the warp threads with a rod: When lining up the warp threads, threads tend to overlap or become attached to one another. A pointed rod is used to separate the threads and line them up properly.

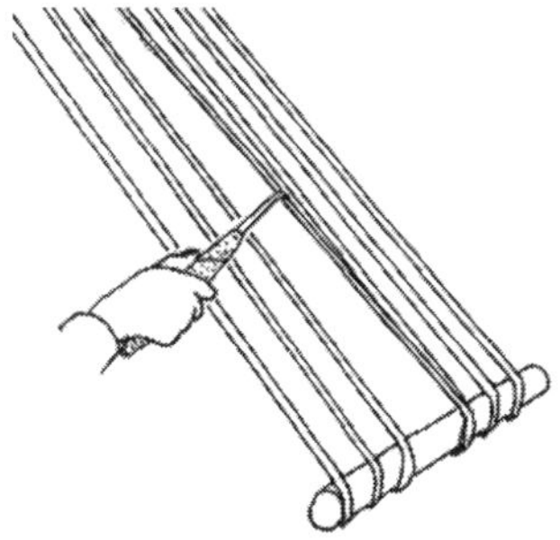

Beating the weft threads: When the weft thread is passed through the warp threads, it must be pulled tight so that it will not hang too loosely on the cloth. However, if it is pulled too tightly, the weft thread will not merge well with the already woven cloth. The weft thread is therefore hit with the pointed rod in a few places to relax the tension and increase the amount of weft thread so that it will not be stretched too tightly; it can then merge neatly with the rest of the cloth.

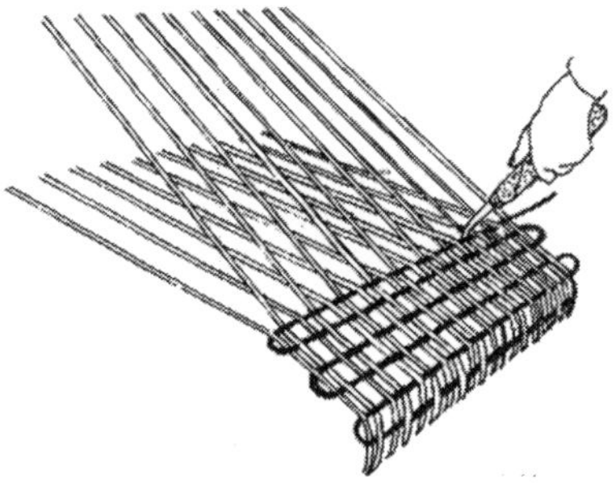

Mounting the warp: This is the act of mounting the warp threads onto the loom to prepare them for weaving.

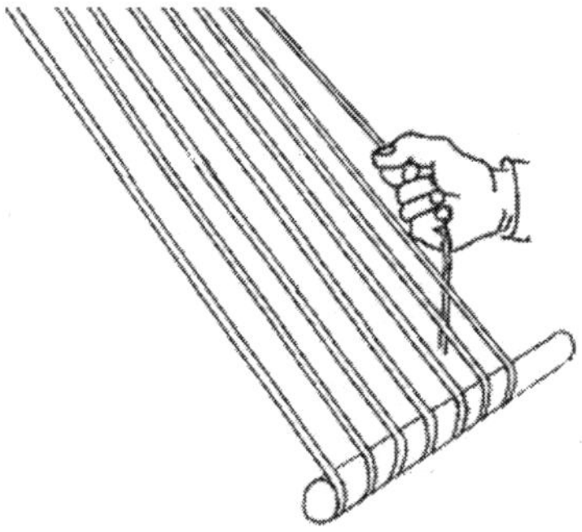

TEXT 2A: **Talmud, *Shabbat* 75b**

Rabbi Yehudah adds lining up and beating.	רַבִּי יְהוּדָה מוֹסִיף אֶת הַשּׁוֹבֵט וְהַמְדַקְדֵק
They [the *Chachamim*] said to him:	אָמְרוּ לוֹ
Lining up the warp threads is included in stretching the threads.	שׁוֹבֵט הֲרֵי הוּא בִּכְלַל מֵיסֵךְ
Beating the weft threads is included in weaving.	מְדַקְדֵק הֲרֵי הוּא בִּכְלַל אוֹרֵג

TEXT 2B: ***Shabbat* 74a, continuation of Tosafot, *VeLo***

And he does not include beating [flax],	וְלֹא חָשִׁיב נַמִּי מְנַפֵּץ
even though they would beat flax in the *Mishkan*	אַף עַל גַּב שֶׁבַּמִּשְׁכָּן הָיוּ מְנַפְּצִין פִּשְׁתָּן
to make curtains and other things,	לַעֲשׂוֹת יְרִיעוֹת וּשְׁאָר דְּבָרִים
since it is exactly the same as threshing,	מִשּׁוּם דְּהַיְינוּ דָּשׁ מַמָּשׁ
only that this is with grain and the other with flax,	אֶלָּא שֶׁזֶּה בִּתְבוּאָה וְזֶה בְּפִשְׁתָּן
but winnowing, selecting and sifting are three [different] things.	אֲבָל זוֹרֶה וּבוֹרֵר וּמְרַקֵּד הֵם שְׁלֹשָׁה דְּבָרִים

Part II

Pounding

TEXT 3: **Talmud, *Shabbat* 74a**

Let him include pounding as well.	וְלִיחֲשֵׁב נַמִי כּוֹתֵשׁ
Abaye said:	אָמַר אַבַּיֵי
Since a poor person eats his bread without pounding [the wheat].	שֶׁכֵּן עָנִי אוֹכֵל פִּתּוֹ בְּלֹא כְּתִישָׁה
Rava said:	רָבָא אָמַר
Who is this [author of our Mishnah]?	הָא מַנִי
It is Rabbi,	רֶבִּי הִיא
who said: the *avot melachot* are forty minus one,	דְאָמַר אָבוֹת מְלָאכוֹת אַרְבָּעִים חָסֵר אַחַת
and if he had included pounding,	וְאִי חָשִׁיב כּוֹתֵשׁ
he would have had forty!	הַוְיָא לֵיה אַרְבָּעִים

The Talmud questions and rejects Rava's answer.

So let him remove one of them	וְלִיפּוֹק חַדָא מֵהַנָךְ
and [instead] include pounding!	וּלְעַיֵּיל כּוֹתֵשׁ
Rather, [the answer] is clearly as Abaye [said].	אֶלָא מַחְוַורְתָּא כִּדְאַבַּיֵי

TEXT 4: **Rashi, *Shabbat* 74a, *Velichashev Nami***

He should also enumerate pounding:	וְלִיחֲשֵׁב נַמִי כּוֹתֵשׁ–
wheat with a mortar	חִטִין בְּמַכְתֶּשֶׁת
to remove its husk;	לְהָסִיר קְלִיפָּתָן
this was performed in the sanctuary with herbs.	דַהֲוָאִי בַּמִקְדָשׁ בְּסַמְמָנִין
But it is not listed because it is similar to threshing,	אֶלָא לַאו מִשׁוּם דְדַמְיָא לְדָשׁ לֹא חָשִׁיב לָהּ
since it too is [an act of] removing a covering.	דְהָא נַמִי מִיפָּרְקָה מַלְבּוּשׁ הִיא

Rabbi Shlomo Yitzchaki (1040–1105). Better known by the acronym *Rashi;* rabbi and famed author of the first comprehensive commentaries on the Talmud and Bible. Born in Troyes, Champagne, Rashi studied in the famed yeshivot of Mainz and Worms. His commentaries, which focus on the simple understanding of the text, are considered fundamental to Torah study. Since their initial printings, they have appeared in virtually every edition of the Talmud and Bible. Amongst Rashi's descendants, were many of the famed Tosafists of France.

TEXT 5: Rashi, *Shabbat* 74a *SheChein Ani Ochel*

Since a poor person eats his bread without pounding—	שֶׁכֵן עָנִי אוֹכֵל פִּתּוֹ בְּלֹא כְּתִישָׁה
therefore, even though it was in the Sanctuary	לְכָךְ אַף עַל גַב דַהֲוָאִי בַּמִקְדָשׁ
and it is an *av melachah,*	וְאַב מְלָאכָה הִיא
when the Tana enumerated threshing, he did not enumerate [pounding].	כֵּיוָן דְתַנָא לֵיה דָשׁ לֹא תַנָא לָה
[On the other hand,] winnowing, selecting and sifting	וְזוֹרֶה וּבוֹרֵר וּמְרַקֵד
belong to the order of making bread	סִידוּרָא דְפַת נִינְהוּ
and since they were performed in the Sanctuary	וְכֵיוָן דְהֲווּ בַּמִקְדָשׁ
and here he started with the order of making bread,	וְהָכָא אַתְחִיל בְּסִידוּרָא דְפַת
he enumerated them [as well].	תַנִינְהוּ
As we say regarding baking,	כִּדְאַמְרִינָן גַבֵּי אוֹפֶה
that he should have enumerated cooking not baking,	דַהֲוָה לֵיה לְמִתְנֵי מְבַשֵׁל וְלֹא אוֹפֶה
since that was not [required] in the Sanctuary's [construction],	דְלֹא הֲוָה בַּמִקְדָשׁ
but since he cites the order of baking bread, he continues with it,	אֶלָא מִשׁוּם סִידוּרָא דְפַת נָקַט וְאָתָא
since baking bread is similar to cooking with herbs.	הוֹאִיל וְאוֹפֶה בְּפַת כִּמְבַשֵׁל בְּסַמְמָנִין
But pounding,	אֲבָל כְּתִישָׁה
it is the rich who moisten and pound	עֲשִׁירִים הוּא דְלַתְתֵי וְכַתְשֵׁי

to make fine flour,	לַעֲשׂוֹת סֹלֶת נְקִיָּה
but the poor don't bother;	אֲבָל עֲנִיִּים לֹא טָרְחֵי
therefore the Tana did not enumerate it.	הִלְכָּךְ לֹא תַּנָא לָהּ
However, it is certainly an *av melachah*	וּמִיהוּ וַדַּאי אַב מְלָאכָה הִיא
and is included in threshing.	וּבִכְלַל דָּשׁ הִיא

TEXT 6: **Rashi, *Shabbat* 74a, *Rabbi Hi***

It is in accordance with Rabbi—	רַבִּי הִיא
who later in chapter *HaZorek* (97b) derives	דְּיָלִיף לְקַמָּן בְּפֶרֶק הַזּוֹרֵק (צז, ב)
the number [of thirty-nine from] "words," "the words," "these are the words."	דְּבָרִים הַדְּבָרִים אֵלֶּה הַדְּבָרִים לְמִנְיָינָא

TEXT 7: **Rashi, *Shabbat*, 74a, *Velipok Chada MeHanach***

Let him remove one of them:	וְלִיפּוֹק חֲדָא מֵהַנָךְ:
either winnowing, selecting or sifting, since they are one.	אוֹ זוֹרֶה אוֹ בּוֹרֵר אוֹ מְרַקֵּד דְּהָווּ חֲדָא
Let him remove one of them and state this one,	לִיפּוֹק מִינַיְיהוּ חֲדָא וְלִיתְנֵי הַךְ
since it is better to teach two of each,	דְּהָכִי עֲדִיף לְמִיתְנֵי תַּרְתֵּי מֵהָא וְתַרְתֵּי מֵהָא
than to teach three examples of one [*melachah*]	מִלְמִיתְנֵי וּלְמִיכְפַּל תְּלָתָא זִימְנֵי בַּחֲדָא
while one is left entirely unrepeated.	וְאִיכָּא חֲדָא דְּלֹא כָּפֵיל בֵּיהּ מִידֵּי

Keys to the Talmud

Keywords in Tosafot—*VeIm Tomar* and *VeYesh Lomar*

These keywords help the reader identify a question and answer in Tosafot. *Ve'im tomar,* literally "and if you will say," introduces a question to which Tosafot normally has an answer. The answer is introduced with the words *veyesh lomar*, literally, "and it can be said." Together they comprise a structure of "if you will say" in question and "it can be said" in answer to the question. These are probably the most common words you will find in Tosafot, emblematic of its system of commentary.

TEXT 8A: **Tosafot, Shabbat 74a, *SheChein***

Since	שֶׁכֵּן
a poor person eats his bread without pounding.	עָנִי אוֹכֵל פִּתּוֹ בְּלֹא כְּתִישָׁה
And if you say (Tosafot questions)	וְאִם תֹּאמַר
nevertheless the pounding of herbs should be counted since it was performed in the *Mishkan*	מִכָּל מָקוֹם לִיחַשֵּׁיב כְּתִישַׁת סַמְמָנִין דַּהֲוָה בְּמִשְׁכָּן
and although a poor person eats his bread without pounding,	וְאַף עַל גַּב דְּעָנִי אוֹכֵל פִּתּוֹ בְּלֹא כְּתִישָׁה
it is [nevertheless considered] an important labor in the case of herbs.	לְעִנְיַן סַמְמָנִים מְלָאכָה חֲשׁוּבָה הִיא
Rabbeinu Yitzchak replies that [the Talmud's statement] refers not only to eating bread,	וְאוֹמֵר רַבֵּינוּ יִצְחָק דְּלַאו דַּוְקָא אוֹכֵל פִּתּוֹ
but rather it applies generally,	אֶלָּא הוּא הַדִּין
for a poor person dyes with herbs without pounding them.	דְּעָנִי צוֹבֵעַ בְּסַמְמָנִים בְּלֹא כְּתִישָׁה
And if you ask,	וְאִם תֹּאמַר
we should not also enumerate sifting [in the Mishnah],	מְרַקֵּד נַמִּי לֹא לִיתְנֵי
since a poor person eats his bread made of impure dough [i.e. unrefined flour]	שֶׁכֵּן עָנִי אוֹכֵל פִּתּוֹ בְּעִיסָּה בְּלוּסָה
as is stated at the end of this chapter (76b)?	כִּדְאָמַר בְּסוֹף פִּרְקִין

Challah

TEXT 8B: **Continuation of Tosafot, *Shabbat* 74a, *SheChein***

You can say that most poor people don't eat [bread] without sifting [its flour].	וְיֵשׁ לוֹמַר דְּרוֹב עֲנִיִּים אֵין אוֹכְלִין בְּלֹא הַרְקָדָה
However, with regard to *challah*, bran is included [in the required measure],	אֶלָּא שֶׁלְּעִנְיַן חַלָּה מִצְטָרְפִין הַסּוּבִּין
as it fulfills the criteria of the verse "from bread of the land,"	דְּקָרֵינַן בֵּיהּ מִלֶּחֶם הָאָרֶץ
since there are poor people who eat bread from bran-filled dough.	כֵּיוָן דְּיֵשׁ עֲנִיִּים שֶׁאוֹכְלִים בְּעִיסָּה בְּלוּסָה
Rabbeinu Tam explained this differently and Rabbeinu Yitzchak was not pleased with his explanation.	וְרַבֵּינוּ תָּם פֵּירֵשׁ בְּעִנְיָן אַחֵר וְלֹא נִתְיַישֵּׁב לְרַבֵּינוּ יִצְחָק

TEXT 9: **Nachmanides, *Chidushim, Shabbat* 74a, *SheChein Ani Ochel Pito***

Rabbeinu Tam of blessed memory gives a troubling answer:	וְרַבֵּינוּ תָּם ז"ל נִדְחַק בָּהּ וּפֵירֵשׁ
Let [the Tanna] also count pounding,	וְלִיחֲשֵׁב נַמִּי כּוֹתֵשׁ
since they would pound barley to test the *techelet* dye.	שֶׁהָיוּ כּוֹתְשִׁין שְׂעוֹרִים לְנִסְיוֹנֵי דִּתְכֵלֶת

Rabbi Moshe ben Nachman (1194–1270). Also known as Nachmanides or by the acronym *Ramban*; considered the foremost authority on Jewish law of his time. Nachmanides authored a popular biblical commentary which includes kabbalistic insights. Born in Spain, he served as leader of Iberian Jewry. He was summoned by King James of Aragon, to a public disputation with Pablo Cristiani, a Jewish apostate, in 1263. Resulting persecution led to his eventual expulsion from Spain. Settling in Israel, Nachmanides helped reestablish communal life in Jerusalem.

Techelet

Continuation of Nachmanides:

They would insert [a strand dyed with *techelet*] in barley bread	שֶׁטוֹמְנִין אוֹתוֹ בְּתוֹךְ פַּת שֶׁל שְׂעוֹרִים
and bake it.	וְאוֹפִין אוֹתוֹ
If its color would change [i.e. fade] it is unfit	אִם נִשְׁתַּנָּה פָּסוּל
and if its color would improve, it is fit for use	וְאִם לְמַעַלְיוּתָא נִשְׁתַּנָּה כָּשֵׁר
and the Talmud's initial thinking was that bread is not baked without pounding.	וְקָא סַלְקָא דַעְתָּךְ שֶׁאֵין אוֹפִין פַּת אֶלָּא בִּכְתִישָׁה
And the Talmud replies: there are many poor people who eat their bread without pounding,	וּפָרִיק הָכִי כַּמָּה עֲנִיִּים אוֹכְלִין פִּיתָּן שֶׁלֹּא בִּכְתִישָׁה
nor did they pound in the *Mishkan*.	וְלֹא הָיוּ כּוֹתְשִׁין גַּם כֵּן בַּמִּשְׁכָּן
Rav Pappa's statement later on poses a difficulty for [Rabbeinu Tam],	וְקַשְׁיָא לֵיהּ הָא דְאָמַר רַב פָּפָּא לְקַמָּן
[for he says] that our Tana left out cooking herbs that were in the *Mishkan* and included baking.	שָׁבִיק תַּנָּא דִידַן בִּשּׁוּל סַמְמָנִין דַּהֲוָה בְּמִשְׁכָּן וְנָקַט אוֹפֶה
From this we see that baking was not performed in the *Mishkan*'s [construction]!	אַלְמָא אַפִיָּיה לֵיתֵיהּ בַּמִּשְׁכָּן
And he replies: The Talmud's question is, the Tana omitted cooking,	וּפָרִיק הָכִי קָאָמַר שָׁבִיק תַּנָּא דִידַן בִּישּׁוּל
which is one of the *melachot* that was necessary for its own sake	שֶׁהוּא מִן הַמְּלָאכוֹת הַצְּרִיכוֹת מֵחֲמַת עַצְמָן
and included baking that was only needed to test the *techelet?*	וְנָקַט אוֹפֶה שֶׁאֵינוֹ אֶלָּא בִּשְׁבִיל נִסָּיוֹן תְּכֵלֶת
I do not agree with this explanation,	וְאֵין הַפֵּירוּשׁ הַזֶּה נָכוֹן אֶצְלִי
as this test is only mentioned in Tractate *Menachot*	לְפִי שֶׁלֹּא נֶאֱמַר נִסָּיוֹן זֶה בִּמְנָחוֹת מ"ג,א
in the case of one who buys [*tzitzit*] already dyed with *techelet*	אֶלָּא בְּלוֹקֵחַ תְּכֵלֶת צָבוּעַ

and out of a concern for *kala ilan* [an unfit *techelet* look-alike],	וּמִשּׁוּם חַשְׁשָׁא דְקָלָא אִילָן
while in the *Mishkan* they would dye it themselves as was taught in [our] *mishnah*, Dyeing.	וּבַמִּשְׁכָּן הֵן עַצְמָן צוֹבְעִין אוֹתוֹ כִּדְתְנַן וְהַצּוֹבֵעַ
Furthermore, had they baked in the *Mishkan* at all,	וְעוֹד שֶׁאִלּוּ הָיוּ אוֹפִין בַּמִּשְׁכָּן כְּלַל
they would have counted forty *avot melachot*,	הָיוּ מוֹנִין אָבוֹת מְלָאכוֹת אַרְבָּעִים
since even though baking and cooking are alike,	שֶׁאַף עַל פִּי שֶׁאוֹפֶה וּמְבַשֵּׁל שָׁוִין
they are not so completely one thing that they both should not be counted.	אֵינָן לְגַמְרֵי דָּבָר אֶחָד עַד שֶׁלֹּא יִמְנוּ שְׁתֵּיהֶן
It would have been more appropriate to count these two than selecting, sifting and winnowing.	וְיוֹתֵר הָיָה רָאוּי לִמְנוֹתָן שְׁתַּיִם מִבּוֹרֵר וּמְרַקֵּד וְזוֹרֶה

Keys to the Talmud

Ka Salka Da'atach* and *Hava Amina

Both of these phrases refer to initial presumptions. The difference between them is that *hava amina*, literally "I would have said," is a hypothesis. In other words, had such and such not been stated, I would have thought such and such. *Ka salka daa'tach*, literally "it has arisen in your mind," refers to an anticipated misperception. The one presenting an argument realizes that people may understand something to be one way, but in the light of the information or argument he is presenting, this misperception will be cleared up.

Part III

Selecting

TEXT 10A: Continuation of Talmud, *Shabbat* 74a

The Rabbis taught [in a *baraita*]:	תָּנוּ רַבָּנָן
If variant types of food were before him,	הָיוּ לְפָנָיו מִינֵי אוֹכְלִין
he may select and eat select and put aside,	בּוֹרֵר וְאוֹכֵל בּוֹרֵר וּמַנִּיחַ
but he may not select	וְלֹא יִבְרוֹר
and if he did select, he is obligated to bring a sin offering.	וְאִם בֵּירֵר חַיָּיב חַטָּאת

TEXT 10B: Rashi, *Shabbat* 74a, *Hayu Lefanav*

If variant types of food were before him—	הָיוּ לְפָנָיו מִינֵי אוֹכְלִין
this is our version, without the word "two."	גַּרְסִינָן וְלֹא גַּרְסִינָן שְׁנֵי

TEXT 10C: Rashi, *Shabbat* 74a. *VeLo Yivror*

He may not select.	וְלֹא יִבְרוֹר
Later [the Talmud] inquires: What is [the *baraita*] saying when	לְקַמֵּיהּ פָּרִיךְ מַאי קָאָמַר
in the beginning it teaches, "He may select"	בְּרֵישָׁא תָּנָא בּוֹרֵר
and later it teaches, "He may not select?"	וְהָדַר תָּנָא לֹא יִבְרוֹר

TEXT 11A: Continuation of Talmud, *Shabbat* 74a

What is [the *baraita*] saying?	מַאי קָאָמַר
Ula says: This is what [the *baraita*] is saying:	אָמַר עוּלָּא הָכִי קָאָמַר

He may select and eat for that day	בּוֹרֵר וְאוֹכֵל לְבוֹ בַּיּוֹם
and he may select and leave [for others to eat] for that day,	וּבוֹרֵר וּמַנִּיחַ לְבוֹ בַּיּוֹם
but for tomorrow, he may not select,	וּלְמָחָר לֹא יִבְרוֹר
and if he selected, he is obligated to bring a sin offering.	וְאִם בֵּירֵר חַיָּיב חַטָּאת

TEXT 11B: Rashi, *Shabbat* 74a, *ULeMachar*

And for tomorrow	וּלְמָחָר
for tomorrow's need.	לְצוֹרֶךְ מָחָר

Discussion Question

What is constructive about selecting?

TEXT 12A: Continuation of Talmud, *Shabbat* 74a

Rav Chisda challenged this [answer]:	מַתְקִיף לָהּ רַב חִסְדָּא
Is it permitted to bake for that day?	וְכִי מוּתָּר לֶאֱפוֹת לְבוֹ בַּיּוֹם
Is it permitted to cook for that day?	וְכִי מוּתָּר לְבַשֵּׁל לְבוֹ בַּיּוֹם

Keys to the Talmud

Matkif Lah

—related to the word *tokif*, meaning forceful or powerful, is used in Talmudic terminology to introduce a question that arises from reason. In the Talmud, there are generally two types of challenges: those that quote a trad

itional source or statement that appears to contradict the statement in question and those that use reason to pose a challenge to the statement in question. *Matkif* always introduces the latter type of question.

TEXT 12B: Rashi, *Shabbat* 74a, *VeChi Mutar Le'efot ULevashel*

Is it permitted to bake and cook for that day?	וְכִי מוּתָּר לֶאֱפוֹת וּלְבַשֵּׁל לְבוֹ בַּיּוֹם
[Selecting] too is considered an *av melachah*,	וְהָכִי נַמִי אַב מְלָאכָה הִיא
since you have said that [if he selects] for tomorrow, he is liable to bring a sin offering.	כֵּיוָן דְּאָמְרַתְּ וּלְמָחָר חַיָּיב חַטָּאת

Part IV

Less-Than-Minimal Transgressions

TEXT 13A: Continuation of Talmud, *Shabbat* 74a

Rather, Rav Chisda says:	אֶלָּא אָמַר רַב חִסְדָּא
One may select and eat less than the amount [for which one is liable];	בּוֹרֵר וְאוֹכֵל פָּחוֹת מִכַּשִּׁיעוּר
one may select and leave [for others to eat] less that the measure [for which one is liable];	בּוֹרֵר וּמַנִּיחַ פָּחוֹת מִכַּשִּׁיעוּר
but the measure itself he may not select	וּכַשִּׁיעוּר לֹא יִבְרוֹר
and if he selected [the measure], he is obligated to bring a sin offering.	וְאִם בֵּירֵר חַיָּיב חַטָּאת

Keys to the Talmud

Ela—Rather and Shiur—a fixed amount

Ela **translates as "rather," but in Talmudic context, its effect is to convey a complete rejection of what was said earlier and instead say something else.**

A *shiur* is a fixed amount, a size that Torah considers to be the measure of significance of an item in the commission of a transgression or the fulfillment of a *mitzvah*. (The common usage of the word *shiur* to refer to a Torah class or lesson originates from a lesson that contains a set amount of Torah

material.) The set measurements of *shiurim* are *halachah leMoshe miSinai*; they were passed down from generation to generation through a direct chain of tradition dating back to Sinai.

What is the Size for Which One is Liable for Selecting?

TEXT 13B: Rashi, *Shabbat* 74a, *Pachot MiKeShi'ur*

Less than the amount—	פָּחוֹת מִכַּשִּׁיעוּר
Less than the size of a dry fig.	פָּחוֹת מִכִּגְרוֹגֶרֶת

Minor Transgressions are Still Transgressions

TEXT 14A: Continuation of Talmud, *Shabbat* 74a

Rav Yosef challenged this [explanation]:	מַתְקִיף לָהּ רַב יוֹסֵף
And is it allowed to bake less than the required amount?	וְכִי מוּתָּר לֶאֱפוֹת פָּחוֹת מִכַּשִּׁיעוּר

Insignificant Prohibitions

Discussion Questions

Before the Great Flood of Noah, people stole insignificant amounts from each other. For example, if one person had a silo of wheat, many people would steal one ear of grain each. While one ear of grain may not be significant in itself, if many thousands of people take just one ear each, they could deplete an entire silo.

Another example: if you hacked into a big bank's computer system and transferred one penny from every account to your personal account, you would have only stolen one penny from each person, but you could have can accrued millions of dollars.

Is stealing a penny the same transgression as stealing a million dollars? Should the significance of the amount of the transgression affect the severity of it? Is there reason to prohibit transgressions of insignificant proportion?

TEXT 14B: **Rashi, *Shabbat* 74a, *VeChi Mutar Le'efot***

Is it permitted to bake less than the measure?	וְכִי מוּתָּר לֶאֱפוֹת פָּחוֹת מִכַּשִּׁיעוּר
True, there is no liability to bring a sin offering,	נְהִי דְחִיּוּב חַטָּאת לֵיכָּא
but there is nevertheless a prohibition,	אִיסוּרָא מִיהָא אִיכָּא
since we have established that a half-measure [of prohibition] is prohibited biblically	דְקַיְימָא לָן חֲצִי שִׁיעוּר אָסוּר מִן הַתּוֹרָה
in the last chapter in of Tractate *Yoma* (74a).	בְּפֶּרֶק בַּתְרָא דְיוּמָא (עד,א)
How then can it rule that he may select [a small amount] in principle?	וְהֵיכִי קָתָּנֵי בּוֹרֵר לְכַתְּחִלָּה

Chatzi Shiur: Half-Measures

TEXT 15: **Talmud, *Yoma* 74a**

[Regarding] half a measure [of a prohibited food,]	חַצִי שִׁיעוּר
Rabbi Yochanan says: It is biblically prohibited,	רַבִּי יוֹחָנָן אָמַר אָסוּר מִן הַתּוֹרָה
[while] Reish Lakish says: It is biblically permitted.	רֵישׁ לָקִישׁ אָמַר מוּתָּר מִן הַתּוֹרָה
Rabbi Yochanan said: It is biblically prohibited,	רַבִּי יוֹחָנָן אָמַר אָסוּר מִן הַתּוֹרָה
since it is fit to combine [with other forbidden food and so meet the measure], he is eating prohibited food.	כֵּיוָן דְחָזֵי לְאִיצְטְרוּפֵי אִיסוּרָא קָא אָכִיל
Reish Lakish says: It is biblically permitted.	רֵישׁ לָקִישׁ אָמַר מוּתָּר מִן הַתּוֹרָה
The Merciful One stated *eating* and there is no [act of eating!]	אַכִילָה אָמַר רַחֲמָנָא וְלֵיכָּא

Is the Glass Half Full or Half Empty?

Do the Prescribed Measures Indicate Significant Quality or Quantity?

TEXT 16: ***Tzafnat Paneach*, Vol. 1, *Laws of Teshuvah*, Chapter 1, Law 2**

Reish Lakish maintains	רֵישׁ לָקִישׁ סְבִירָא לֵיהּ
that the measure is the essence [of the prohibition]	דְּהַשִּׁיעוּר הוּא עֶצֶם
and less than it is nothing at all,	וּפָחוֹת מִזֶּה לַאו כְּלוּם הוּא
whereas Rabbi Yochanan maintains	וְרַבִּי יוֹחָנָן סְבִירָא לֵיהּ
that since it combines [with other prohibited food to become prohibited],	דְּהַוּ מִצְטָרֵף
then less than it is also defined [as prohibition].	וּפָחוֹת מִזֶּה גַּם כֵּן שְׁמוֹ עָלָיו

Rabbi Yosef Rosen (1858–1936). Also known as the "Rogatchover *Gaon*"; one of the prominent Talmudic scholars of the early 20th century. Born in Rogachev, Belarus, to a Chassidic family, his unusual capabilities were noticed at a young age. At thirteen he was brought to Slutsk to study with Rabbi Yosef Ber Soloveichik. For a full year he remained there studying primarily with the rabbi's son, the legendary Rabbi Chaim Soloveitchik. Later, he studied with Rabbi Moshe Yehoshua Leib Diskin. He was the Rabbi of the Chasidic community in Dvinsk, Latvia. His works, titled *Tzafnat Pa'neach*, are famed for both their depth and difficulty.

Table 1

Shiurim—Prescribed Measures	
Rabbi Yochanan	**Reish Lakish**
determine significant **quantity** (even less than the measure has the quality of prohibition)	determine significant **quality** (less than the prescribed measurement is nothing at all)

Chatzi Shiur/Chatzi Melachah: A Half-Measure or Half a *Melachah?*

Learning **Activity**

(Write/Pair/Share)

In Lesson Three, we learned that the *melachah* of transferring an object from one domain to another is comprised of two components: 1) *akirah*, uprooting the object from the original domain and 2) *hanachah*, placing the object in a different domain.

According to Rabbi Yochanan, who maintains that there is no biblical prohibition against a half-measure, would it be biblically permissible to do *akirah* without *hanachah*? Explain your logic:

Circle One:	Yes	No
Briefly explain your logic		

Key Points

1. The *Mishnah* lists *melachot* that were performed in the *Mishkan* even when similar *melachot* were also mentioned, provided they are not the same.

Pounding: Pounding is not listed in the *Mishnah,* since it is not essential to the baking of bread, since poor people bake bread without pounding the wheat.

Rashi: Pounding is still an *av melachah*, since it was performed with the dyes in the *Mishkan*. It is not listed in the *Mishnah*, since the *Mishnah* only lists activities that are essential to the baking of bread.

Tosafot: Pounding is not an *av melachah*, even though it was performed in the *Mishkan*, because it was not essential, since a poor man does not pound his dyes.

Rabbeinu Tam: Pounding was performed in the baking of barley bread to test the *techelet* dye and is not listed as an *av melachah*, since a poor man does not pound his wheat before baking bread.

2. Selecting is a productive *melachah* when it is done in large quantities for storage.

3. Half-measures of prohibited acts:

Reish Lakish: they are biblically permitted since quantity defines quality.

Rabbi Yochanan: they are biblically prohibited since measure only defines quantity, whereas even the smallest quantity contains the entire quality of prohibition.

4. Half-*melachot* are different from half-measures, in that half a *melachah* contains no quality of *melachah*, even according to Rabbi Yochanan.

Rav Chisda: permits selecting half-measures, since he compares it to half a *melachah*, since selecting is a *melachah* defined by its quantity.

Rav Yosef: compares selecting to any other measure that only defines the quantity (according to Rabbi Yochanan) and not the quality.

Terms to Retain

And if you will say [in question] (introduces a question in Tosafot)	וְאִם תֹּאמַר
And it can be said [in answer] (introduces an answer in Tosafot)	וְיֵשׁ לוֹמַר
You might have assumed	קָא סָלְקָא דַּעְתָּךְ
I might have said (in theory)	הֲוָא אַמִינָא
Challenged it [based on reason]	מַתְקֵיף לָהּ
Rather, reject what was said earlier and say as follows (lit. "rather")	אֶלָּא
A prescribed measure	שִׁיעוּר

Optional Appendix
Keys to the Talmud

Rabbi Akiva Eiger's Questions

TEXT 17: *Chidushei Rabbi Akiva Eiger*, Vol. 3, *Shabbat* 74a, *Ela Machavarta KeDeAbaye*

Rather, [the answer] is clearly as Abaye [said]—	אֶלָא מַחְוַורְתָּא כִּדְאַבַּיֵי—
I still find it difficult.	וַעֲדַיִין קָשֶׁה לִי
For Rabbi, who derives [from the verse] that there are only thirty-nine *melachot*,	לְרַבִּי דְדָרִישׁ דְהָוֵי רַק ל"ט מְלָאכוֹת
could have removed either pounding or sifting [to retain the count of thirty-nine].	הָיָה מַפִּיק אִם כּוֹתֵשׁ אוֹ מְרַקֵד
And this requires further investigation.	וְצָרִיךְ עִיוּן

Rabbi Akiva Eiger (1761–1837). Born in Eisenstaedt, Hungary; an outstanding Talmudic scholar and influential halachic decisor. Authored commentaries on the Talmud and the *Shulchan Aruch*. Was rabbi of the city Posen. His daughter married the *Chatam Sofer*.

Lesson 8

Introduction

What makes sorting food from waste a constructive activity? What is the origin of *gefilte* fish, a traditional Shabbat food? What is the difference between cooking and kindling a fire? Can you cook metal? In this lesson, we will learn how the sages of the Talmud debated the definition of sorting and cooking, two central *melachot* of Shabbat. As we do so, we will find answers to the questions above as well as understand the development of what is Shabbat observance today!

The Apparently Self-Contradictory *Baraita*

TEXT 1: **Talmud, *Shabbat* 74a**

The Rabbis taught [in a *baraita*]:	תָּנוּ רַבָּנַן
If different types of food were before him,	הָיוּ לְפָנָיו מִינֵי אוֹכְלִין
he may select and eat and select and leave [for others to eat],	בּוֹרֵר וְאוֹכֵל בּוֹרֵר וּמַנִּיחַ
but he may not select,	וְלֹא יִבְרוֹר
and if he did select, he is obligated to bring a sin offering.	וְאִם בֵּירֵר חַיָּיב חַטָּאת

Part I

By Hand Alone vs. With a Utensil

TEXT 2: **Talmud, *Shabbat* 74a**

Rather, Rav Yosef said:	אֶלָּא אָמַר רַב יוֹסֵף
He may select by hand and eat,	בּוֹרֵר וְאוֹכֵל בְּיַד
he may select by hand and leave [for others to eat].	בּוֹרֵר וּמַנִּיחַ בְּיַד
However, he may not select with a funnel or with a large plate,	בְּקָנוֹן וּבְתַמְחוּי לֹא יִבְרוֹר
and if he did select [with one of these utensils], he is exempt [from bringing a sin offering], but it is nonetheless forbidden.	וְאִם בֵּירֵר פָּטוּר אֲבָל אָסוּר
Furthermore, he may not select with a fine sieve or with a coarse sieve	וּבְנָפָה וּבִכְבָרָה לֹא יִבְרוֹר
and if he did select [with one of these utensils], he is obligated to bring a sin offering.	וְאִם בֵּירֵר חַיָּיב חַטָּאת

Selecting with a Funnel

TEXT 3: **Rashi, *Shabbat* 74a, *BiKanon***

With a funnel—	בְּקָנוֹן
a wooden utensil that is carved like a pipe,	כְּלִי עֵץ שֶׁעוֹשִׂין כְּעֵין צִינוֹר
that is wide at its back part and narrow at its front part	רָחָב מִלְאַחֲרָיו וְקָצָר מִלְּפָנָיו
and it is made by smiths.	וּבַעֲלֵי מַטְבֵּעַ עוֹשִׂים אוֹתוֹ
One who separates [impurities from] legumes with it	וְהַבּוֹרֵר בּוֹ קִטְנִית
places the legumes in the wide part and shakes it [around in circles]	נוֹתֵן קִטְנִית בְּמָקוֹם הָרָחָב וּמְנַעְנְעוֹ

and because the legumes are round,	וְהַקִּטְנִית מִפְּנֵי שֶׁהוּא סְגַלְגַּל
they roll down through the narrow opening	מִתְגַּלְגֵּל וְיוֹרֵד דֶּרֶךְ פִּיו הַקָּצָר
and the impurities remain in the utensil.	וְהַפְּסוֹלֶת נִשְׁאָר בַּכְּלִי

Rabbi Shlomo Yitzchaki (1040–1105). Better known by the acronym *Rashi;* rabbi and famed author of the first comprehensive commentaries on the Talmud and Bible. Born in Troyes, Champagne, Rashi studied in the famed yeshivot of Mainz and Worms. His commentaries, which focus on the simple understanding of the text, are considered fundamental to Torah study. Since their initial printings, they have appeared in virtually every edition of the Talmud and Bible. Amongst Rashi's descendants, were many of the famed Tosafists of France.

Exempt but Prohibited

TEXT 4: Rashi, *Shabbat* 74a, *Patur Aval Asur*

He is exempt, but it is nonetheless forbidden.	פָּטוּר אֲבָל אָסוּר
It is not permissible to be done in principle,	מוּתָּר לְכַתְּחִלָּה לֹא הָוֵי
since it is similar to selecting.	דְדָמִי לִבְרֵירָה
However, it does not make one liable to bring a sin offering,	וְחַיָּיב חַטָּאת לֹא הָוֵי
since it is performed in a backhanded manner,	דִּכְלְאַחֵר יַד הוּא
as selecting is primarily performed with a fine sieve or with a coarse sieve.	דְעִיקָּר בְּרֵירָה בְּנָפָה וּכְבָרָה
However, [selecting] by hand is not at all similar to [the *melachah* of] selecting.	אֲבָל בְּיַד לֹא דָמִי לְבוֹרֵר כְּלָל

Is it in the *Baraita*?

TEXT 5: Talmud, *Shabbat* 74a

Rav Hamnuna challenged this [explanation of Rav Yosef]:	מַתְקִיף לָהּ רַב הַמְנוּנָא
Does the *baraita* teach anything about a funnel or wide plate?	מִידִי קָנוֹן וְתַמְחוּי קָתָנֵי

TEXT 6: **Rashi, *Shabbat* 74a, *Midi Kenon VeTamchui Katani***

Does the baraita teach anything about a funnel or a wide plate?	מִידֵי קָנוֹן וְתַמְחוּי קָתָנֵי
He could have equally asked	הוּא הַדִּין נַמִּי דְּפָרִיךְ
"Does the *baraita* teach anything about a fine sieve and a coarse sieve?"	מִידֵי נָפָה וּכְבָרָה קָתָנֵי
but he chose only one of them.	אֶלָּא חֲדָא מִינַּיְיהוּ נָקַט

Food from Waste

TEXT 7: **Talmud, *Shabbat* 74a**

Rather, Rav Hamnuna said:	אֶלָּא אָמַר רַב הַמְנוּנָא
One may select the food from the waste and eat [or]	בּוֹרֵר וְאוֹכֵל אוֹכֶלמִתּוֹךְ הַפְּסוֹלֶת
one may select the food from the waste and leave it [for others to eat].	בּוֹרֵרוּמַנִּיחַאוֹכֶלמִתּוֹךְ הַפְּסוֹלֶת
However, he may not select the waste from the food	פְּסוֹלֶתמִתּוֹךְאוֹכֶללֹא יִבְרוֹר
and if he did select [the waste from the food] he is liable for a sin offering.	וְאִם בֵּירֵר חַיָּיב חַטָּאת

TEXT 8: **Rashi, *Shabbat* 74a, *Ochel Mitoch HaPesolet***

Food from waste—	אוֹכֶל מִתּוֹךְ הַפְּסוֹלֶת
Such is not the manner of selecting.	לֹא דֶּרֶךְ בְּרֵירָה הִיא

For Immediate Consumption

TEXT 9: **Talmud, *Shabbat* 74a**

Abaye challenged [this explanation]:	מַתְקִיף לָהּ אַבַּיֵי
Does the *baraita* teach anything about [removing] food from waste?	מִידֵי אוֹכֶל מִתּוֹךְ פְּסוֹלֶת קָתָנֵי
Rather, Abaye said:	אֶלָּא אָמַר אַבַּיֵי
one may select and eat immediately,	בּוֹרֵר וְאוֹכֵל לְאַלְתַּר
and one may select and leave [for others to eat] immediately.	וּבוֹרֵר וּמַנִּיחַ לְאַלְתַּר
However, he may not select for [later] that day	וּלְבוֹ בַּיּוֹם לֹא יִבְרוֹר
and if he did select, it becomes as if he selected for storage	וְאִם בֵּירֵר נַעֲשֶׂה כְּבוֹרֵר לְאוֹצָר
and he is liable for a sin offering.	וְחַיָּיב חַטָּאת
The Rabbis stated this [explanation] before Rava.	אַמְרוּהָ רַבָּנָן קַמֵּיהּ דְּרָבָא
He said to them: Nachmani said well.	אֲמַר לְהוּ שַׁפִּיר אָמַר נַחְמָנִי

The Manner of Seleting

TEXT 10: **Rashi, *Shabbat* 74a, *UVoreir UMeniach LeAltar***

One may select [to eat] and leave [for others to eat] immediately.	וּבוֹרֵר וּמַנִּיחַ לְאַלְתַּר
To eat immediately,	לֶאֱכוֹל לְאַלְתַּר
since this is not the way people select.	שֶׁאֵין זֶה דֶּרֶךְ בּוֹרְרִין

TEXT 11: **Rashi, *Shabbat* 74a, *LeOtzar***

For storage	לְאוֹצָר
To set aside.	לְהַצְנִיעַ

TEXT 12A: **Rashi, *Shabbat* 74a, *Nachmani***

Nachmani	נַחְמֵנִי
[is]Abaye	אַבַּיֵי

TEXT 12B: **Rashi, *Gitin* 34b, *VeHilcheta KeNachmani***

It appears to me	וְנִרְאֶה בְּעֵינַי
that [the name Nachmani] was for Rabbah bar Nachmani,	דְעַל שֵׁם שֶׁרַבָּה בַּר נַחְמֵנִי
who raised Abaye in his home	גִידֵל אַבַּיֵי בְּבֵיתוֹ
and taught him Torah.	וְלִמְדוֹ תּוֹרָה
Since he was an orphan,	שֶׁהָיָה יָתוֹם
he made him carry the name of his father, Nachmani.	הִשִּׂיאוֹ אֶת שֵׁם אָבִיו נַחְמֵנִי

TEXT 12C: **Rashi, *Horayot* 14a, *Nachmani Patach***

Others say	וְאִיכָּא דְאַמְרֵי
that he was called Nachamani out of disrespect,	דִבְלָשׁוֹן גְנַאי קָרֵי לֵיהּ נַחְמֵנִי
as if saying, "You are still a disciple of Rav Nachman."	כְּלוֹמַר עֲדַיִין אַתָּה תַּלְמִידוֹ שֶׁל רַב נַחְמָן

TEXT 12D: ***Chatam Sofer, Gitin* 34a**

See *Sefer Yuchasin* under the name Abaye,	עַיֵּין בְּסֵפֶר יוּחָסִין בְּשֵׁם אַבַּיֵי
who wrote the opposite,	שֶׁכָּתַב בְּהֵיפּוּךְ
that his name was Nachmani like the name of Rabbah's father	שְׁמוֹ הָיָה נַחְמֵנִי כְּשֵׁם אָבִיו שֶׁל רַבָּה
and [Rabbah] did not want to call him by his name ,	וְלֹא רָצָה לִקְרוֹתוֹ בִּשְׁמוֹ
as it was the same as his father's name and	שֶׁהוּא כְּשֵׁם אָבִיו
he therefore gave him the name Abaye from the word Av (father) since his name was the same as his father's.	עַל כֵּן הֵסִיב שְׁמוֹ אַבַּיֵי לְשׁוֹן אָב שֶׁשְּׁמוֹ כְּשֵׁם אָבִיו
Abaye is an acronym for*Asher Becha Yerucham Yatom, "For in you the fatherless find mercy"* (Hoshea 14:4).	וְאַבַּיֵי רָאשֵׁי תֵּיבוֹת אֲשֶׁר בְּךָ יְרוּחַם יָתוֹם

Rabbi Moshe Sofer (Schreiber) (1762–1839). Also known by the title of his main work, *Chatam Sofer,* a collection of responsa literature. One of the leading rabbinical authorities of the nineteenth century, his policies and decisions helped shape Austria-Hungarian Jewry. Born in Frankfurt am Main, Germany, he entered the yeshiva of Rabbi Natan Adler, at the age of nine. After declining various offers for the rabbinate, he ultimately accepted a position in Pressburg (now Bratislava), Slovakia. Serving as rabbi, and head of the Yeshiva he established, Rabbi Sofer maintained a strong traditionalist perspective, fighting all deviations from tradition.

Table 1

Opinions on Permissibility

Amora	Selecting is Permitted	Selecting is Prohibited	Objection
Ulla	For today	For tomorrow	Is one allowed to bake for today?
Rav Chisda	Incomplete measure	Complete measure	Is an incomplete measure of baking permitted?
Rav Yosef	By hand	Funnel/wide plate (not liable) Fine/coarse sieve (liable)	Does a funnel or wide plate appear in the *baraita*?
Rav Hamnuna	Food from waste	Waste from food	Is food from waste stated in the *baraita*?
Abaye	For immediate consumption	For later consumption	None

Learning Activity

Please answer these questions:

Under what conditions are you allowed to select on Shabbat, according to all opinions?

Under what conditions would you be liable for selecting on Shabbat according to all opinions?

Discussion Question

In his final response, Abaye posits that selecting for immediate consumption is permitted. Normally, there is at least a rabbinic prohibition against performing a *melachah* in an irregular manner. Why in this instance is it different?

Introduction to *Shulchan Aruch HaRav*

An Act of Eating

TEXT 13: ***Shulchan Aruch*** **of Rabbi Schneur Zalman of Liadi 319:1**

Anyone who selects waste from food,	כָּל הַבּוֹרֵר פְּסוֹלֶת מִתּוֹךְ הָאוֹכֶל
even with one hand	אֲפִילוּ בְּיָדוֹ אַחַת
and even to eat immediately,	וַאֲפִילוּ כְּדֵי לֶאֱכוֹל לְאַלְתַּר
is liable [for a sin offering].	חַיָּיב
However, one who selects food from waste	אֲבָל הַבּוֹרֵר אוֹכֶל מִתּוֹךְ הַפְּסוֹלֶת
in order to eat immediately	כְּדֵי לֶאֱכוֹל לְאַלְתַּר
is not liable	אֵינוֹ חַיָּיב
unless he selects with a fine sieve or a coarse sieve,	אֶלָּא אִם כֵּן בּוֹרֵר בְּנָפָה אוֹ כְּבָרָה
since this is the normal method of selecting.	שֶׁזֶּהוּ דֶּרֶךְ בְּרֵירָתוֹ
However, if one selected with a funnel or wide plate,	אֲבָל אִם בֵּירֵר בְּקָנוֹן אוֹ תַּמְחוּי
he is biblically exempt;	פָּטוּר מִן הַתּוֹרָה
however it is prohibited by the rabbis	אֲבָל אָסוּר מִדִּבְרֵי סוֹפְרִים
as a decree so that [one will not select] using a fine sieve or a coarse sieve.	גְּזֵרָה מִשּׁוּם נָפָה וּכְבָרָה
And if he selects the food by hand to eat immediately	וְאִם בּוֹרֵר הָאוֹכֶל בְּיָדוֹ כְּדֵי לֶאֱכוֹל לְאַלְתַּר
it is permitted,	מוּתָּר
since removing the food from the waste to eat immediately	מִפְּנֵי שֶׁנְּטִילַת הָאוֹכֶל מִתּוֹךְ הַפְּסוֹלֶת כְּדֵי לְאָכְלוֹ מִיַּד

is not a type of *melachah* at all	אֵין זֶה מֵעֵין מְלָאכָה כְּלָל
as such is the way of one who eats,	שֶׁדֶּרֶךְ אֲכִילָה כָּךְ הוּא
since it is not possible to eat everything,	שֶׁהֲרֵי אִי אֶפְשָׁר לֶאֱכוֹל הַכֹּל
the food with the waste.	הָאוֹכֶל עִם הַפְּסוֹלֶת
And Torah only prohibited	וְלֹא אָסְרָתוֹ תּוֹרָה
[selecting] it with a utensil that is designed for such a purpose,	אֶלָּא לַעֲשׂוֹתוֹ בִּכְלִי הַמְיוּחָד לְכָךְ
i.e. with a fine sieve or a coarse sieve.	דְּהַיְינוּ נָפָה וּכְבָרָה
But removing the waste	אֲבָל נְטִילַת הַפְּסוֹלֶת
is not the manner of one who eats,	אֵין זוֹ דֶּרֶךְ אֲכִילָה
but a way of preparing the food	אֶלָּא דֶּרֶךְ תִּיקּוּן הָאוֹכֶל
to be suitable for eating.	שֶׁיְּהֵא רָאוּי לַאֲכִילָה
It is a complete *melachah.*	הֲרֵי זוֹ מְלָאכָה גְמוּרָה
Therefore, even when there is more food than waste	וּלְפִיכָךְ אֲפִילוּ אִם הָאוֹכֶל מְרוּבֶּה עַל הַפְּסוֹלֶת
and it is more difficult to remove the food,	וְיֵשׁ טוֹרַח יוֹתֵר בִּבְרֵירַת הָאוֹכֶל
nevertheless, he should not select the waste	אַף עַל פִּי כֵן לֹא יִבְרוֹר הַפְּסוֹלֶת
even to eat immediately.	אֲפִילוּ כְּדֵי לֶאֱכוֹל לְאַלְתַּר:

Rabbi Shne'ur Zalman of Liadi (1745–1812). Known as "the Alter Rebbe" and "the Rav"; Born in Liozna, Belarus; buried in Hadiach, Ukraine; Chassidic Rebbe and founder of the Chabad movement; among the principle students of the *Magid* of Mezeritch. His numerous works include the *Tanya,* an early classic of Chassidism; *Torah Or* and *Likutei Torah,* and *Shulchan Aruch HaRav*, a rewritten code of Jewish law. He was succeeded by his son, Rabbi Dovber of Lubavitch.

Table 2

Selecting for immediate consumption is permitted because . . .

Rashi	*Shulchan Aruch HaRav*
Shinui: It is not the normal manner of selecting.	*Derech Achilah*: It is not an act of selecting, but an act of eating.
Negative: Not considered selecting	Positive: Considered an act of eating

Learning Activity

Part A

Check off the opinions that are presented as law in the *Shulchan Aruch*

	Ulla—today/tomorrow
	Rav Chisda—incomplete/complete measure
	Rav Yosef—by hand/with utensil
	Rav Hamnuna—Food from waste/waste from food
	Abaye—Immediate/later consumption

Part B

Can you differentiate between the objections to the solutions that are cited in *Shulchan Aruch* and the objections that that are not?

The objections to the solutions cited in Shulchan Aruch are . . .	The objections to the solutions that are **not** cited in *Shulchan Aruch* are . . .

Did You Know?

***Gefilte* Fish**

Gefilte fish is a minced fish loaf that is traditionally eaten on Shabbat. How did this tradition develop? The *melachah* of *borer* (selecting) presented a problem with regard to eating fish on Shabbat. Removing the bones from the fish is considered removing waste from food and is prohibited even by hand and even for immediate use. The solution: *gefilte* fish! Because it has no bones, it presents no problems of selecting on Shabbat. This is the reason why *gefilte* fish became the traditional Shabbat fish!

Part II

Baking and Cooking

The Order of Bread

TEXT 14A: **Talmud, *Shabbat* 74b**

Kneading and baking:	וְהַלָּשׁ וְהָאוֹפֶה
Rav Pappa said	אָמַר רַב פָּפָּא
Our Tana left aside	שָׁבַק תַּנָּא דִידַן
the cooking of herbs that was performed in the *Mishkan* [construction]	בִּישׁוּל סַמְמָנִין דַּהֲוָה בְּמִשְׁכָּן
and mentioned baking?	וְנָקַט אוֹפֶה
Our Tana chose the order of baking bread.	תַּנָּא דִידַן סִידּוּרָא דְפַת נָקַט

TEXT 14B: **Rashi, *Shabbat* 74b, *VeNakat Ofeh***

And mentioned baking—	וְנָקַט אוֹפֶה
which did not belong at all among the activities of the Tabernacle's construction.	דְלֹא שַׁיָיךְ בִּמְלֶאכֶת הַמִשְׁכָּן כְּלַל

Cooking was performed in the *Mishkan*, as they would cook herbs to make dyes. Baking was not performed in the construction of the *Mishkan*. What troubled Rav Pappa is why baking was mentioned in the *mishnah* as the *av melachah* and not cooking?

TEXT 14C: **Rashi, *Shabbat* 74b, *Sidura DePat***

The order of baking bread—	סִידוּרָא דְפַּת
with which he started,	שֶׁהִתְחִיל בּוֹ
he chose to mention	נָקַט
and baking is in place of cooking the herbs,	וְאוֹפֶה בְּמָקוֹם בִּישׁוּל דְסַמְמָנִין הוּא
[for baking] is the *cooking* of bread.	דְהוּא בִּישׁוּל דְפַּת

Defining the *Melachah* of Cooking

Discussion Questions

What is the definition of cooking/baking? Is it applicable outside of the realm of food preparation? If you baked bricks on Shabbat, did you transgress the *melachah* of cooking/baking? What effect must cooking have on the cooked item to transgress the prohibition of cooking?

TEXT 15A: **Talmud, *Shabbat* 74b**

Rav Acha bar Rav Avira said:	אָמַר רַב אַחָא בַּר רַב עֲוִירָא
One who throws a peg into an oven	הַאי מַאן דְּשָׁדָא סִיכְתָא לְאַתּוּנָא
is liable on account of cooking.	חַיָּיב מִשּׁוּם מְבַשֵּׁל
Is it not obvious?	פְּשִׁיטָא
But you might have said	מַהוּ דְּתֵימָא
that he intends only to strengthen the utensil.	לְשָׁרוּרֵי מָנָא קָא מִיכַּוֵּין
He therefore informs us:	קָא מַשְׁמַע לָן
that it first softens and then hardens.	דְּמֵירְפָּא רָפֵי וְהָדַר קָמִיט

TEXT 15B: **Rashi, *Shabbat* 74b, *DeShada***

Throws a peg—	דְּשָׁדָא סִיכְתָא
He threw a moist [earthenware] peg into the oven to dry it	שֶׁהִשְׁלִיךְ יָתֵד לַח לַתַּנּוּר חַם לְיַבְּשׁוֹ
so that it would harden.	שֶׁיִּתְקַשֶּׁה

Keys to the Talmud

Peshita—Is it not obvious?
and Mahu DeTeima—You might have said

Peshita **is a question that is normally asked in astonishment over a particular statement of *Tannaim* (Sages of the Mishnah) or *Amoraim* (Sages of the Talmud). Its implication is that since the concept seems to be simple and easily understood, what could have been the *Tana* or *Amora's* intention in teaching something so obvious? The question of *peshita* is based upon the premise that the Talmud will not mention teachings that are superfluous. Therefore, if it appears that a particular teaching contains no innovation, the Talmud will object with *peshita*, "It is obvious! Why must it be stated?"**

The question *peshita* is normally asked for one of two primary reasons:

a. Logic: If something is common sense and self-evident, why must it be stated?

b. Common knowledge: If a teaching is known from elsewhere, why must it be taught again here?

TEXT 15C: Rashi, *Shabbat* 74b, *Lisherurei*

To strengthen to toughen,	לְשָׁרוּרֵי חָזָק
and there is no [instance of] cooking here!	וְאֵין כָּאן בִּישׁוּל

TEXT 15D: Rashi, *Shabbat* 74b, *DeMarpi Rafi*

It softens—	דְּמִירְפָּא רָפֵי
from the heat of the fire	עַל יְדֵי חוֹם הָאוּר
and the water inside it is released	וְהַמַּיִם שֶׁבְּתוֹכוֹ יוֹצְאִין
and after the water leaves,	וּלְאַחַר שֶׁיָּצְאוּ מֵימָיו
it contracts and hardens	קָמִיט מִתְקַשֶּׁה
and when it initially softened, that was its cooking.	וְכִי רָפֵי בְּרֵישָׁא הָוֵי בִּישׁוּלוֹ

TEXT 16: Talmud, *Shabbat* 74b

Rabbah bar Rav Huna said:	אָמַר רַבָּה בַּר רַב הוּנָא
Someone who heats tar	הַאי מַאן דְּאַרְתַּח כּוּפְרָא
is liable on account of cooking.	חַיָּיב מִשּׁוּם מְבַשֵּׁל
Is it not obvious?	פְּשִׁיטָא
What you might have said was	מַהוּ דְּתֵימָא
That since it subsequently hardens, I would say that he is not [liable].	כֵּיוָן דְּהָדַר וְאִיקּוּשָׁא אֵימָא לֹא
He therefore informs us [that he is nevertheless liable].	קָא מַשְׁמַע לָן.

Discussion Questions

If you heat up a sheet of metal on Shabbat, are you liable for the *melachah* of lighting a fire or for cooking? What is the basic difference between cooking and kindling a fire?

Between Cooking and Burning

TEXT 17: Rogatchover Gaon, *Tzafnat Paneach* Second Ed., Laws of Idolatry 3:3

Kindling a fire is [a *melachah*]	הַבְעָרָה הוּא
on account of the consumption of the item,	מֵחֲמַת כִּלְיוֹן הַדָּבָר
whereas cooking is [a *melachah* on account of]	וּבִישׁוּל הוּא
the improvement of the item.	תִּיקּוּן הַדָּבָר

Rabbi Yosef Rosen (1858–1936). Also known as the "Rogatchover *Gaon*"; one of the prominent Talmudic scholars of the early 20th century. Born in Rogachev, Belarus, to a Chassidic family, his unusual capabilities were noticed at a young age. At thirteen he was brought to Slutsk to study with Rabbi Yosef Ber Soloveichik. For a full year he remained there studying primarily with the rabbi's son, the legendary Rabbi Chaim Soloveitchik. Later, he studied with Rabbi Moshe Yehoshua Leib Diskin. He was the Rabbi of the Chasidic community in Dvinsk, Latvia. His works, titled *Tzafnat Pa'neach*, are famed for both their depth and difficulty.

Softening the Hard and Hardening the Soft

TEXT 18: Maimonides, *Laws of Shabbat* 9:6

One who cooks earthenware utensils	הַמְבַשֵּׁל כְּלֵי אֲדָמָה
until they become pottery	עַד שֶׁיַּעֲשׂוּ חֶרֶס
is liable on account of cooking.	חַיָּיב מִשּׁוּם מְבַשֵּׁל
The general rule is:	כְּלָלוֹ שֶׁל דָּבָר
Whether one softens a hard substance	בֵּין שֶׁרִיפָּה גוּף קָשֶׁה בָּאֵשׁ
or hardens a soft substance,	אוֹ שֶׁהִקְשָׁה גוּף רַךְ
he is liable on account of cooking.	הֲרֵי זֶה חַיָּיב מִשּׁוּם מְבַשֵּׁל

Rabbi Moshe ben Maimon (1135–1204). Better known as Maimonides or by the acronym, the *Rambam*. Born in Cardoba, Spain. After the conquest of Cardoba by the Almohads, who sought to forcibly convert the Jews to Islam, he fled and eventually settled in Cairo. There he became the leader of the Jewish community and served as court physician to the vizier of Egypt. His rulings on Jewish law are considered integral to the formation of Halachic consensus. He is most noted for authoring the *Mishneh Torah,* an encyclopedic arrangement of Jewish law. His philosophical work, *Guide to the Perplexed,* is also well-known.

TEXT 19: ***Lechem Mishneh, Laws of Shabbat*** **9:6**

[The Talmud] implies that if the peg would not initially soften,	מַשְׁמַע דִּבְסִיכְתָּא אִי לַאו דְּרָפֵי בִּתְחִלָּה
he would not be liable.	לֹא הֲוָה חַיָּיב
How does [Maimonides] write that in every instance	וְאֵיךְ כָּתַב שֶׁבְּכָל מָקוֹם
that one hardens a soft item, that he is liable?	שֶׁהִקְשָׁה גוּף הָרַךְ שֶׁחַיָּיב
It could be said [in answer]	וְיֵשׁ לוֹמַר
that he maintains that every soft item that is cooked,	דְּהוּא סוֹבֵר דְּכָל דָּבָר לַח שֶׁמִּתְבַּשֵּׁל
even though it hardens,	אַף עַל פִּי שֶׁמִּתְקַשֶּׁה
makes one liable on account of cooking	חַיָּיב מִשּׁוּם בִּישּׁוּל
similar to baking.	דּוּמְיָא דְּאוֹפֶה

Rabbi Avraham ben Moshe di Buton (ca. 1545–1588). Born and lived in Salonika, Greece and served in its Rabbinate; a disciple of Rabbi Shmuel di Modena. He is famous for his authorship of a commentary on Maimonides' code of law which is widely used and very popular. We also have a collection of his responsa, *Lechem Rav.*

Cooking vs. Baking

TEXT 20: **Rogatchover Gaon, *Dvinsk Responsa* vol. 2, Page 8c**

There are two definitions [of the *melachah*]:	בְּאֵשׁ יֵשׁ ב' גְּדָרִים
one is ***to soften the item***	אֶחָד לְרַכֵּךְ הַדָּבָר
and the second is ***to harden it and to bake it.***	וְהַשֵּׁנִי לְיַבְּשׁוֹ וְלֶאֱפוֹת

And this is the difference between roasting and cooking,	וְזֶה נַפְקָא מִינָהּ בֵּין צָלִי לְבִישּׁוּל
that roasting bakes and dries the item	דְצָלִי אוֹפֶה וּמְיַבֵּשׁ הַדָּבָר . . .
whereas cooking softens.	אֲבָל בִּישּׁוּל מְרַכֵּךְ

Cooking in our Service of G-d

TEXT 21: ***Torat Menachem,* Vol. 11 pg. 78 *(Parshat Mishpatim 5714)***

Physical cooking and roasting	בְּגַשְׁמִיּוּת בְּבִישּׁוּל וּצְלִיָּה
make the item suitable to be eaten,	שֶׁעַל יְדֵי זֶה נַעֲשֶׂה הַדָּבָר רָאוּי לַאֲכִילָה
which is a change of the substance,	שֶׁזֶּהוּ עִנְיָן שֶׁל שִׁינּוּי הַמְּהוּת
since the flavor of the food	שֶׁהֲרֵי הַטַּעַם שֶׁל הַמַּאֲכָל
is not the physical component, but the spirit that is in it,	אֵינוֹ הַגַּשְׁמִי שֶׁל הַדָּבָר אֶלָּא הָרוּחָנִי שֶׁבּוֹ
and the effect of cooking is that the physical is minimized and the spirit is felt.	וּפְעוּלַּת הַבִּישּׁוּל הִיא שֶׁנִּתְמַעֵט הַגַּשְׁמִי וְנִרְגָּשׁ הָרוּחָנִי

Rabbi Menachem Mendel Schneerson (1902–1994). Known as "the Lubavitcher Rebbe," or simply as "the Rebbe." Born in southern Ukraine. Rabbi Schneerson escaped from the Nazis, arriving in the US in June 1941. The towering Jewish leader of the twentieth century, the Rebbe inspired and guided the revival of traditional Judaism after the European devastation, and often emphasized that the performance of just one additional good deed could usher in the era of Mashiach.

Key Points

1. There are three distinctions in the *melachah* of selecting:

a. with a utensil, not by hand
b. waste from food, not food from waste
c. for long term storage, not for immediate consumption

2. Selecting is permitted on Shabbat only when three conditions are met:

a. One selects by hand
b. One selects food from waste
c. One selects for immediate consumption

3. Selecting for immediate consumption is permitted because:

Rashi: it is not the normal manner of selecting
Rabbi Shneur Zalman of Liadi: it is an act of eating, not selecting

4. When removing the evil to reveal the sparks of G-dliness in this world, one must:

a. use special techniques (utensils) to remove the evil and elevate good to holiness
b. first remove oneself from evil before doing good (waste from food)
c. make sure it will be a long-lasting transformation, not a temporary one

5. The *melachah* of cooking is listed in the *Mishnah* as baking because the *Mishnah* follows the order of making bread.

6. Cooking also applies to non-food substances.

7. Cooking improves the item, whereas burning consumes the item.

8. Cooking is a process of softening. According to Maimonides, it also includes hardening a soft substance.

9. Baking and cooking represent two definitions of the *melachah* of cooking: hardening and softening.

10. Cooking alters the physical and brings out the spiritual (flavor and aroma).

In our service of building a Tabernacle for G-d, it represents deemphasizing the physical and stressing the spiritual.

Terms to Retain

Sorting/selecting	בּוֹרֵר
Food	אוֹכֶל
Waste	פְּסוֹלֶת
Baking	אֲפִיָּה
Cooking	בִּישׁוּל
It is obvious	פְּשִׁיטָא
You might have said	מַהוּ דְתֵימָה
He therefore informs us	קָא מַשְׁמַע לָן

Lesson 9

Introduction

When you use extraordinary talents in the performance of *melachah*, is it considered normative? Is there any difference in terms of the deviation from the norm between skilled craftsmen and ordinary people displaying extraordinary talent? Does tying your shoelaces or your tie constitute the *melachah* of tying a knot? How would you define the *melachah* of tying a knot?

In this lesson, we will explore *melachot* that the Talmud defines by intent of the person doing the *melachah*. We will also learn that the appearance of an action plays an important role even when we define the act by its intent.

Part I

Extraordinary Craftsmanship

Spinning on the Goat

TEXT 1: Talmud, *Shabbat* 74b

Shearing wool and whitening it—	הַגּוֹזֵז אֶת הַצֶּמֶר וְהַמְלַבְּנוֹ
Rabbah bar bar Chanah said in the name of Rabbi Yochanan:	אָמַר רַבָּה בַּר בַּר חַנָה אָמַר רַבִּי יוֹחָנָן
One who spins wool on the back of an animal on Shabbat	הַטּוֹוֶה צֶמֶר שֶׁעַל גַּבֵּי בְּהֵמָה בְּשַׁבָּת
is liable to bring three sin offerings:	חַיָּיב שָׁלֹשׁ חַטָּאוֹת
one on account of shearing,	אַחַת מִשּׁוּם גּוֹזֵז
one on account of combing	וְאַחַת מִשּׁוּם מְנַפֵּץ
and one on account of spinning.	וְאַחַת מִשּׁוּם טוֹוֶה
Rav Kahana said: This is not the manner of shearing,	רַב כַּהֲנָא אָמַר אֵין דֶּרֶךְ גְּזִיזָה בְּכַךְ
this is not the manner of combing	וְאֵין דֶּרֶךְ מְנַפֵּץ בְּכַךְ
and this is not the manner of spinning.	ואין דֶּרֶךְ טִוּוּי בְּכַךְ
Is it not?	וְלֹא
Was it not taught in a *baraita* in the name of Rabbi Nechemiah:	וְהָתַנְיָא מִשְּׁמֵיהּ דְּרַבִּי נְחֶמְיָה
They washed [the hair] on the goats and they spun [it] on the goats?	שָׁטוּף בָּעִזִּים וְטָווּ בָּעִזִּים
Thus we see that spinning on the back of an animal is considered spinning.	אַלְמָא טְוִויָה עַל גַּבֵּי בְּהֵמָה שְׁמָהּ טְוִויָה
[An act performed with] extraordinary craftsmanship is different.	חָכְמָה יְתֵירָה שַׁאנִי

Biblical Source

TEXT 2A: **Rashi, *Shabbat* 74b, *Shatuf Be'Izim***

They washed [the hair] on the goats and they spun [it] on the goats.	שָׁטוּף בָּעִזִּים וְטָווּ בָּעִזִּים
[The *baraita*] expounds upon a verse (Exodus 35:26): *spun* et *the goats [hair].*	קְרָא קָדָרִישׁ טָווּ אֶת הָעִזִּים (שמות לה)
[The verse] implies [that they spun it] on the body of the goats.	בְּגוּפָן שֶׁל עִזִּים מַשְׁמַע

Rabbi Shlomo Yitzchaki (1040–1105). Better known by the acronym *Rashi;* rabbi and famed author of the first comprehensive commentaries on the Talmud and Bible. Born in Troyes, Champagne, Rashi studied in the famed yeshivot of Mainz and Worms. His commentaries, which focus on the simple understanding of the text, are considered fundamental to Torah study. Since their initial printings, they have appeared in virtually every edition of the Talmud and Bible. Amongst Rashi's descendants, were many of the famed Tosafists of France.

Keys to the Talmud

Et את

With 3450 mentions, the word *et* is the word that appears most frequently in the Torah. The word *et* surprisingly has no translation in the English language (save for the few times it is used to mean "with"). It is the sign of the accusative or in other words, a particle of the objective case. (For those who are not familiar with complex grammatical terminology, it precedes the word that is the direct object of the verb if that object is definite, i.e. preceded by the definite article, defined by a suffix or a proper noun.) Interestingly, this is indicated by the construct of the word; it is comprised of the first and last letters of the Hebrew alphabet, *alef* and *tav,* indicating that it connotes the entirety or the essence of the object to which the verb refers. *Et* is often understood in biblical exegesis to include something. In the following *baraita* from Tractate *Pesachim*, we find that every mention of the word *et* in the Torah teaches us something new.

Text 2B: ***Baraita, Pesachim* 22b**

Shimon HaAmsoni, and some say it was Nechemiah HaAmsoni,	שִׁמְעוֹן הָעַמְסוּנִי וְאַמְרִי לָהּ נְחֶמְיָה הָעַמְסוּנִי
would expound every *et* written in the Torah.	הָיָה דוֹרֵשׁ כָּל אֶתִים שֶׁבַּתּוֹרָה
However, once he reached the words (Deuteronomy 6:13): "You shall revere *et* the L-rd your G-d", he withdrew.	כֵּיוָן שֶׁהִגִּיעַ לְאֶת ה׳ אֱלֹקֶיךָ תִּירָא פֵּירֵשׁ
His students said to him:	אָמְרוּ לוֹ תַּלְמִידָיו
Teacher, what will become of all the *et*s that you expounded?	רַבִּי כָּל אֶתִים שֶׁדָּרַשְׁתָּ מַה תְּהֵא עֲלֵיהֶן
He said to them:	אָמַר לָהֶם
Just as I received reward for expounding,	כְּשֵׁם שֶׁקִּבַּלְתִּי שָׂכָר עַל הַדְּרִישָׁה
so I will receive reward for refraining (from expounding).	כַּךְ אֲנִי מְקַבֵּל שָׂכָר עַל הַפְּרִישָׁה
[So it was] until Rabbi Akiva came along and expounded:	עַד שֶׁבָּא רַבִּי עֲקִיבָא וְדָרַשׁ
You shall revere *et* the L-rd your G-d.	אֶת ה׳ אֱלֹקֶיךָ תִּירָא
[Here, the *et*] comes to include Torah scholars.	לְרַבּוֹת תַּלְמִידֵי חֲכָמִים

Extraordinary Talent or Irregularity?

Text 3A: **Rashi, *Shabbat* 74b, *Chochmah Yeteirah***

Extraordinary craftsmanship.	חָכְמָה יְתֵירָה
As the verse states (Exodus 35:25), *And all the women that were wise hearted . . .*	כְּדִכְתִיב וְכָל אִשָּׁה חָכְמַת לֵב
But for the ordinary person,	אֲבָל לְהֶדְיוֹט
it is not the regular manner for him	אֵין דַּרְכּוֹ בְּכַךְ
and it is considered as if it were done in an unusual (lit. backhanded) manner.	וְהָוֵי כִּלְאַחַר יָד

Different Strokes for Different Folks?

TEXT 3B: **Tosafot, *Shabbat* 74b, *Chochmah Yeteirah Shani***

[An act performed with] extraordinary craftsmanship is different.	חָכְמָה יְתֵירָה שַׁאנִי
and those who do it [in such a manner], their outlook is nullified before that of most [lit. all] people,	וְהָעוֹשִׂים אוֹתָם בָּטְלָה דַעְתָּם אֵצֶל כָּל אָדָם
as is stated in chapter *HaMatznia (Shabbat* 92b*)* regarding the people of Hutzal.	כִּדְאַמְרִינַן בְּהַמַּצְנִיעַ (לְקַמָּן דַּף צב:) גַּבֵּי אַנְשֵׁי הוּצַל

Tosafot (10th-13th centuries). A collection French and German Talmudic commentaries in the form of critical and explanatory glosses; written during the twelfth and thirteenth centuries. Among the most famous authors of Tosafot are Rabbi Yaakov Tam, Rabbi Shimshon ben Avraham of Sens, and Rabbi Shmuel ben Meir. Printed in almost all editions of the Talmud, these commentaries are fundamental to basic Talmudic study.

Keys to the Talmud

Rov—Majorities

In Torah there is a principle (Exodus 23:2) אַחֲרֵי רַבִּים לְהַטּוֹת when the judges are in disagreement in a court of law, we follow the majority opinion and disregard the minority. This principle does not only apply in a court of law, but in almost all areas of Jewish law, we also follow the majority and disregard the minority. Therefore, even when there is a normative practice in a minority group, Torah agrees with the majority and disregards the minority in establishing the norm.

Minority Customs

TEXT 3C: **Talmud, *Shabbat* 92a-b**

One who transfers a load on his head—is exempt.	—הַמּוֹצִיא מַשּׂוֹי עַל רֹאשׁוֹ פָּטוּר
And if you will say	וְאִם תִּימְצָא לוֹמַר
the people of Hutzal do this,	אַנְשֵׁי הוּצַל עוֹשִׂין כֵּן
their thoughts are negated before the view of most people.	בָּטְלָה דַעְתָּן אֵצֶל כָּל אָדָם

TEXT 3D: **Rashi, *Shabbat* 92a, *Anshei Hutzal***

The people of Hutzal—	—אַנְשֵׁי הוּצַל
They would carry jugs of water and wine on their heads	הָיוּ נוֹשְׂאִין כַּדֵּי מַיִם וָיַיִן עַל רָאשֵׁיהֶן
and would not hold them in their hands.	וְאֵין אוֹחֲזִין אוֹתָם בְּיָדַיִם

Discussion Questions

1. A right-handed person who writes with his left hand is not liable for writing on Shabbat, whereas a left-handed person is liable for writing with his left hand (Tractate *Shabbat* 103a). When do we say that a minority group follows the majority with regard to the laws of Shabbat and when do we consider people on an individual basis?

2. Rav Kahana answered that spinning wool while it is still on the animal is not considered shearing, combing or spinning since it is not the normal method of doing the *melachah* (i.e. it is a case of *keleachar yad*). Why does Rashi wait until the Talmud concludes that it was a *chochmah yeteirah* to explain that this manner

Part II

Permanence

Lasting Significance

Tying in the *Mishkan*

TEXT 4A: **Talmud, *Shabbat* 74b**

Tying and untying—	הַקּוֹשֵׁר וְהַמַּתִּיר
Where was there tying in the *Mishkan*?	קְשִׁירָה בַּמִּשְׁכָּן הֵיכָא הֲוָאִי
Rava said: For indeed they would tie onto the tent pegs.	אָמַר רָבָא שֶׁכֵּן קוֹשְׁרִין בְּיִתְדוֹת אֹהָלִים
[Abaye responded:] It is tying in order to untie.	אָמַר לֵיהּ אַבַּיֵי] הַהוּא קוֹשֵׁר עַל מְנָת לְהַתִּיר הוּא]

TEXT 4B: **Rashi, *Shabbat* 74b, *BiYeteidot***

Onto the tent pegs—	בְּיִתְדוֹת אֹהָלִים
They would thrust pegs into the ground,	נוֹעֲצִים יְתֵידוֹת בַּקַּרְקַע
as the verse states (Exodus 35:18), *the pegs of the Mishkan*,	כְּדִכְתִיב יִתְדוֹת הַמִּשְׁכָּן
and would tie them onto to the curtains, to the [curtains'] cords.	וְקוֹשְׁרִין הַיְרִיעוֹת בָּהֶן בְּמֵיתְרֵיהֶם

TEXT 4C: **Rashi, *Shabbat* 74b, *Kosheir***

It is tying in order to untie	קוֹשֵׁר עַל מְנָת לְהַתִּיר הוּא
Further on, we have held someone in such a situation as exempt,	וְכִי הַאי גַּוְונָא פַּטְרִינָן לֵיהּ לְקַמָּן

as it was taught in a *mishnah* (*Shabbat* 113a),	דִּתְנַן
Any knot that is not permanent,	כָּל קֶשֶׁר שֶׁאֵינוֹ שֶׁל קַיָּימָא
one is not liable for it.	אֵין חַיָּיבִין עָלָיו

Knotted Curtains

TEXT 5A: **Talmud, *Shabbat* 74b**

Rather, Abaye said:	אֶלָּא אָמַר אַבַּיֵי
For indeed, the curtain weavers who had a thread break on them	שֶׁכֵּן אוֹרְגֵי יְרִיעוֹת שֶׁנִּפְסְקָה לָהֶן נִימָא
would tie it.	קוֹשְׁרִים אוֹתָהּ
Rava responded:	אָמַר לֵיהּ רָבָא
You have resolved tying; what is there to say about untying?	תֵּרַצְתָּ קוֹשֵׁר מַתִּיר מַאי אִיכָּא לְמֵימַר
And if you should say	וְכִי תֵּימָא
that if two knots happened to be side-by-side on two strings,	דְּאִי מִתְרַמֵּי לֵיהּ תְּרֵי חוּטֵי קִיטְרֵי בַּהֲדֵי הֲדָדֵי
he would untie one and tie the other one,	שָׁרֵי חַד וְקָטַר חַד
if before a king of flesh and blood we would not do so,	הַשְׁתָּא לִפְנֵי מֶלֶךְ בָּשָׂר וָדָם אֵין עוֹשִׂין כֵּן
would we do so before the King of kings, the Holy One, blessed be he?	לִפְנֵי מֶלֶךְ מַלְכֵי הַמְּלָכִים הַקָּדוֹשׁ בָּרוּךְ הוּא עוֹשִׂין

TEXT 5B: **Rashi, *Shabbat* 74b, *BeHadei Hadadi***

Side by side—	בַּהֲדֵי הֲדָדֵי
With two strings next to each other.	בִּשְׁנֵי חוּטִין זֶה אֵצֶל זֶה

TEXT 5C: **Rashi, *Shabbat* 74b, *Shari Chad***

He would untie one—	שָׁרֵי חַד
After weaving them, he would untie one	לְאַחַר אֲרִיגָתָן מַתִּיר הָאֶחָד
since they protrude and are visible.	מִפְּנֵי שֶׁבּוֹלְטִין וְנִרְאִין

TEXT 5D: **Rashi, *Shabbat* 74b, *VeKatar Chad***

And tie one—	וְקָטַר חַד
As if to say, leave it as is.	כְּלוֹמַר מַנִּיחַ כְּמוֹ שֶׁהוּא

TEXT 5E: **Rashi, *Shabbat* 74b, *Hashta***

Now . . . we would not do so—	הַשְׁתָּא כו' אֵין עוֹשִׂין –
When he unties it, a[n obvious] hole is seen in the curtain,	שֶׁכְּשֶׁמַּתִּירוֹ נִרְאֶה הַנֶּקֶב בַּיְרִיעָה
since [each of] its strings consisted of six threads and were thick.	שֶׁחוּטֶיהָ הָיוּ כְּפוּלִין שִׁשָּׁה וְהָיוּ גַּסִּין
Initially, they were careful about it (avoiding two knots in the same place on adjacent strings)	וּמִתְּחִלָּה הָיוּ זְרִיזִין בְּכָךְ
and when it happened that there were two knots [on adjacent strings in the same place],	וְכִי מִתְרַמּוּ לָהּ תְּרֵי קִיטְרֵי
they would tie one of them	קוֹשְׁרִין הָאֶחָד
and cut out the second string from the bottom and the top	וְנוֹתְקִין הַחוּט הַשֵּׁנִי מִלְּמַטָּה וּלְמַעְלָה
and replace it with a long string	וּמְסַפְּקָן בְּחוּט אָרוֹךְ
and tie it above and below	וְקוֹשְׁרִין לְמַעְלָה וּלְמַטָּה
and there would not be two knots near each other.	וְאֵין שָׁם שְׁנַיִם קְשָׁרִים סְמוּכִין

TEXT 6A: **Talmud, *Shabbat* 74b**

Rather, Rava said (and some say it was Rabbi Ilai),	אֶלָּא אָמַר רָבָא וְאִיתֵּימָא רַבִּי עִילָאִי
The *chilazon* hunters would tie and untie.	שֶׁכֵּן צָדֵי חִלָּזוֹן קוֹשְׁרִין וּמַתִּירִין

TEXT 6B: **Rashi, *Shabbat* 74b, *Tzadei Chilazon***

The chilazon *hunters*—	צָדֵי חִלָּזוֹן
To dye the *techeilet* with its blood.	לִצְבּוֹעַ הַתְּכֵלֶת בְּדָמוֹ
It is a small fishlike creature	וְהוּא כְּמִין דָּג קָטָן
that emerges [is spewed out of the sea] once in seventy years.	וְעוֹלֶה אַחַת לְשִׁבְעִים שָׁנָה

TEXT 6C: **Rashi, *Shabbat* 74b, *Koshrin UMatirin***

Tie and untie—	קוֹשְׁרִין וּמַתִּירִין –
All nets are made of [ropes] tied together	שֶׁכָּל רְשָׁתוֹת עֲשׂוּיוֹת קְשָׁרִים קְשָׁרִים
with permanent knots.	וְהֵן קִשְׁרֵי קַיָּימָא
Sometimes it is necessary [to extend a net by] taking ropes from one net	וּפְעָמִים שֶׁצָּרִיךְ לִיטּוֹל חוּטִין מֵרֶשֶׁת זוֹ
and adding them to another,	וּלְהוֹסִיף עַל זוֹ
untying from this [net] and tying [it] to that [net].	מַתִּיר מִכָּאן וְקוֹשֵׁר מִכָּאן

Defining a Knot

Learning Exercise

(Write/Pair/Share)

To define the *melachah* of tying a knot we need to define what a knot is. There is debate about whether the tying of several types of knots constitutes the biblical *melachah* of tying a knot (examples: string tangles, bowknots, slipknots, shoelace knots, tie knots). Bearing in mind that a *melachah* is a creative, constructive and innovative activity, how would you define the act of tying a knot?

prohibited to tie on Shabbat.

Table 1

Knot	To Remain Permanently	To Last Longer than a Week	To be Untied Within 24 Hours
Loose Knot	Biblical	Rabbinic	Permitted
Tight Knot	Biblical	Rabbinic	Rabbinic

Discussion Questions

What is the fundamental difference between tying a permanent and a temporary knot? Why is tying a temporary knot permitted, while you are liable for tying a permanent knot? The difference between a temporary knot and a permanent knot is only in the intent of how long you plan for it to last; the knot and the action of tying the knot is the same. Normally, the Rabbis prohibit doing a partial *melachah* in the fear that you might complete the *melachah*. Why did they not prohibit tying a loose knot for temporary use in the fear that you might have the intent of leaving it permanently?

TEXT 7: ***Likutei Sichot*, vol. 14, pg. 16**

Without the intent that the knot will last,	בִּלְעֲדֵי הַדַּעַת שֶׁיִּתְקַיֵּים הַקֶּשֶׁר
it is not only that there is lacking	הֲרֵי אֵין הָעִנְיָן שֶׁנֶּחְסַר חֵלֶק
a part of the completion of the act of the *melachah*,	מִשְׁלֵימוּת פְּעוּלַת הַמְּלָאכָה
rather there is absent to begin with,	אֶלָּא שֶׁנֶּעֱדַר מִלְּכַתְּחִילָּה
the primary aspect of the *melachah* of tying,	הָעִיקָּר שֶׁבִּמְלֶאכֶת הַקְּשִׁירָה
since the strings are not truly tied and united.	שֶׁהֲרֵי הַחוּטִים אֵינָם קְשׁוּרִים וּמְאוּחָדִים בֶּאֱמֶת
For it was only an act	וְאֵין זֹאת כִּי אִם פְּעוּלָּה
of bringing the strings nearer and touching them together and the like;	שֶׁל קִירוּב וּנְגִיעַת הַחוּטִים בִּלְבַד וְכַיּוֹצֵא בָּזֶה
since this does not include even a small part	וּמִכֵּיוָן שֶׁאֵין בָּזֶה אֲפִילוּ מִקְצַת וְחֵלֶק
of the *melachah* that the Torah prohibited,	שֶׁל אוֹתָהּ הַמְּלָאכָה שֶׁאָסְרָה הַתּוֹרָה
they therefore did not decree against it,	לָכֵן לֹא גָּזְרוּ בָּהּ
lest he comes to do the entire act	שֶׁמָּא יָבוֹא מִמִּקְצָתָהּ לַעֲשׂוֹת כּוּלָּהּ
and transgress a biblical prohibition.	וְיַעֲבוֹר עַל אִיסּוּר מִן הַתּוֹרָה

Rabbi Menachem Mendel Schneerson (1902–1994). Known as "the Lubavitcher Rebbe," or simply as "the Rebbe." Born in southern Ukraine. Rabbi Schneerson escaped from the Nazis, arriving in the US in June 1941. The towering Jewish leader of the twentieth century, the Rebbe inspired and guided the revival of traditional Judaism after the European devastation, and often emphasized that the performance of just one additional good deed could usher in the era of Mashiach.

Judging Action, Not Intent

TEXT 8A: **Numbers 15:32-36**

The Children of Israel were in the wilderness	וַיִּהְיוּ בְנֵי יִשְׂרָאֵל בַּמִּדְבָּר
and they found a man gathering wood on the Shabbat day.	וַיִּמְצְאוּ אִישׁ מְקֹשֵׁשׁ עֵצִים בְּיוֹם הַשַּׁבָּת
Those who found him gathering wood brought him	וַיַּקְרִיבוּ אֹתוֹ הַמֹּצְאִים אֹתוֹ מְקֹשֵׁשׁ עֵצִים
to Moshe and Aaron and to the entire assembly.	אֶל מֹשֶׁה וְאֶל אַהֲרֹן וְאֶל כָּל הָעֵדָה:
They placed him in custody,	וַיַּנִּיחוּ אֹתוֹ בַּמִּשְׁמָר
for it had not been clarified what should be done to him.	כִּי לֹא פֹרַשׁ מַה יֵּעָשֶׂה לוֹ:
G-d said to Moshe, "The man shall be put to death;	וַיֹּאמֶר ה׳ אֶל מֹשֶׁה מוֹת יוּמַת הָאִישׁ
the entire assembly shall pelt him with stones outside of the camp."	רָגוֹם אֹתוֹ בָאֲבָנִים כָּל הָעֵדָה מִחוּץ לַמַּחֲנֶה:
The entire assembly removed him to the outside of the camp;	וַיֹּצִיאוּ אֹתוֹ כָּל הָעֵדָה אֶל מִחוּץ לַמַּחֲנֶה
they pelted him with stones and he died,	וַיִּרְגְּמוּ אֹתוֹ בָּאֲבָנִים וַיָּמֹת
as G-d had commanded Moshe.	כַּאֲשֶׁר צִוָּה ה׳ אֶת מֹשֶׁה:

TEXT 8B: *Targum Yonatan/Yerushalmi,* Numbers 15:32

The Children of Israel sojourned in the wilderness	וַהֲווֹ בְּנֵי יִשְׂרָאֵל שַׁרְיָין בְּמַדְבְּרָא
and they were informed of the decree of Shabbat.	גְּזֵירַת שַׁבְּתָא אִשְׁתְּמוֹדַע לְהוֹן
However, they were not informed of the punishment of Shabbat.	בְּרַם קְנָסָא דְשַׁבְּתָא לָא אִשְׁתְּמוֹדַע לְהוֹן
A man arose from the house of Yosef and said,	קָם גַּבְרָא מִדְּבֵית יוֹסֵף אָמַר בְּמֵימְרֵיהּ
"I will go and pluck twigs on the day of Shabbat	אֵיזִיל וְאֶתְלוֹשׁ קֵיסִין בְּיוֹמָא דְשַׁבְּתָא
and witnesses will see me and testify to Moshe	וְיֶחֱמוּן יָתִי סַהֲדַיָּא וִיתַנּוּן לְמֹשֶׁה
and Moshe will seek instruction from before G-d and will judge me	וּמֹשֶׁה יִתְבַּע אוּלְפַן מִן קֳדָם יְיָ וְיִדּוֹן יָתִי
and thus the punishment will be made known to the entire house of Israel."	וּבְכֵן אִשְׁתְּמוֹדַע קְנָסָא לְכָל בֵּית יִשְׂרָאֵל
And witnesses found a man who was plucking	וְאַשְׁכְּחוּ סַהֲדָא יַת גַּבְרָא כַּד תָּלִישׁ
and uprooting twigs on the day of Shabbat.	וְעָקַר קֵיסִין בְּיוֹמָא דְשַׁבְּתָא:

TEXT 8C: Maharsha, *Chidushei Agadot*, Talmud, *Bava Batra* 119a

Some have asked about this [explanation] in *Targum Yonatan*:	וְיֵשׁ שָׁאֲלוּ בָּזֶה בְּתַּ"י
How did he [permit himself to] sin by violating a Shabbat prohibition	הֵיאַךְ חָטָא בְּאִיסוּר שַׁבָּת
to make known by which death penalty a Shabbat desecrator is executed?	כְּדֵי לֵידַע בְּאֵיזֶה מִיתָה דָּנִין הַמְחַלֵּל שַׁבָּת
It could be said [in answer]	וְיֵשׁ לוֹמַר
that since he only needed this *melachah*	כֵּיוָן שֶׁלֹּא הָיָה צָרִיךְ לִמְלָאכָה זוֹ
to make known which death, etc.,	אֶלָּא לֵידַע בְּאֵיזוֹ מִיתָה כו'
it is a *melachah* that is not required in its own right,	הֲוֵה לֵיהּ מְלָאכָה שֶׁאֵינָהּ צְרִיכָה לְגוּפָהּ

like one who digs a hole and only requires its dirt	כְּמוֹ חוֹפֵר גּוּמָא וְאֵין צָרִיךְ אֶלָּא לַעֲפָרָה
who is exempt according to Rabbi Shimon.	שֶׁהוּא פָּטוּר לְרַבִּי שִׁמְעוֹן
However, he was certainly liable to receive the death penalty according to human law,	וּמִיהוּ הוּא וַדַּאי דְּהָיָה חַיָּיב מִיתָה בְּדִינֵי אָדָם
since the witnesses that warned him	שֶׁלֹּא יָדְעוּ הָעֵדִים שֶׁהִתְרוּ בּוֹ
did not know that he did so with this intent,	שֶׁהוּא עָשָׂה עַל דַּעַת זוֹ
[since] they are only matters of the heart	וְאֵינָן אֶלָּא דְּבָרִים שֶׁבְּלֵב
and they judged him for death based on this testimony.	וְדָנִין הָיוּ אוֹתוֹ לְמִיתָה עַל פִּי הָעֵדוּת

Rabbi Shmuel Eliezer ben Yehudah HaLevi Eidel's (1555–1632). Commonly known by the acronym Maharsha; born in Cracow. Rabbi, head of Yeshivah and popular commentator of the Talmud. He established a yeshiva in Posen, the hometown of his wife, which was supported by his mother-in-law Eidel. After her death, he served as a rabbi in a number of cities in Poland. He is primarily known for his *Chidushei Halachot,* his commentary encompassing the entire Talmud, in which he dealt with difficulties in the Talmud, Rashi, and Tosafot; and for his *Chidushei Aggadot,* his commentary on the Aggadic material of the Talmud. Both commentaries have for many years been published with the standard version of the Babylonian Talmud.

Keys to the Talmud

***Devarim SheBeLev*—Matters of the heart**

The responsibility of judges in Torah as well as in a secular court is to follow sound reasoning. Judges shouldn't follow hunches, sorcery or supernatural gifts. Torah instructs the judge to accept as evidence the testimony of witnesses and nothing less. In Jewish law, hypotheses about motive and probability, however plausible, do not prove guilt or innocence. There must be clear testimony of an eyewitness of what transpired for a judge to be able to pass judgment. For this reason, what the witness sees is the only factor in determining the law and thus ***devarim shebelev einam devarim*****, matters of the heart are not reckoned with.**

Key Points

1. In constructing the *Mishkan*, they would spin goats' hair while still attached to the goats.

2. An act that requires extraordinary skill is considered to be performed in an irregular manner and is not a *melachah.*

3. For a *melachah* to be considered *melechet machshevet*, it must have a certain degree of permanence.

4. The *avot melachot* of tying and untying are derived from the tying and untying of knots to catch a sea creature called the *chilazon* in order to produce the *techeilet* dye for the *Mishkan*'s coverings and tapestries.

5. The difference between a permanent knot and a temporary knot is in the intent of how long it should last.

6. Although acts of *melachot* on Shabbat are primarily defined by their intent, the judgment and physical penalty for doing *melachah* is determined by the act alone.

Terms to Retain

Extraordinary talent	חָכְמָה יְתֵירָה
Particle of the objective case (sometimes "with")	אֶת
Majority	רוֹב
Knot	קֶשֶׁר
Lasting (permanence)	קַיָּימָא
Matters of the heart are not matters (i.e. not reckoned with)	דְבָרִים שֶׁבְּלֵב אֵינָם דְבָרִים

Lesson 10

Introduction

Melechet machshevet is the term used to define the work that the Torah prohibits on Shabbat as deliberate and intentional activity. Suppose, then, you are playing catch and the ball is accidentally thrown into the street. Deliberately throwing the ball into the street would clearly have been a violation of the Shabbat *melachah* of *ha'avarah* (making an object go from a private to a public domain or vice versa). But here, the act was unintentional. Can *melachot* that are unintended by-products of non-*melachot* be considered *melachot*?

In this lesson, we will study *melachot* that are variously inevitable, unintended or inadvertent consequences of non-*melachah* activity. We will learn from this how intent plays a role in one's service of building a tabernacle for G-d. Is intent a necessary component of fulfilling a mitzvah? Must a mitzvah be performed deliberately to count as a mitzvah? How can non-mitzvot play an important role in building a tabernacle for G-d?

Part I

Mitasek and *Eino Mitkaven*: Inadvertent Acts and Unintended Consequences

TEXT 1: **Talmud, *Shabbat* 75a**

One who captures a deer, etc.—	הַצָד צְבִי וכו'
The Rabbis taught [in a *tosefta*]: One who captures a *chilazon* and crushes it	תָּנוּ רַבָּנָן הַצָד חִלָּזוֹן וְהַפּוֹצְעוֹ
is only liable for one [transgression].	אֵינוֹ חַיָּיב אֶלָּא אַחַת
Rabbi Yehudah says: He is liable for two;	רַבִּי יְהוּדָה אוֹמֵר חַיָּיב שְׁתַּיִם
as Rabbi Yehudah would say:	שֶׁהָיָה רַבִּי יְהוּדָה אוֹמֵר
Crushing is included in threshing.	פְּצִיעָה בִּכְלַל דִּישָׁה
They said to him: Crushing is not included in threshing.	אָמְרוּ לוֹ אֵין פְּצִיעָה בִּכְלַל דִּישָׁה
Rava said: What is our Rabbis' reasoning?	אָמַר רָבָא מַאי טַעְמָא דְרַבָּנָן
They maintain: Threshing only applies to that which grows from the ground.	קָסַבְרִי אֵין דִּישָׁה אֶלָּא לְגִדּוּלֵי קַרְקַע
Let him also be liable for taking a life!	וְלִיחַיֵּיב נַמִּי מִשּׁוּם נְטִילַת נְשָׁמָה
Rabbi Yoachanan answers: Since he crushed it after it was already dead.	אָמַר רַבִּי יוֹחָנָן שֶׁפְּצָעוֹ מֵת
Rava says: Even say that he crushed it while it was alive,	רָבָא אָמַר אֲפִילוּ תֵּימָא שֶׁפְּצָעוֹ חַי
he was only incidentally occupied in taking a life.	מִתְעַסֵּק הוּא אֵצֶל נְטִילַת נְשָׁמָה

TEXT 2A: **Rashi, *Shabbat* 75a, *HaPotzeo***

One who crushes it—	הַפּוֹצְעוֹ
Squeezes it in his hands to extract its blood.	דּוֹחֲקוֹ בְּיָדָיו שֶׁיֵּצֵא דָּמוֹ

Rabbi Shlomo Yitzchaki (1040–1105). Better known by the acronym *Rashi;* rabbi and famed author of the first comprehensive commentaries on the Talmud and Bible. Born in Troyes, Champagne, Rashi studied in the famed yeshivot of Mainz and Worms. His commentaries, which focus on the simple understanding of the text, are considered fundamental to Torah study. Since their initial printings, they have appeared in virtually every edition of the Talmud and Bible. Amongst Rashi's descendants, were many of the famed Tosafists of France.

Keys to the Talmud

Tana Kama*—The First *Tana

When the first opinion in a *mishnah* is anonymous, its author is referred to as the *tana kama*, literally, the first sage of the *mishnah*. Often, the Talmud will state: "The *tana kama* maintains . . ." (*Bava Batra* 4b et al).

Many *mishnayot* are anonymous, without a named author. Such a *mishnah* is called a *stam mishnah.* The Talmud will often try to determine who the author of the *mishnah* is. In most instances, the author of a *stam mishnah* is Rabbi Meir.

TEXT 2B: **Rashi, *Shabbat* 75a, *Eino Chayav***

Is only liable —	אֵינוֹ חַיָּב
for one [transgression]	אֶלָּא אַחַת
for capturing.	מִשּׁוּם צֵידָה
However, for the crushing, there is no liability.	אֲבָל אַפְּצִיעָה לֵיכָּא חִיּוּב

TEXT 2C: **Rashi, *Shabbat* 75a, *BiChlal Dishah***

Is included in threshing—	בִּכְלַל דִּישָׁה—
since he extracts its blood from it,	שֶׁמְּפָרֵק דָּמוֹ הֵימֶנּוּ
as one extracts grain from its husk.	כִּמְפָרֵק תְּבוּאָה מִקַּשִּׁין שֶׁלָּהּ

Optional Section

Chilazon: Why Trapping?

TEXT 3: **Tosafot, *Shabbat* 75a, *HaTzad Chilazon***

***One who captures* a chilazon**—	הַצָּד חִלָּזוֹן
According to the opinion which establishes that he crushed it alive,	לְמַאן דְּמוֹקֵי לָהּ בְּשֶׁפְּצָעוֹ חַי
it is understood why it mentions one who captures a *chilazon*,	אָתֵי שַׁפִּיר הָא דְּנָקַט הַצָּד חִלָּזוֹן
as is it customary to crush it immediately after capturing it	דְּדֶרֶךְ לְפוֹצְעוֹ מִיַּד אַחַר צֵידָה
while it is still alive.	כָּל זְמַן שֶׁהוּא חַי
It teaches us that although he crushed it alive,	וְקָא מַשְׁמַע לָן דְּאַף עַל פִּי שֶׁפְּצָעוֹ חַי
he is not liable on account of taking a life.	לֹא מִיחַיֵּיב מִשּׁוּם נְטִילַת נְשָׁמָה

Tosafot (10th-13th centuries). A collection French and German Talmudic commentaries in the form of critical and explanatory glosses; written during the twelfth and thirteenth centuries. Among the most famous authors of Tosafot are Rabbi Yaakov Tam, Rabbi Shimshon ben Avraham of Sens, and Rabbi Shmuel ben Meir. Printed in almost all editions of the Talmud, these commentaries are fundamental to basic Talmudic study.

And even according to the opinion that he crushed it after it was dead,
וַאֲפִילוּ לְמַאן דְּמוֹקֵי לָהּ
כְּשֶׁפְּצָעוֹ מֵת

it teaches us that he is not liable in his capturing
קָא מַשְׁמַע לָן דלֹא מִיחַיֵּיב בְּצֵידָה שֶׁלוֹ

for taking a life.
מִשּׁוּם נְטִילַת נְשָׁמָה

TEXT 4: **Talmud, *Shabbat* 107b**

Shmuel said: If one removes a fish from the sea,
אָמַר שְׁמוּאֵל הַשּׁוֹלֶה דָּג מִן הַיָּם

as soon as there is a dry spot on it the size of a *sela*, he is liable [for taking a life].
כֵּיוָן שֶׁיָּבֵשׁ בּוֹ כְּסֶלַע חַיָּיב

Tosafot Continue . . .

Even though we say in chapter *Shemoneh Sheratzim*,
דְּאַף עַל גַּב דְּאָמְרִינַן בְּפֶרֶק שְׁמוֹנָה שְׁרָצִים

"If one takes a fish from the sea . . ."
הַשּׁוֹלֶה דָּג מִן הַיָּם כֵּיוָן שֶׁיָּבֵשׁ בּוֹ כו'

here, perhaps the *chilazon* is accustomed to squirm and hasten its death.
הָכָא שֶׁמָּא חִלָּזוֹן דַּרְכּוֹ
לְפַרְכֵּס וּלְקָרֵב מִיתָתוֹ

Capturing the *Chilazon*

Tosafot Conclude . . .

However, further examination is required, for the Jerusalem Talmud implies
וְצָרִיךְ עִיּוּן
דְּבִירוּשַׁלְמִי מַשְׁמַע

that one who captures a *chilazon* is not liable on account of capturing.
דְּצָד חִלָּזוֹן
לֹא מִיחַיֵּיב מִשּׁוּם צֵידָה

Keys to the Talmud

Mitasek—Doing a *Melachah* Inadvertently

For one to be liable for doing a *melachah*, there must be intent. Otherwise it constitutes a *davar she'eino mitkaven*, an unintentional act.

For there to be liability, one must:

- do the act of *melachah* that he intended to do,
- do it with the object that he had in mind to do it,
- do it in the forbidden manner that he had in mind to do it and
- do it in the same sequence in which he intended it to happen.

If one of these details is not met, even accidentally, he is not liable and it is considered a *mitasek*.

Keys to the Talmud

Davar She'eino Mitkaven—Unintentional Act

Davar she'eino mitkaven includes any instance in which one does a non-*melachah* and there is a possibility (but not a certainty) that a *melachah* may unintentionally result from it. In this instance, it is permissible to do the non-*melachah,* despite the chance that a *melachah* will result from it, since he does not intend to do the *melachah* and it is not definite that a *melachah* will result from it.

Learning Activity

Which of the following definitions do you think best describe Rava's exemption for taking a life while crushing the *chilazon* in order to extract its blood? Circle your answer and explain your reasoning.

Mitasek—accidental *melachah*   *Davar she'eino mitkaven*—unintended *melachah*

TEXT 5: **Rashi, *Shabbat* 75a, *Mitasek Hu***

He is only incidentally occupied in taking a life,	מִתְעַסֵּק הוּא אֵצֶל נְטִילַת נְשָׁמָה
meaning, in regard to taking a life,	כְּלוֹמַר לְגַבֵּי נְטִילַת נְשָׁמָה
he is preoccupied with something else	הֲוֵי מִתְעַסֵּק בְּדָבָר אַחֵר
and it is not considered calculated labor,	וְלֹא הָוְיָא מְלֶאכֶת מַחְשֶׁבֶת
since he does not intend that it should die.	שֶׁאֵינוֹ מִתְכַּוֵּין שֶׁיָּמוּת

TEXT 6: **Tosafot, *Shabbat* 75a, *Mitasek Hu***

Shortened Version of Tosafot

He is incidentally occupied in taking a life;	מִתְעַסֵּק הוּא אֵצֶל נְטִילַת נְשָׁמָה
preoccupation here is not meant literally . . .	הַאי מִתְעַסֵּק לָאו דַּוְקָא . . .
Preoccupation here means an unintended *melachah* (*davar sheèino mitkaven*),	וּמִתְעַסֵּק דְּהָכָא הַיְינוּ דָּבָר שֶׁאֵין מִתְכַּוֵּין
since he did not intend at all to perform the *melachah*.	כֵּיוָן דְּאֵין מִתְכַּוֵּין כְּלָל לִמְלָאכָה

TEXT 7A: **Tosafot, *Shabbat* 75a, *Mitasek Hu***

He is only incidentally occupied in taking a life.	מִתְעַסֵּק הוּא אֵצֶל נְטִילַת נְשָׁמָה
Preoccupation here is not meant literally,	הַאי מִתְעַסֵּק לָאו דַּוְקָא
for one who makes a wound while being preoccupied is liable according to Rabbi Shimon.	דְּהָא מִתְעַסֵּק בְּחַבּוּרָה חַיָּיב לְרַבִּי שִׁמְעוֹן
Who said at the end of chapter *Safek Achal* (*Keritot* 19b):	דְּאָמַר בְּסוֹף פֶּרֶק סָפֵק אָכַל (כריתות יט:)
Leave the case of infants alone,	הַנַּח לְתִינוֹקוֹת

since one who acts destructively while making a wound is liable.	הוֹאִיל וּמְקַלְקֵל בְּחַבּוּרָה חַיָּיב
A *mitasek* is also liable;	מִתְעַסֵק נַמִי חַיָּיב
the reason [the *mitasek* is liable] we derive in chapter *HaOreg* (*Shabbat* 106a)	וְטַעֲמָא כִּדְיַלִיף בְּהָאוֹרֵג (לקמן קו.)
from the fact that [the Torah] needs to permit circumcision.	מִדְאִיצְטְרִיךְ לְמִישְׁרֵי מִילָה
We can deduce that one who acts destructively while making a wound is liable	מִכְּלַל דְמְקַלְקֵל בְּחַבּוּרָה חַיָּיב
and we are not concerned about it being a calculated labor (*melechet machshevet*),	וְלֹא חַיְישִׁינָן לִמְלֶאכֶת מַחֲשֶׁבֶת
since destructive acts would only be exempt	דִמְקַלְקֵל דְעָלְמָא לֹא מִיפְטַר
because of the requirement of calculated labor (*melechet machshevet*),	אֶלָא מִשּׁוּם מְלֶאכֶת מַחֲשֶׁבֶת
as stated at the end of the first chapter of *Chagigah*.	כִּדְאָמַר בְּסוֹף פֶּרֶק קַמָא דְחַגִיגָה (דף י:)

TEXT 7B: Tosafot, *Shabbat* 75a, *Mitasek Hu,* continued

Preoccupation here means an unintended *melachah* (*davar sheeino mitkaven*).	וּמִתְעַסֵק דְהָכָא הַיְינוּ דָבָר שֶׁאֵין מִתְכַּוֵין
Since he did not intend at all to perform the *melachah*,	כֵּיוָן דְאֵין מִתְכַּוֵין כְּלַל לִמְלָאכָה
even making a wound is permitted,	מוּתָּר אֲפִילוּ בְּחַבּוּרָה
even though it does not require the specification of calculated labor (*melechet machshevet*),	אַף עַל פִּי דְלֹא בָּעֵי מְלֶאכֶת מַחֲשֶׁבֶת
as in all [other] prohibitions of Torah,	כְּמוֹ כָּל אִיסוּרִים שֶׁבַּתּוֹרָה
for calculated labor (*melechet machshevet*) does not apply	דְלֹא שַׁיָּיךְ בְּהוּ מְלֶאכֶת מַחֲשֶׁבֶת
and unintended [prohibitions] are permitted,	וְשָׁרוּ אֵין מִתְכַּוֵין

as is stated: "Vendors of clothes may sell clothes [made of *kilayim*] in accordance with their trade custom,	כִּדְאָמַר מוֹכְרֵי כְּסוּת מוֹכְרִין כְּדַרְכָּן
so long as they when they are in the sun, they do not have the intention [to protect themselves] from the sun, etc" (*Kilayim* 9:2).	וּבִלְבַד שֶׁלֹּא יִתְכַּוֵין בַּחַמָּה מִפְּנֵי הַחַמָּה כו' (כלאים פ"ט משנה ה)

TEXT 7C: **Tosafot, *Shabbat* 75a, *Mitasek Hu*, continued**

And the same is evident in the first chapter of *Ketubot* (5b),	וְכֵן מוּכַח בְּפֶרֶק קַמָּא דִכְתוּבוֹת (ד' ה:)
where it is states: If you say that the blood is attached,	דְאָמַר אִם תִּמְצָא לוֹמַר דָם חִבּוּרֵי מִיחַבַּר
is it the blood that he needs or is it his own pleasure that he seeks ?	לְדָם הוּא צָרִיךְ אוֹ לַהֲנָאַת עַצְמוֹ הוּא צָרִיךְ
And if you say that he seeks only his own pleasure,	וְאִם תִּמְצָא לוֹמַר לַהֲנָאַת עַצְמוֹ הוּא צָרִיךְ
is the law in accordance with Rabbi Yehudah	הֲלָכָה כְּרַבִּי יְהוּדָה
or is the law in accordance with Rabbi Shimon	אוֹ הֲלָכָה כְּרַבִּי שִׁמְעוֹן
(i.e. concerning an unintended *melachah* (*davar she'eino mitkaven*))?	פֵּירוּשׁ בְּדָבָר שֶׁאֵין מִתְכַּוֵין
And even if you say that the law is in accordance with Rabbi Yehudah with regard to an unintended *melachah* (*davar she'eino mitkaven*),	וְאִם תִּמְצָא לוֹמַר הֲלָכָה כְּרַבִּי יְהוּדָה בְּדָבָר שֶׁאֵין מִתְכַּוֵין
with regard to an act of destruction, in accordance to whom does the law seem to be?	בִּמְקַלְקֵל הֲלָכָה כְּמַאן מַשְׁמַע
For if the law is in accordance with Rabbi Shimon with regard to an unintended *melachah* (*davar she'eino mitkaven*),	דְאִי הֲלָכָה כְּרַבִּי שִׁמְעוֹן בְּדָבָר שֶׁאֵין מִתְכַּוֵין
there is no more room for doubt concerning acts of destruction.	תוּ לֵיכָּא לִסְפּוּקֵי בִּמְקַלְקֵל
For even if one is liable for acts of destruction by afflicting a wound,	דַאֲפִילוּ מְקַלְקֵל בְּחַבּוּרָה חַיָּיב
since it is unintended (*eino mitkaven*), it is permitted.	כֵּיוָן דְאֵין מִתְכַּוֵין מוּתָּר

Part II

Pesik Reisha: Inevitable Consequence

Discussion Questions

The Talmud concluded thus far that one who crushes a *chilazon* to extract its blood is not liable for taking a life because its death is unintended. But even when the person who crushes the *chilazon* has no intention to kill it, he still knows that it will inevitably die.

Is it possible to crush a snail or a fish and extract its blood without intending to kill it? What is the significance of intent when one actively does something that has a well-known and inevitable outcome? Can you cut off the head of a chicken and be exempt for killing it because you did not intend for it die? By extension, does a well-known, inevitable consequence not indicate intent? Can one intentionally chop off the head of a living thing and then credibly claim, "I did not intend to kill it?"

TEXT 8: **Continuation of Talmud, *Shabbat* 75a**

But Abaye and Rava have both said:	וְהָא אַבַּיֵי וְרָבָא דְּאָמְרִי תַּרְוַיְיהוּ
Rabbi Shimon concedes [to Rabbi Yehudah] concerning inevitable consequence (literally: if you sever its head, will it not die?).	מוֹדֶה רַבִּי שִׁמְעוֹן בִּפְסִיק רֵישָׁא וְלֹא יָמוּת

Keys to the Talmud

***Pesik Reisha*—Inevitable Consequence**

Rabbi Shimon accepts that intent is a requirement of *melechet machshevet* and disagrees with Rabbi Yehudah who maintains that unintended *melachot* are prohibited on Shabbat. Nonetheless, Rabbi Shimon concedes to Rabbi Yehudah that taking an action with a well-known, unavoidable consequence is tantamount to intending to bring about that consequence. One is liable for doing even an unintended *melachah* if it is an inevitable and known consequence of his deliberate actions.

It is different here,	שַׁאנֵי הָכָא
for the longer it stays alive, the more he is pleased,	דְּכַמָּה דְאִית בֵּיה נְשָׁמָה טְפֵי נִיחָא לֵיהּ
since the dye should be clearer.	כִּי הֵיכִי דְלֵיצִיל צִיבְעֵיהּ

Table 1

Summary of the *Sugya*

***Baraita*: One who captures *chilazon* and crushes it to remove its dye . . .**	
Rabbanan: Violates one transgression: Capturing	**Rabbi Yehudah:** Violates two transgressions Capturing/Threshing (crushing to extract blood)
Rava: Rabbis don't include threshing because it only applies to things that grow from the ground, not to sea creatures	
Question: Why does his act of crushing (to extract blood) not also make him liable for taking a life?	
Rabbi Yochanan: He crushed it once it was already dead	**Rava:** His taking of a life was only incidental
Challenge to Rava: Abaye and Rava both say that in the case of inevitable consequence (*pesik reisha*) he is liable	
Answer: This case is different in that even as he crushes the *chilzaon*, he wants it to remain alive so that the dye produced from it will be clear and therefore even in a case of *pesik reisha* he is exempt	

TEXT 9: Rashi, *Shabbat* 75a, *Tefei Neicha Lei*

***He is more pleased*—**	טְפֵי נִיחָא לֵיה
for blood of the living is better than blood of the dead	שֶׁדַּם הַחַי טוֹב מִדַּם הַמֵּת
and since his entire being intends and labors to guard it,	וְכֵיוָן דְּכָל עַצְמוֹ מִתְכַּוֵין וְטוֹרֵחַ לְשׁוֹמְרוֹ
so that it not die in his hands,	שֶׁלֹּא יָמוּת בְּיָדוֹ
[therefore,] even when it dies, it is only considered an unintended consequence (*mitasek*).	אֲפִילוּ מֵת אֵין כַּאן אֶלָּא מִתְעַסֵּק
And in what circumstance does Rabbi Shimon concede?	וְכִי מוֹדֶה רַבִּי שִׁמְעוֹן
Only regarding that which does not bother him if it occurs,	בְּמִידִי דְלֹא אִיכְפַּת לֵיה אִי מִיתְרַמֵי
provided that he does not intend it.	וּמִיהוּ אִיכַּוְונִי לֹא מִיכַּוֵין

TEXT 10: *Kovetz Shiurim* (Rabbi Elchonon Wasserman), Vol. 1 pg. 76

The reasoning behind Rabbi Shimon's concession in the case of *pesik reisha*	בְּטַעֲמָא דְמוֹדֶה רַבִּי שִׁמְעוֹן בִּפְסִיק רֵישָׁא
could be explained in two ways:	דְיֵשׁ לְפָרֵשׁ בָּזֶה שְׁנֵי טְעָמִים
1) In the case of (the Mishnah (*Nazir* 42a)): *A Nazarite may shampoo his hair . . . but not comb it,*[1]	א) כְּגוֹן בְּנָזִיר חוֹפֵף אֲבָל לֹא סוֹרֵק
since combing constitutes *pesik reisha,*	דִסְרִיקָה הִיא פְּסִיק רֵישָׁא
for we can say that since he knows that by combing he will pluck hairs,	דְיֵשׁ לוֹמַר כֵּיוָן שֶׁיוֹדֵעַ דִּבְסְרִיקָתוֹ יִתְלוֹשׁ שְׂעָרוֹת
it is considered intending to pluck.	מִיקְרֵי מְכַוֵין לִתְלִישָׁה
However, when [the plucking] doesn't please him,	אֲבָל הֵיכָא דְלֹא נִיחָא לֵיה
he certainly does not intend it.	עַל כָּרְחָךְ אֵינוֹ מְכַוֵין
2) Since combing will inevitably result in plucking [hairs],	ב) כֵּיוָן דִסְרִיקָה הִיא פְּסִיק רֵישָׁא לִתְלִישָׁה
consequently, plucking is included in combing	נִמְצָא דִתְלִישָׁה בִּכְלַל סְרִיקָה

and his intention to comb is enough (to make him liable) . . .	. . . וְסַגִּי בְּמַה שֶׁמְּכַוֵּין לִסְרִיקָה
This is the meaning of, "One does not require intent for the *melachah* itself	וְהַיְינוּ דְּאֵין צָרִיךְ כַּוָּנָה לְגוּף הַמְּלָאכָה
and it suffices that he intends to do that action,"	אֶלָּא סַגִּי בְּמַה שֶּׁמִּתְכַּוֵּין לְהַמַּעֲשֶׂה
since the *melachah* is inevitably included in it.	שֶׁהַמְּלָאכָה נִכְלֶלֶת בָּהּ בְּהֶכְרֵחַ

Rabbi Elchanan Bunim Wasserman (1874–1941). A disciple of Rabbis Shimon Shkop, Rabbi Chaim Brisker and the Chofetz Chaim; a preeminent Talmudic genius; renowned founder and head of yeshiva in Baranovitch, Poland. He authored works on Talmudic thought, most notably *Kovetz Shiurim,* a penetrative analysis of Talmudic discussions which remain today very popular. In the summer of 1941, he was murdered by the Nazis and their Lithuanian accomplices near Kovna. His immortal words of belief and destiny, uttered moments before this tragedy, expressed his strength of character and unwavering spirit.

Nafka Mina: The Practical Difference

Optional Text

TEXT 11: Tosafot, *Shabbat* 75a, *Tefei Neicha Lei*

The more he is pleased in that his dye will be clear—	כִּי הֵיכִי דְּלֵיצִיל צִיבְעֵיהּ טְפֵי נִיחָא לֵיהּ
This means that although it is a case of inevitable consequence	פֵּירוּשׁ אַף עַל גַּב דְּהָוֵי פְּסִיק רֵישֵׁיהּ
in which Rabbi Shimon would [usually]concede [that he is liable],	דְּמוֹדֶה רַבִּי שִׁמְעוֹן
here he is exempt	הָכָא מִיפְּטַר
because it is a *melachah* that is not required for its designated purpose.	מִשּׁוּם דְּהָוֵי מְלָאכָה שֶׁאֵינָהּ צְרִיכָה לְגוּפָהּ
For even in a case of destruction, Rabbi Shimon maintains an exemption	דַּאֲפִילּוּ בִּמְקַלְקֵל פָּטַר רַבִּי שִׁמְעוֹן
in the case of a *melachah* that is not required for its designed intent,	בִּמְלָאכָה שֶׁאֵינָהּ צְרִיכָה לְגוּפָהּ

as is stated in chapter *HaNechenakin* (*Sanhedrin* 84b):	כִּדְאָמַר בְּפֶּרֶק הַנֶּחֱנָקִין (סנהדרין פד:)
"Who have you heard is of the opinion that one who performs a destructive act of wounding is liable?	מַאן שָׁמְעַתְּ לֵיהּ דְּאָמַר מְקַלְקֵל בְּחַבּוּרָה חַיָּיב
It is Rabbi Shimon,	רַבִּי שִׁמְעוֹן
for he maintains that anyone who performs a *melachah* that is not required for its designed intent is exempt."	הָא אָמַר מְלָאכָה שֶׁאֵינָהּ צְרִיכָה לְגוּפָהּ פָּטוּר עָלֶיהָ

When does Rabbi Shimon concede with regard to inevitable consequence?	וְכִי מוֹדֶה רַבִּי שִׁמְעוֹן בִּפְסִיק רֵישֵׁיהּ
Only regarding things that he is pleased if they occur,	הָנֵי מִילֵּי בְּמִידֵּי דְּנִיחָא לֵיהּ אִי מִתְרַמֵּי
which constitute its designed intent.	דַּהֲוֵי צְרִיכָה לְגוּפָהּ
However, regarding things that do not bother him [one way or the other],	אֲבָל בְּמִידֵּי דְּלָא אִיכְפַּת לֵיהּ
he does not concede.	לֹא מוֹדֶה

Rashi explained that Rabbi Shimon's concession in the case of inevitable consequence	ורש"י פֵּירֵשׁ דְּהָא דְּמוֹדֶה רַבִּי שִׁמְעוֹן בִּפְסִיק רֵישֵׁיהּ
is with regard to things by which he is not bothered if they occur.	הַיְינוּ בְּמַאי דְּלָא אִיכְפַּת לֵיהּ אִי מִתְרַמֵּי
However, this is not so,	וְלֵיתָא
for in the case of one who prunes reeds on the land of his fellow,	דְּהָא מְזָרֵד זְרָדִין בְּאַרְעָא דְּחַבְרֵיהּ
Rabbi Shimon maintains that he is exempt in chapter *HaBoneh* (*Shabbat* 103a)	פָּטַר רַבִּי שִׁמְעוֹן בְּפֶרֶק הַבּוֹנֶה (לקמן קג.)
and there he is not bothered if it will occur.	וְהָתָם לֹא אִיכְפַּת לֵיהּ אִי מִתְרַמֵּי
Rather, it is as I have already explained.	אֶלָּא כִּדְפֵירַשְׁתִּי

And this is puzzling,	וְתֵימָה
for the end of the first chapter of Tractate *Chagigah* (10b) implies	דִּבְסוֹף פֶּרֶק קַמָּא דַחֲגִיגָה (דף י:) מַשְׁמַע
that Rabbi Shimon's exemption of someone who performs a *melachah* not needing what it is intended to produce	דְּהָא דְּפָטַר רַבִּי שִׁמְעוֹן מְלָאכָה שֶׁאֵינָהּ צְרִיכָה לְגוּפָהּ
is because intentional labor (*melechet machshevet*) is required.	הַיְינוּ מִשּׁוּם דְּבָעֵי מְלֶאכֶת מַחֲשֶׁבֶת
Therefore, in the case of wounding, in which intentional labor (*melechet machshevet*) is not required,	וְאִם כֵּן בְּחַבּוּרָה דְּלֹא בָּעֵי מְלֶאכֶת מַחֲשֶׁבֶת
should he maintain liability for a *melachah* not performed for its designed intent?	לִיחַיֵּיב בָּהּ מְלָאכָה שֶׁאֵינָהּ צְרִיכָה לְגוּפָהּ

TEXT 12: Rashi, *Shabbat* 75a, *Deleitzil Tziv'ei*

The correct version is: *that his dye will be clear,*	דְּלֵיצִיל צִיבְעֵיהּ גַּרְסִינַן
so that the appearance of his dye will be clearer.	שֶׁתְּהֵא מַרְאִית צִבְעוֹ צְלוּלָה

TEXT 13: Tosafot, *Shabbat* 75a, *Ki Heichei*

In that his dye will be clear—	כִּי הֵיכִי דְּלֵיצִיל צִיבְעֵיהּ
This presents a difficulty for Rabbeinu Yitzchak,	קָשֶׁה לְרַבֵּינוּ יִצְחָק
since he should be liable anyway for extracting the blood	דְּמִכָּל מָקוֹם עַל נְטִילַת הַדָּם לִיחַיֵּיב
on account of taking a life	מִשּׁוּם נְטִילַת נְשָׁמָה
and it appears to be like the second understanding in Rashi	וְנִרְאֶה כְּלָשׁוֹן אַחֵר שֶׁפֵּירֵשׁ בְּקוּנְטְרֵס

at the beginning of chapter *Shemoneh Sheratzim*,	בְּרֵישׁ שְׁמוֹנָה שְׁרָצִים (לקמן קז.)
[that] one who bruises [one of the eight *sheratzim*] is liable	דְחוֹבֵל בָּהֶן חַיָּיב
because it is a *toladah* of slaughtering	מִשּׁוּם דְהָוֵי תּוֹלָדָה דְשׁוֹחֵט
and his liability is on account of taking a life.	וְחַיָּיב מִשּׁוּם נְטִילַת נְשָׁמָה
And removing the blood is [the act of] taking a life;	וּנְטִילַת הַדָּם הַיְינוּ נְטִילַת נְשָׁמָה
as the verse states: *For the blood is the life.*	כְּדִכְתִיב כִּי הַדָּם הוּא הַנָּפֶשׁ
Therefore, in the case of the eight *sheratzim* that have hides,	וּלְכַךְ שְׁמוֹנָה שְׁרָצִים שֶׁיֵּשׁ לָהֶם עוֹר
one is liable when the blood collects even though it does not emerge,	חַיָּיב בְּנִצְרַר הַדָּם אַף עַל פִּי שֶׁלֹּא יָצָא
for since it has been collected it is destined to emerge, it is	דְּכֵיוָן שֶׁנִּצְרַר סוֹפוֹ לָצֵאת
only that right now the hide impedes it.	אֶלָּא שֶׁעַתָּה הָעוֹר מְעַכְּבוֹ
However, for other *sheratzim* that have no hide,	וּשְׁאָר שְׁרָצִים שֶׁאֵין לָהֶם עוֹר
one is not liable until blood [actually] emerges from them,	אֵינוֹ חַיָּיב עַד שֶׁיֵּצֵא מֵהֶם דָּם
but when the blood [only] collects and does not emerge, it does not make one liable,	אֲבָל בְּנִצְרַר הַדָּם וְלֹא יָצָא לֹא מִיחַיֵּיב
for since it did not emerge, it is destined to return [and be absorbed back into the *sheretz*],	דְּכֵיוָן שֶׁלֹּא יָצָא סוֹפוֹ לַחֲזוֹר
for if it were destined to emerge, it would emerge immediately,	דְּאִם הָיָה סוֹפוֹ לָצֵאת הָיָה יוֹצֵא מִיָּד
since the hide does not impede it.	שֶׁאֵין הָעוֹר מְעַכְּבוֹ
Rabbeinu Tam replied	וְהֵשִׁיב לוֹ רַבֵּינוּ תָּם
that the blood of the *chilazon* that is used for dyeing is stored [in a special chamber]	דְּדַם חִלָּזוֹן הָרָאוּי לִצְבִיעָה מִיפְקַד פָּקִיד

and for [extracting] that blood, one is not liable on account of taking a life	וְלֹא מִיחַיֵּיב עַל אוֹתוֹ הַדָּם מִשּׁוּם נְטִילַת נְשָׁמָה
and for other blood that emerges with it one is also not liable,	וְעַל דַּם אַחֵר הַיּוֹצֵא עִמּוֹ נַמִּי לֹא מִיחַיֵּיב
for it is not pleasing to him, for [he wants] the color of his dye to be clear.	דְּלָא נִיחָא לֵיהּ כִּי הֵיכִי דְּלֵיצִיל צִיבְעֵיהּ
However, you cannot explain	אֲבָל אֵין לְפָרֵשׁ
that taking a life means weakening the thing that one bruises,	דִּנְטִילַת נְשָׁמָה הַיְינוּ שֶׁמַּחְלִישׁ אוֹתוֹ דָּבָר שֶׁחוֹבֵל בּוֹ
because regarding virginal blood, is the weakening of the woman a requirement? [Obviously not!]	דְּגַבֵּי דַּם בְּתוּלִים מַה צָּרִיךְ לַחֲלִישׁוּת הָאִשָּׁה
And regarding circumcision, is the weakening of the infant a requirement? [Obviously not!]	וְגַבֵּי מִילָה מַה צָּרִיךְ לַחֲלִישׁוּת הַתִּינוֹק
Only the drawing of blood is called taking a life, as I have explained.	אֶלָּא לִנְטִילַת הַדָּם קָרֵי נְטִילַת נְשָׁמָה כִּדְפֵירַשְׁתִּי.

Learning **Activity**

Match the following activities with the principles that explain why they are excluded from being *melechet machshevet* by writing its letter in the box to the left of the activity.

A	פְּסִיק רֵישָׁא—***pesik reisha*** **inevitable consequence (Lesson 10)**		Digging a hole solely to retrieve its earth
B	דָּבָר שֶׁאֵינוֹ מִתְכַּוֵּין—***davar she'eino mitkaven*** **unintended consequence (Lesson 10)**		Tying shoelaces (to untie them before the end of the day)
C	מְלָאכָה שֶׁאֵינָהּ צְרִיכָה לְגוּפָהּ ***melachah she'einah tzerichah legufah*** **substitute purpose (Lesson 4)**		Igniting a fire to destroy his house (for no constructive reason, not even out of rage)
D	מִתְעַסֵּק—***mitasek*** **inadvertent *melachah* (Lesson 10)**		Severing the head of a chicken without intending to kill it because he needs a chicken head
E	כַּוָּנָה לִמְלָאכָה—***kavanah limelachah*** **intent to be *melachah* (Lesson 10)**		Roasting an egg in the sun
F	שִׁינּוּי—***shinui*** **unusual or backhanded manner (Lesson 5)**		Walking in tall grass where one might tear out grass
G	גְּרָמָא—***gerama*** **indirect act of *melachah* (Lesson 10)**		Uprooting an object in a private domain to hand to someone else to place in the public domain
H	מְקַלְקֵל—***mekalkel*** **destructive act (Lesson 4)**		Selecting waste that is collectively less than the size of a fig from food
I	אֵינוֹ מִתְקַיֵּים—***eino mitkayem*** **temporary effect (Lesson 9)**		Opening the refrigerator to retrieve food lets out cold air and causes the thermostat to turn on the compressor
J	חֲצִי שִׁיעוּר—***chatzi shi'ur*** **incomplete measure (Lesson 7)**		Selecting peanuts from raisins when he doesn't prefer one over the other
K	חֲצִי מְלָאכָה—***chatzi melachah*** **incomplete *melachah* (Lesson 7)**		Accidentally brushing the light switch and turning it on

Key Points

1. For the Tabernacle, the Israelites would trap a sea creature called the *chilazon* from which they would extract the *techeilet* dye; this is the source for the *melachah* of capturing.

2. Although the death of the *chilazon* is unintended, the lack of intent alone does not exempt one from punishment for the *melachah* of taking its life, since crushing is known to cause its death inevitably.

3. Crushing the *chilazon* to extract its dye does not constitute the *melachah* of taking a life, since the person is not pleased by its death, because he wants it to remain alive so that its dye will be a clear color and not become murky.

4. The liability for even an unintended, inevitable consequence can be explained in two ways: the well-known inevitability of such a consequence is reason enough for us believe that it was intended; or all inevitable consequences of a particular action are included in that action and all that is needed for liability is for that action to be intended.

5. The difference: If one is displeased by the consequence, there is no reason to believe that it was intended; however, it is still included in the intent for the action that led up to it.

6. Building a dwelling for G-d is the inevitable consequence of doing a *mitzvah*, but to transform mundane routine activities such as eating and sleeping into a tabernacle for G-d requires specific intent.

7. Although a mitzvah is still a mitzvah when it is done without specific intent, it still needs to be a deliberate deed for it to be a mitzvah; it is not a mitzvah if it was just an accident.

Terms to Retain

The first sage (who is mentioned anonymously in a *mishnah* or *baraita*)	תַּנָּא קַמָּא
Acting while preoccupied (doing *melachah* inadvertently or accidentally)	מִתְעַסֵּק
Unintended *melachah*	דָּבָר שֶׁאֵינוֹ מִתְכַּוֵּין
Inevitable consequence	פְּסִיק רֵישָׁא
Indirect cause	גְּרָמָא
Intent to be *melachah*	כַּוָּנָה לִמְלָאכָה

NOTES

The **Rohr Jewish Learning Institute**

An affiliate of
Merkos L'Inyonei Chinuch
The Educational Arm of
The Chabad Lubavitch Movement
822 Eastern Parkway, Brooklyn, NY 11213

Printing
Shimon Leib Jacobs
Point One Communications
Montreal, CA

Accounting
Mrs. Shaina B. Mintz
Mrs. Nechama Shmotkin

JLI Departments
JLI Flagship
Rabbi Yisrael Rice
Chairman
S. Rafael, CA

Dr. Chana Silberstein
Director of Curriculum
Ithaca, NY

Mrs. Rivka Sternberg
Administrator
Brooklyn, NY

Mrs. Chana Lightstone
Research Associate
Brooklyn, NY

Mrs. Ya'akovah Weber
Copy Editor
Brooklyn, NY

Nachman Levine
Research Editor
Detroit, MI

Dr. Michael Akerman, MD
Consultant
Continuing Medical Education
Associate Professor of Medicine,
SUNY–Downstate Medical Center

Bernard Kanstoroom, Esq.
Consultant
Continuing Legal Education
Bethesda, MD

JLI For Teens
in partnership with
CTeeN: Chabad Teen Network

Rabbi Chaim Block
Chairman
San Antonio, TX

Rabbi Benny Rapoport
Director
Clarks Summit, PA

Rabbi Beryl Frankel
Director, CTeeN
Yardley, PA

JLI International Desk
Rabbi Avrohom Sternberg
Chairman
New London, CT

Rabbi Moshe Heber
Coordinator

JLI Supplementary Courses
Rabbi Levi Kaplan
Director
Brooklyn, NY

Authors
Mrs. Chani Abehsera
Los Angeles, CA

Rabbi Zalman Abraham
Brooklyn, NY

Rabbi Levi Jacobson
Toronto, ON

Mrs. Malka Touger
Jerusalem, Israel

Mrs. Shimonah Tzukernik
Brooklyn, NY

JLI Teacher Training
Rabbi Berel Bell
Director
Montreal, QC

National Jewish Retreat
Rabbi Hesh Epstein
Chairman
Columbia, SC

Rabbi Yoni Katz
Director

Bruce Backman
Coordinator

Rabbi Avrumy Epstein
Liaison

Sinai Scholars Society
in partnership with
Chabad on Campus

Rabbi Menachem Schmidt
Chairman
Philadelphia, PA

Rabbi Moshe Chaim Dubrowski
Chabad on Campus

Rabbi Yitzchok Dubov
Director

Rabbi Lev Cotlar
Affiliate Liaison

Torah Café Online Learning
Rabbi Levi Kaplan
Director

Rabbi Simcha Backman
Consultant

Rabbi Mendel Bell
Webmaster

Getzy Raskin
Filming and Editing

Rabbi Mendy Elishevitz
Website Design

Moshe Raskin
Video Editing

Torah Studies
Rabbi Yossi Gansburg
Chairman
Toronto, ON

Rabbi Meir Hecht
Director

Rabbi Yechezkel Deitsch
Mrs. Nechama Shmotkin
Administrators

JLI Academy
Rabbi Hesh Epstein
Chairman

Rabbi Shmuel Wolvovsky
Director

Beis Medrosh L'Shluchim
in partnership with
Shluchim Exchange
Steering Committee
Rabbi Simcha Backman
Rabbi Mendy Kotlarsky
Rabbi Efraim Mintz

Rabbi Sholom Zirkind
Administrator

Rabbi Yitzchok Steiner
Coordinator

Rabbi Mendel Margolin
Producer

Advisory Board
Rabbi Yisroel Altein
Pittsburgh, PA

Rabbi Mendel Cohen
Sacramento, CA

Rabbi Mordechai Farkash
Bellevue, WA

Rabbi Mendel Lipsker
Sherman Oaks, CA

JLI Central
Founding Department Heads
Rabbi Zalman Charytan
Acworth, GA

Rabbi Mendel Druk
Cancun, Mexico

Rabbi Menachem Gansburg
Toronto, ON

Rabbi Chaim Zalman Levy
New Rochelle, NY

Rabbi Elchonon Tenenbaum
Napa Valley, CA

myShiur Affiliates

Share the **Rohr JLI** experience with friends and relatives worldwide

ARIZONA

Chandler
Rabbi Menachem Lipskier
480.855.4333

Scottsdale
Rabbi Yossi Bryski
480.443.5362

CALIFORNIA

Laguna Miguel
Rabbi Mendy Paltiel
949.831.8475

Los Angeles
Rabbi Mordechai Zaetz
310.826.4453

Marina del Rey
Rabbi Mendy Avtzon
310.859.0770

Sacramento
Rabbi Mendy Cohen
916.455.1400

S. Monica
Rabbi Boruch Rabinowitz
310.394.5699

CONNECTICUT

West Hartford
Rabbi Yosef Kulek
860.232.1116

KANSAS

Overland Park
Rabbi Mendy Wineberg
913.649.4852

MARYLAND

Baltimore
Rabbi Shmuel Kaplan
301.983.4200

Rabbi Elchonon Lisbon
Rabbi Uri Feldman
410.358.4787

Gaithersburg
Rabbi Sholom Rachik
301.926.3632

MASSACHUSETTS

Andover
Rabbi Asher Bronstein
978.470.2288

Boston
Rabbi Shmuel Posner
718.221.6900

Newton
Rabbi Moshe Lieberman
718.221.6900

Swampscott
Rabbi Yoli Kranz
Rabbi Yossi Lipsker
781.581.3833

NEW JERSEY

Cherry Hill
Rabbi Mendy Mangel
856.874.1500

Morganville
Rabbi Levi Wolosow
732.972.3687

Rockaway
Rabbi Mordechai Baumgarten
973.625.1525

Tenafly
Rabbi Mordechai Shain
201.871.1152

NEW YORK

Brooklyn
Rabbi Zalman Abraham
718.221.6900

Dix Hills
Rabbi Levi Kaplan
718.221.6900 x18

Great Neck
Rabbi Yoseph Geisinsky
516.487.4554

Long Beach
Rabbi Anchelle Perl
516.739.3636

Rochester
Rabbi Dovid Mochkin
585.271.0330

OREGON

Lake Oswego
Rabbi Motti Wilhelm
503.977.9947

OHIO

Cleveland Heights
Rabbi Osher Kravitsky
216.570.0289

PENNSYLVANIA

Kingston
Rabbi Uri Pearlman
570.239.4348

WASHINGTON

Olympia
Rabbi Cheski Edelman
360.584-4306

AUSTRALIA

Brisbane
Rabbi Chanoch Sufrin
61 7.3342.6326

Sydney
Dover Heights
Rabbi Benzion Milecki
612.9371.7300 Ext 4

New South Wales
Rabbi Nochum Schapiro
612.9488.9548

BELGIUM

Antwerp
Rabbi Mendy Gurary
32.3.239.6212

BRAZIL

S. Paulo
Rabbi Avraham Steinmetz
55.11.3081.3081

CANADA

ONTARIO
Nepean
Rabbi Menachem M. Blum
Rabbi Yisroel Simon
613.843.7770

Thornhill
Rabbi Yossi Gansburg
905.731.7000

QUEBEC
Montreal
Rabbi Ronnie Fine
514.342.3554

TURKEY

Izmir
Rabbi Yisahar Aaron Izak
0090.530.3206551

UNITED KINGDOM

Liverpool
Rabbi Avremi Kievman
+441517290443

Explorations in Talmud

Tractate Shabbat

שַׁבָּת

These are the Talmud pages we will study and explore in Tractate *Shabbat*.

Reprinted with kind permission from **Tuvia's**.

אַבָּא שַׁלָּחָא הֲוָה ואָמַר הָבִיאוּ שְׁלָחִין וְנֵשֵׁב עֲלֵיהֶן מֵיתִיבֵי נְסָרִין שֶׁל בעה"ב מְטַלְטְלִין אוֹתָן וְשֶׁל אוּמָּן אֵין מְטַלְטְלִין אוֹתָן וְאִם חִישֵּׁב לָתֵת עֲלֵיהֶן פַּת לְאוֹרְחִין בֵּין כָּךְ וּבֵין כָּךְ מְטַלְטְלִין שָׁאנֵי נְסָרִים דְּקָפִיד עֲלַיְיהוּ ת"ש עוֹרוֹת בֵּין עֲבוּדִין וּבֵין שֶׁאֵין עֲבוּדִין מוּתָּר לְטַלְטְלָן בְּשַׁבָּת לֹא אָמְרוּ עֲבוּדִין אֶלָּא לְעִנְיַן טוּמְאָה בִּלְבַד מַאי לָאו לֹא שְׁנָא שֶׁל בַּעַל הַבַּיִת וְלֹא שְׁנָא שֶׁל אוּמָּן לֹא שֶׁל בעה"ב אֲבָל שֶׁל אוּמָּן מַאי אֵין מְטַלְטְלִין אִי הָכֵי הָא דְּתָנֵי וְלֹא אָמְרוּ עֲבוּדִין אֶלָּא לְעִנְיַן טוּמְאָה בִּלְבַד לִפְלוֹג וְלִיתְנֵי בְּדִידָהּ בד"א בְּשֶׁל בעה"ב אֲבָל בְּשֶׁל אוּמָּן לֹא כּוּלָּהּ בְּבַעַל הַבַּיִת קָמַיְירֵי כְּתַנָּאֵי עוֹרוֹת שֶׁל בעה"ב מְטַלְטְלִין אוֹתָן וְשֶׁל אוּמָּן אֵין מְטַלְטְלִין אוֹתָן ר' יוֹסֵי אוֹמֵר אֶחָד זֶה וְאֶחָד זֶה מְטַלְטְלִין אוֹתָן: הֲדוּר יָתְבֵי וְקָמִיבַּעְיָא לְהוּ הָא *דִּתְנַן אָבוֹת מְלָאכוֹת אַרְבָּעִים חָסֵר אַחַת כְּנֶגֶד מִי אָמַר לְהוּ ר' חֲנִינָא בַּר חָמָא כְּנֶגֶד עֲבוֹדוֹת הַמִּשְׁכָּן אָמַר לְהוּ ר' יוֹנָתָן בְּר' אֶלְעָזָר כָּךְ אָמַר רַבִּי שִׁמְעוֹן בְּרַבִּי יוֹסֵי בֶּן לָקוּנְיָא כְּנֶגֶד *מְלָאכָה מְלַאכְתּוֹ וּמְלֶאכֶת שֶׁבַּתּוֹרָה אַרְבָּעִים חָסֵר אַחַת בָּעֵי רַב יוֹסֵף וַיָּבֹא הַבַּיְתָה לַעֲשׂוֹת מְלַאכְתּוֹ מִמִּנְיָנָא הוּא אוֹ לֹא א"ל אַבַּיֵי וְלַיְתֵי סֵפֶר תּוֹרָה וְלִימְנֵי מִי לֹא *אָמַר רַבָּה בַּר בַּר חָנָה א"ר יוֹחָנָן לֹא זָזוּ מִשָּׁם עַד שֶׁהֵבִיאוּ סֵפֶר תּוֹרָה וּמְנָאוּם אָמַר לֵיהּ כִּי קָא מְסַפְּקָא לִי מִשּׁוּם דִּכְתִיב וְהַמְּלָאכָה הָיְתָה דַיָּם מִמִּנְיָנָא הוּא וְהָא כְּמַאן דְּאָמַר* לַעֲשׂוֹת צְרָכָיו נִכְנַס אוֹ דִילְמָא וַיָּבֹא הַבַּיְתָה לַעֲשׂוֹת מְלַאכְתּוֹ מִמִּנְיָנָא הוּא וְהַאי וְהַמְּלָאכָה הָיְתָה דַיָּם הָכֵי קָאָמַר דִּשְׁלִים לֵיהּ עֲבִידְתָּא תֵּיקוּ תַּנְיָא כְּמַאן דְּאָמַר כְּנֶגֶד עֲבוֹדוֹת הַמִּשְׁכָּן דְּתַנְיָא אֵין חַיָּיבִין אֶלָּא עַל מְלָאכָה שֶׁכַּיּוֹצֵא בָּהּ הָיְתָה בַּמִּשְׁכָּן הֵם זָרְעוּ וְאַתֶּם לֹא תִּזְרְעוּ הֵם קָצְרוּ וְאַתֶּם לֹא תִּקְצְרוּ הֵם הֶעֱלוּ אֶת הַקְּרָשִׁים מִקַּרְקַע לָעֲגָלָה וְאַתֶּם לֹא תַּכְנִיסוּ מרה"ר לרה"י הֵם הוֹרִידוּ אֶת הַקְּרָשִׁים מֵעֲגָלָה לַקַּרְקַע וְאַתֶּם לֹא תוֹצִיאוּ מרה"י לרה"ר הֵם הוֹצִיאוּ מֵעֲגָלָה לַעֲגָלָה וְאַתֶּם לֹא תוֹצִיאוּ מרה"י לרה"י מרה"י לִרְשׁוּת הַיָּחִיד מַאי קָא עָבֵיד אַבַּיֵי וְרָבָא דְּאָמְרֵי תַּרְוַיְיהוּ וְאִיתֵּימָא רַב אַדָּא בַּר אַהֲבָה מֵרְשׁוּת הַיָּחִיד לרה"י דֶּרֶךְ רְשׁוּת הָרַבִּים: בְּגִיזֵּי צֶמֶר וְאֵין מְטַלְטְלִין: אָמַר רָבָא לֹא שָׁנוּ אֶלָּא שֶׁלֹּא טָמַן בָּהֶן אֲבָל טָמַן בָּהֶן מְטַלְטְלִין אוֹתָן אֵיתִיבֵיהּ הַהוּא מֵרַבָּנָן בַּר יוֹמֵיהּ לְרָבָא טוֹמְנִין בְּגִיזֵּי צֶמֶר וְאֵין מְטַלְטְלִין אוֹתָן כֵּיצַד הוּא עוֹשֶׂה

נוֹטֵל

(תורה אור: בראשית לט; שמות לו)

רש"י

שַׁלָּחָא הֲוָה. אוּמָּן לְעַבֵּד עוֹרוֹת: **וְאָמַר.** בְּחוֹל: **הָבִיאוּ שְׁלָחִין וְנֵשֵׁב עֲלֵיהֶן.** אַלְמָא לֹא קָפִיד: **דְּקָפִיד עֲלַיְיהוּ.** שֶׁמָּא יִתְקַלְקְלוּ: **וְלֹא אָמְרוּ עֲבוּדִין.** לֹא הוּזְכְּרוּ לְחַלֵּק בֵּין עֲבוּדִין לְשֶׁאֵינָן עֲבוּדִין: **אֶלָּא לְעִנְיַן טוּמְאָה.** דַּעֲבוּדִין מְקַבְּלִין טוּמְאָה וְלֹא שֶׁאֵינָן עֲבוּדִין: **לִיפְלוֹג בְּדִידָהּ.** בְּטַלְטוּל גּוּפֵיהּ אִיכָּא לְפַלּוּגֵי בְּשֶׁל אוּמָּן בֵּין עֲבוּדִין לְשֶׁאֵינָן עֲבוּדִין דַּעֲבוּדִין קָפִיד עֲלַיְיהוּ: **בד"א.** דַּעֲבוּדִין מוּתָּר לְטַלְטְלָן בְּשֶׁל בעה"ב אֲבָל שֶׁל אוּמָּן מֵאַחַר שֶׁעִבְּדָן קָפִיד עֲלַיְיהוּ: **כּוּלָּהּ בְּבעה"ב אַיְירֵי.** וּמְהַדַּר לְפַלּוּגֵי בְּבעה"ב דְּאַיְירֵי בֵּיהּ וְלֹא אַשְׁכַּח לְפַלּוּגֵי אֶלָּא לְעִנְיַן טוּמְאָה וְאִי שַׁבְקֵיהּ לְבעה"ב דְּאַיְירֵי בֵּיהּ וְנָקַט אוּמָּן *מִפְסְקָה לְמִילְּתֵיהּ טְפֵי מִדְּהַשְׁתָּא: **הֲדוּר יָתְבֵי.** הַנָּךְ רַבָּנָן דִּלְעֵיל: **כְּנֶגֶד עֲבוֹדוֹת הַמִּשְׁכָּן.** אוֹתָן הַמְּנוּיוֹת שָׁם בְּפֶרֶק כְּלָל גָּדוֹל הָיוּ צְרִיכִין לַמִּשְׁכָּן וּפָרָשַׁת שַׁבָּת נִסְמְכָה לְפָרָשַׁת מְלֶאכֶת הַמִּשְׁכָּן לִלְמוֹד הֵימֶנָּה: **שֶׁבַּתּוֹרָה.** שֶׁכְּתוּבִים בְּכָל הַתּוֹרָה וְהָכֵי קָאָמַר קְרָא (שמות כ) לֹא תַעֲשֶׂה כָל מְלָאכָה כְּמִנְיַן כָּל מְלָאכָה שֶׁבַּתּוֹרָה: **לֹא זָזוּ מִשָּׁם.** לֹא יָדַעְנָא הֵיכָא אִיתְּמַר וּמִיהוּ [אֶפְשָׁר] לְעִנְיַן וָי"ו דְּגָחוֹן אִתְּמַר מִדְּפָרְכִינַן לָהּ נַמִּי בְּקִדּוּשִׁין *גַּבֵּי וָי"ו דְּגָחוֹן וּמְתָרְצִינַן אִינְהוּ הֲווּ בְּקִיאֵי בַּחֲסֵרוֹת וִיתֵרוֹת ש"מ לְעִנְיַן אוֹתִיּוֹת אִיתְּמַר וְהָכָא לֵיכָּא לְשַׁנּוּיֵי הָכֵי: **מִשּׁוּם דִּכְתִיב וְהַמְּלָאכָה הָיְתָה דַיָּם.** וְאִי מָנִינַן לְתַרְוַיְיהוּ הֲווּ אַרְבָּעִים וּמִדִּתְנַן אָבוֹת מְלָאכוֹת אַרְבָּעִים חָסֵר אַחַת אִיכָּא חַד דְּלָא מִמִּנְיָנָא וּבְהָנֵי תְּרֵי דְּאִיכָּא לְמֵימַר דְּלָא מְלָאכָה נִינְהוּ וְלָא יָדַעְנָא הֵי מִינַּיְיהוּ נָפֵיק וְהָכֵי קָא מִיבַּעְיָא לֵיהּ וְהַמְּלָאכָה הָיְתָה דַיָּם מִמִּנְיָנָא הִיא וּמְלָאכָה מַמָּשׁ קָאָמַר וְהָכֵי קָאָמַר הַמְּלָאכָה שֶׁהָיוּ עוֹשִׂין הָיוּ עוֹשִׂין דַּי לֹא פָּחוֹת מִן הַצּוֹרֶךְ וְלֹא יוֹתֵר מִן הַצּוֹרֶךְ כְּגוֹן רִידּוּדֵי טַסִּין לְצִיפּוּי הַקְּרָשִׁים לְדַי הָיוּ מְרַדְּדִין אוֹתָם וְכֵן בְּטַוּוּי שֶׁל יְרִיעוֹת וְהַאי לַעֲשׂוֹת מְלַאכְתּוֹ הוּא דְּמַפֵּיק וּמְסַיֵּיעַ לְמַאן דְּאָמַר בְּמַסֶּכֶת סוֹטָה לַעֲשׂוֹת צְרָכָיו נִכְנַס לִשְׁכַּב עִמָּהּ אֶלָּא שֶׁנִּרְאֲתָה לוֹ דְּמוּת דְּיוֹקְנוֹ שֶׁל אָבִיו וְאָמַר לוֹ עֲתִידִין אַחֶיךָ לִיכָּתֵב עַל אַבְנֵי אֵפוֹד רְצוֹנְךָ שֶׁיִּמָּחֶה שִׁמְךָ מִבֵּינֵיהֶם כו' אוֹ דִּילְמָא הַאי לַעֲשׂוֹת מְלַאכְתּוֹ מְלָאכָה מַמָּשׁ הוּא וּמְסַיֵּיעַ לָהּ לְאִידָךְ: **וְהַאי וְהַמְּלָאכָה הָיְתָה דַיָּם.** לָאו מְלָאכָה הִיא אֶלָּא כִּדְמַשְׁמַע קְרָא בַּהֲבָאַת נְדָבָה וּכְמַאן דְּאָמַר שְׁלִימָא לֵיהּ עֲבִידְתָּא מְלֶאכֶת הַהֲבָאָה שֶׁלֹּא הָיוּ צְרִיכִין עוֹד וְכָל מִידֵי דְּרָמֵי עֲלֵיהּ דְּאִינָשׁ קָרֵי לֵיהּ עֲבִידְתָּא כְּדַאֲמְרִינַן בְּמַסֶּכֶת סוֹטָה (דף לג.) בְּטִילַת עֲבִידְתָּא דַּאֲמַר סַנְאָה לְאַיְיתוּאָה לְהֵיכְלָא וְאֵינוֹ אֶלָּא צָבָא מִלְחָמָה לְהַחֲרִיב: **הֵם זָרְעוּ וְקָצְרוּ סַמָּנִין.** לִצְבּוֹעַ תְּכֵלֶת וְעוֹרוֹת אֵילִים וְטָחֲנוּ וְלָשׁוּ נַמִּי סַמָּנִין לִצְבּוֹעַ וְאוֹפֶה דְּקָתָנֵי בְּמַתְנִי' בְּאָבוֹת מְלָאכוֹת הוּא בִּישּׁוּל סַמָּנִין אֶלָּא דְּנָקַט סִידּוּרָא דְּפַת וְהָכֵי מְפָרֵשׁ בְּפֶרֶק כְּלָל גָּדוֹל (לקמן דף עד:): **קַרְקַע.** רְשׁוּת הָרַבִּים: **עֲגָלָה.** רְשׁוּת הַיָּחִיד שֶׁגְּבוֹהָה י' וּרְחָבָה ד': **דֶּרֶךְ רְשׁוּת הָרַבִּים.** דַּאֲוִיר שֶׁבֵּין הָעֲגָלוֹת רְשׁוּת הָרַבִּים: **אֲבָל טָמַן בָּהֶן מְטַלְטְלִין אוֹתָן.** קס"ד הַשְׁתָּא דְּמִילֵּי מִילֵּי קָתָנֵי מַתְנִיתִין וְלָאו אַהַנָּךְ דְּטָמַן בָּהֶן קָאֵי: **הַהוּא מֵרַבָּנָן בַּר יוֹמֵיהּ.** אוֹתוֹ הַיּוֹם בָּא לְבֵית מִדְרָשׁוֹ תְּחִלָּה*:

נוֹטֵל

תוספות

אַבָּא שַׁלָּחָא. פר"ח וְאָמַר הָבִיאוּ לִי שְׁלָחִין בְּשַׁבָּת וַהֲלָכָה כְּר' יוֹסֵי דְּקי"ל מַעֲשֶׂה רַב וְכֵן נִרְאֶה דְּאִי בְּחוֹל מַיְירֵי כִּדְפֵי' בְּקוּנְט' וְלֹא מַיְיתֵי רְאָיָה אֶלָּא דְּאוּמָּן נַמִּי לֹא קָפִיד טְפֵי הֲוָה לֵיהּ לְאַתּוּיֵי דְּר' יוֹסֵי אֲבוּהּ דְּשָׁרֵי לְקַמָּן בְּכַדְיָא שֶׁל אוּמָּן: **לֹא אָמְרוּ עֲבוּדִין אֶלָּא לְעִנְיַן טוּמְאָה בִּלְבַד.** פרש"י שֶׁאֵין עוֹר מְקַבֵּל טוּמְאָה עַד לְאַחַר עִיבּוּד וְאִם תֹּאמַר וְהָא אָמַר בִּזְבָחִים בְּפ' דַּם חַטָּאת (דף צג: ושם) מִנַּיִין לְרַבּוֹת עוֹר מִשֶּׁהוּפְשַׁט תַּלְמוּד לוֹמַר אֲשֶׁר יִזֶּה עָלֶיהָ תְּכַבֵּס יָכוֹל אַף עוֹר שֶׁלֹּא הוּפְשַׁט תַּלְמוּד לוֹמַר בֶּגֶד מַה בֶּגֶד מְקַבֵּל טוּמְאָה אַף כָּל דָּבָר הַמְקַבֵּל טוּמְאָה מַשְׁמַע דְּעוֹר מִשֶּׁהוּפְשַׁט מְקַבֵּל טוּמְאָה וְיֵשׁ לוֹמַר דְּהָתָם כְּשֶׁיִּחֲדוּ לִישִׁיבָה וְהָכָא כְּשֶׁלֹּא יִחֲדוּ וַאֲפ"ה מוּתָּר לְטַלְטְלוֹ בְּשַׁבָּת וְהָא דְּאָמַר רַבָּה בְּרֵישׁ כָּל הַכֵּלִים (לקמן קכג.) מִדִּלְעִנְיַן טוּמְאָה לָאו מָנָא הוּא לְעִנְיַן שַׁבָּת נַמִּי לָאו מָנָא הוּא גַּבֵּי מַחַט שֶׁנִּיטַּל חֻרָהּ אוֹ עוּקְצָהּ ה"פ מִדִּלְעִנְיַן טוּמְאָה לָאו מָנָא הוּא אֲפִי' ע"י יִחוּד דְּנִיטַּל חֻרָהּ אוֹ עוּקְצָהּ טְהוֹרָה וְלֹא מְהַנֵּי בָּהּ יִחוּד וְהָא דִּתְנַן בְּמַסֶּכֶת כֵּלִים בְּפֶרֶק י"ג (משנה ה) מַחַט שֶׁנִּיטַּל חֻרָהּ אוֹ עוּקְצָהּ טְהוֹרָה וְאִם הִתְקִינָהּ לְמִיתּוּחַ טְמֵאָה אוֹמֵר ר"י דְּהָתָם מַיְירֵי כְּשֶׁעָשָׂה בָּהּ שׁוּם שִׁינּוּי וְתִיקּוּן לְמִיתּוּחַ אֲבָל בְּיִחוּד בְּעָלְמָא לְמִיתּוּחַ אֵינָהּ טְמֵאָה אֲבָל הֵיכָא דַּהֲוֵי מָנָא לְעִנְיַן טוּמְאָה ע"י יִחוּד לְגַבֵּי שַׁבָּת הָוֵי מָנָא בְּלֹא יִחוּד וְכֵן מַשְׁמַע הָתָם דְּקָאָמַר תַּרְגְּמָא אַבַּיֵי אַלִּיבָּא דְּרַבָּה בְּגָלְמֵי דְּזִימְנִין דְּמִימְלִיךְ עֲלַיְיהוּ וּמְשַׁוֵּי לְהוּ מָנָא לְהָכֵי מוּתָּר לְטַלְטְלָהּ אע"ג דַּאֲכַתִּי לֹא אִימְּלִיךְ עֲלָהּ וְהִיא טְהוֹרָה: **אַרְבָּעִים אָבוֹת מְלָאכוֹת חָסֵר אַחַת כְּנֶגֶד מִי.** דְּהַרְבֵּה מְלָאכוֹת יֵשׁ דְּדָמְיָין לַהֲדָדֵי וַהֲוָה לָן לְמֶחְשְׁבִינְהוּ כּוּלָּן כְּאַחַת כִּדְפָרֵיךְ בְּפֶרֶק כְּלָל גָּדוֹל (לקמן עג:) הַיְינוּ זוֹרֶה הַיְינוּ בּוֹרֵר הַיְינוּ מְרַקֵּד וּמִשּׁוּם חִילּוּק מוּעָט שֶׁבֵּינֵיהֶם לֹא הֲוָה מְחַלְּקִינַן לְהוּ אִי לָאו דְּקִים לְהוּ דל"ט מְלָאכוֹת הֵן כְּנֶגֶד שׁוּם דָּבָר לְכָךְ בָּעֵי כְּנֶגֶד מִי: **כְּנֶגֶד כָּל מְלָאכָה שֶׁבַּתּוֹרָה.** לִכְאוֹרָה נִרְאֶה דְּיָלִיף נַמִּי מִמִּשְׁכָּן שֶׁהֲרֵי לְכָךְ נִסְמְכָה פָּרָשַׁת שַׁבָּת לְפָרָשַׁת מִשְׁכָּן וְעוֹד דְּאִי לֹא יָלִיף מִמִּשְׁכָּן א"כ הֵיכִי יָדְעִינַן לְדִידֵיהּ הֵי נִינְהוּ אָבוֹת מְלָאכוֹת וְהֵי תּוֹלָדוֹת דְּאֵין סְבָרָא לוֹמַר שֶׁמִּדַּעְתָּם בֵּירְרוּ מְלָאכוֹת הַחֲשׁוּבוֹת וַעֲשָׂאוּם אָבוֹת וְעוֹד דִּבְהֶדְיָא תְּנַן לְקַמָּן בְּהַזּוֹרֵק* הַמּוֹשִׁיט חַיָּיב שֶׁכָּךְ הָיְתָה עֲבוֹדַת הַלְוִיִּם [דף צו.] אֶלָּא לְפִי שֶׁיֵּשׁ מְלָאכוֹת דּוֹמוֹת זוֹ לְזוֹ וְאָנוּ עוֹשִׂין שְׁתֵּיהֶן אָבוֹת כְּגוֹן מְרַקֵּד וּבוֹרֵר לְכָךְ חִלְּקוּם חֲכָמִים לְהַשְׁלִים מִנְיַן מְלָאכוֹת שֶׁבַּתּוֹרָה הוֹאִיל וַחֲלוּקוֹת קְצָת זוֹ מִזּוֹ וְאִי אֶפְשָׁר לוֹמַר כֵּן דְּלֹא פָּלִיג מִדְּקָאָמַר בְּסָמוּךְ תַּנְיָא כְּמ"ד כְּנֶגֶד עֲבוֹדוֹת הַמִּשְׁכָּן מַשְׁמַע דִּפְלִיגֵי וְעוֹד לְמַאן דְּלֵית לֵיהּ דְּרָשָׁא דִּמְלֶאכֶת וּמְלָאכָה מְנָא לֵיהּ דְּחָשֵׁיב זוֹרֶה וּבוֹרֵר בִּשְׁתַּיִם וְעוֹד לְקַמָּן מַשְׁמַע דְּמִטַּעַם דִּכְנֶגֶד עֲבוֹדוֹת הַמִּשְׁכָּן גְּרֵידָא אִית לָן לְאַחְשׁוּבִינְהוּ בְּתַרְתֵּי דְּקָאָמַר אַבַּיֵי וְרָבָא בְּפֶרֶק כְּלָל גָּדוֹל (לקמן עג:) כָּל מִילְּתָא דַּהֲוָאי בַּמִּשְׁכָּן אע"ג דְּאִיכָּא דְּדָמְיָא לַהּ חָשֵׁיב לַהּ: **הֵם הֶעֱלוּ קְרָשִׁים כו'.** אֲפִילּוּ רַבָּנָן דִּפְלִיגֵי אַדְּרַבִּי יוֹסֵי בְּרַבִּי יְהוּדָה גַּבֵּי *) נָעַץ קָנֶה בִּרְשׁוּת הָרַבִּים וּבְרֹאשׁוֹ טְרַסְקָל וְלֵית לְהוּ גּוּד אַחֵית מוֹדוּ בַּעֲגָלָה שֶׁהִיא רְשׁוּת הַיָּחִיד כֵּיוָן דַּעֲגָלָה גּוּפָהּ יֵשׁ אוֹרֶךְ בִּזְקִיפָה עֲשָׂרָה וְרוֹחַב אַרְבָּעָה אע"פ שֶׁתַּחְתֶּיהָ רְשׁוּת הָרַבִּים וּבְרֵישׁ כָּל גַּגּוֹת (עירובין פט.) [ד"ה במחיצות] הֶאֱרַכְתִּי יוֹתֵר: **וְאַתֶּם אַל תַּכְנִיסוּ.** וַאֲפ"ה לֹא הָוְיָא אָב כִּדְפָרֵישִׁית לְעֵיל (דף ג.) [ד"ה פשט]:

אֶלָּא

*) [לעיל ה. לקמן קא.]

רבינו חננאל

פושט עורות היה וקבלנו מרבותינו דהלכתא כר' יוסי דקי"ל מעשה רב ואמר ר' ישמעאל בר' יוסי אבא שלחא הוה ואמר הביאו שלחין ונשב עליהן. נמצא כי עשה מעשה כשמועתו דתניא עורות של בעל הבית מטלטלין אותן. של אומן אין מטלטלין אותן. ר' יוסי אומר זה וזה מטלטלין הלכך עורות של אומן הואיל וראויין לישב עליהן ואין נפסדין אינו מקפיד עליהן ומותר לטלטלן. אבל נסרין של אומן הואיל ואם ישב עליהן נפגמין הלכך קפיד עליהן ואסור לטלטלן: **אמר** ר' חנינה הא דתנן אבות מלאכות ארבעים חסר אחת כנגד עבודות המשכן. ותניא כוותיה אין חייבין אלא על מלאכה שכיוצא בה היתה במשכן כיצד הן זרעו וקצרו והעלו קרשים מקרקע לעגלה אתם לא תזרעו ולא תקצרו כו' הא דתנן אבות מלאכות ארבעים חסר אחת כו'. וא"ר יונתן בן אלעזר כנגד מלאכת ומלאכה שבתורה*) והן ס"א. כשתוציא ג' מלאכות הכתובין ביכולו השמים וד' שכתוב בהן ועשית ויעשה ותעשה ולרגל המלאכה וי"ג שכתב כל מלאכת עבודה הרי כ"א נשארו מ' ובכללם ששת ימים וכו' לא תעשה מלאכה. ולמה (זכה) כי בפירוש אמרו בתלמוד א"י שבא זה הכתוב להשלים ל"ט מלאכות בתורה ויש מי שמוציא מכלל אלו מ' ויבא יוסף הביתה לעשות מלאכתו. ונשארו ל"ט ויש מי שמוציא והמלאכה היתה דים ולדברי הכל נשארים ל"ט מלאכות: **פים'** בגיזי צמר ואין מטלטלין אותן. וקיי"ל

*) עי' ראב"ן סימן ש"ע שמבאר היטב דברי הר"ח כמ"ש כאן ורמב"ן ורשב"א ע"ש:

רב נסים גאון

ולא אמרו עבודין אלא לענין טומאה בלבד. עיקר דיליה משתכח במסכת חולין בפ' העור והרוטב (דף קכב) וכולן שעיבדן או שהילך בהן כדי עבודה טהורין ובתוספתא וכולן שעיבדן ושהילך בהן כדי עבודה טהורין משום עור: **אותיביה** ההוא מרבנן בר יומיה לרבא זה התלמיד אמרו עליו באותו היום נכנס לבית המדרש על כן קרו ליה בר יומיה וכיוצא בו אמרנו בשחיטת קדשים (זבחים פ"ה דף נז) היה שם תלמיד אחד שבא לשמש לבית המדרש ור' יוסי הגלילי שמו וכבר היה רב אידי אבוה דר' יעקב בר אידי הוו קרי ליה בר בי רב דחד יומא כמו שאמרו (חגיגה דף ה) רב אידי אבוה דר' יעקב בר אידי הוה רגיל דהוה אתי תלתא ירחין באורחא והוה קאי חד יומא בבי רב והדר אזיל תלתא ירחין באורחא הוה קאי חד יומא באושפיזיה והדר אתי הוה קא קרו ליה בר בי רב דחד יומא חלש דעתיה קרי אנפשיה (איוב יב) שחוק לרעהו אהיה אמר ליה ר' יוחנן במטותא מינך לא תעניש רבנן נפק ר' יוחנן ודרש (ישעיה נח) ואותי יום יום ידרשון וכי ביום דורשין אותו ובלילה אין דורשין אותו אלא לומר לך כל העוסק בתורה אפילו יום אחד בשנה מעלה עליו הכתוב כאילו עוסק כל השנה כולה:

עין משפט נר מצוה

טז א מיי' פכ"ו מהלכות שבת הלכה יב סמג לאוין סה טוש"ע או"ח סימן שח סעיף כה:

יז ב שם סעיף כו:

יח ג מיי' פכ"ו מהלכות שבת שם סמג שם טור שו"ע או"ח סימן רנט סעיף א:

מסורת הש"ס

ס"א מספקא

ב"ק ג. לקמן עג. וש"נ

[דף ל.]

[ועי' תוי"ט שבת פ"ז מ"ב סד"ה אבות ועי' חידושי רמב"ן ורשב"א בשם פיר"ח]

קידושין ל. ע"ש

סוטה לו:

[פי' אחר רב אידי הוה דהוה קרי לי' בר בי רב דחד יומא בחגיגה ה: ערוך]

גליון הש"ס

רש"י ד"ה לא זזו לא ידענא כו'. עיין ברכות דף כה ע"ב רש"י ד"ה מאן שמעת ליה וש"נ:

ראשי תיבות

א"כ – אִם כֵּן
א"ל – אָמַר לֵיהּ
א"ר – אָמַר רַבִּי
אע"ג – אַף עַל גַּב
אע"פ – אַף עַל פִּי
ואפ"ה – וַאֲפִילּוּ הָכֵי
בד"א – בַּמֶּה דְּבָרִים אֲמוּרִים
בעה"ב – בַּעַל הַבַּיִת
בבעה"ב – בְּבַעַל הַבַּיִת
לבעה"ב – לְבַעַל הַבַּיִת
ה"פ – הָכֵי פֵּירוּשׁוֹ
כמ"ד – כְּמַאן דְּאָמַר
ע"י – עַל יְדֵי
פר"ח – פֵּירֵשׁ רַבֵּינוּ חֲנַנְאֵל
פרש"י – פֵּירֵשׁ רַשִׁ"י
דקי"ל – דְּקַיְימָא לָן
קס"ד – קָא סָלְקָא דַּעְתָּךְ
לרה"י – לִרְשׁוּת הַיָּחִיד
מרה"י – מֵרְשׁוּת הַיָּחִיד
לרה"ר – לִרְשׁוּת הָרַבִּים
מרה"ר – מֵרְשׁוּת הָרַבִּים
ת"ש – תָּא שְׁמַע

אלא לאו רישא בעכו"ם וסיפא בשאר מצות ושגג בלא מתכוין בשאר מצות ה"ד דסבור דשומן הוא ואכלו משא"כ בשבת דפטור דנתכוון לחתוך את התלוש וחתך את המחובר פטור ואביי שגג בלא מתכוין ה"ד דסבור רוק הוא ובלעו משא"כ בשבת דפטור דנתכוון להגביה את התלוש וחתך את המחובר פטור אבל נתכוון לחתוך את התלוש וחתך את המחובר חייב: איתמר *נתכוון לזרוק שתים וזרק ארבע *רבא אמר פטור אביי אמר חייב רבא אמר פטור (א) דלא קמיכוין לזריקה דארבע אביי אמר חייב דהא קמיכוין לזריקה בעלמא כסבור רשות היחיד ונמצאת רשות הרבים רבא אמר פטור ואביי אמר חייב רבא אמר פטור דהא לא מיכוין לזריקה דאיסורא ואביי אמר חייב דהא קא מיכוין לזריקה בעלמא וצריכא דאי אשמעינן קמייתא בההוא קאמר רבא דהא לא קמיכוין לחתיכה דאיסורא אבל נתכוון לזרוק שתים וזרק ארבע דארבע בלא תרתי לא (ב) מיזדרקא ליה אימא מודה ליה לאביי ואי אשמעינן בהא בהא קאמר רבא דהא לא קמיכוין לזריקה דארבע אבל כסבור רה"י ונמצא רה"ר דמכוין לזריקה דארבע אימא מודי ליה לאביי צריכא *תנן אבות מלאכות ארבעים חסר אחת והוינן בה מנינא למה לי וא"ר יוחנן שאם עשאן כולם בהעלם אחד חייב על כל אחת ואחת בשלמא לאביי דאמר כי האי גוונא חייב משכחת לה דידע דאיסורא (ג) שבת וידע לה איסור מלאכות וקא טעה בשיעורין אלא לרבא דאמר פטור היכי משכחת לה בזדון שבת ושגגת מלאכות הניחא אי סבר לה כר' יוחנן דאמר כיון ששגג בכרת אע"פ שהזיד בלאו משכחת לה דידע לה לשבת בלאו אלא אי סבר לה כרשב"ל דאמר עד שישגוג בלאו וכרת דידע לה לשבת במאי *דידע לה בתחומין ואליבא דר"ע:

מתני' (א) אבות *מלאכות ארבעים חסר אחת הזורע והחורש והקוצר והמעמר והדש והזורה הבורר הטוחן והמרקד והלש והאופה הגוזז את הצמר המלבנו והמנפצו והצובעו והטווה *והמיסך והעושה שתי בתי נירין והאורג שני חוטין והפוצע שני חוטין הקושר והמתיר *והתופר שתי תפירות הקורע על מנת לתפור [שתי תפירות] הצד צבי השוחטו והמפשיטו המולחו והמעבד את עורו והממחקו והמחתכו הכותב שתי אותיות והמוחק על מנת לכתוב שתי אותיות הבונה והסותר המכבה והמבעיר המכה בפטיש *המוציא מרשות לרשות הרי אלו אבות מלאכות ארבעים חסר אחת:

גמ'

(א) ס"א אלו אבות

רש"י

דסבור שומן הוא ואכלו. והיינו דשגג דסבור שומן הוא ולא נתכוין לאכול חלב וחייב ואף על פי דמתעסק הוא לרבא דהא לא מתכוין לאכילת איסור חייב דאמר שמואל בכריתות (פ"ד דף יט:) בחלבי' ועריות מתעסק חייב שכן נהנה אבל בשבת פטור דלא נהנה והיינו סייעתא לדידיה דאמר נתכוין לחתוך את התלוש וחתך את המחובר פטור: ואביי. אמר לך לעולם כי האי גוונא אף בשבת חייב דלאו מתעסק הוא והיכי דמי מתעסק דשאר מצות חייב קסבר רוק הוא שהיה חלב נימוח ובלעו דלא איכוין לאכילה דרוק לאו בר אכילה הוא אלא בליעה דכתיב (איוב ז) עד בלעי רוקי ועלתה בידו אכילה דהא לא איכוין לאכילה ודכוותייהו דשבת דפטור נתכוין להגביה ועלתה בידו חתיכה: דהא לא איכוין לזריקה דאיסור. ויהא שוגג בשבת או במלאכה אבל זה אינו שוגג לא בשבת ולא במלאכות אלא מתעסק בדבר אחד של היתר ועלתה בידו איסור: וצריכא. לאיפלוגי בכולהו אף על גב דדמי להדדי: דארבע בלא תרתי לא מזדריק. וזה שנתכוין לשתים וזרק ארבע נעשית מחשבתו דהא יש בכלל ד' שתים הלכך לאו מתעסק הוא: דלא איכוין לזריקה דארבע. ובליר מהני לא שם זריקה עלה: אבל כסבור רה"י הוא וכו'. דנתכוין לזריקה גמורה: משכחת לה. להאי שנשתכחה תורת כל הלכות שבת ממנו ואפילו הכי חשיבא ליה כזדון שבת ושגגת מלאכות לחיוביה אכל חדא כגון דידע ליה לשבת באיסורין וטעה בשיעורין שנתכוין לפחות מכשיעור ועשה כשיעור דלכולן יש שיעור: אלא לרבא דאמר פטור היכי משכחת לה. דמיחייב שוס אדם על כל מלאכה ומלאכה שבהעלם אחד על כרחך בזדון שבת ושגגת מלאכות הוא דבעית לאשכוחיה והכא דאיעלימו כולהו מיניה מאי זדון שבת איכא במה ניכר לו שבת משאר ימים:

מתני' הזורה. ברחת לרוח: הבורר. פסולת בידיו: המרקד. בנפה ובגמ' פריך הני כולהו חדא היא דלהפריש פסולת מתוך אוכל נעשות שלשתן: האופה. לא הוה במשכן דלא שייך אלא בפת ופת לא שייכא במלאכת המשכן אבל כולהו קמייתא הואי בסממנין של צבע תכלת וארגמן ותולעת שני ובגמרא פריך דשביק תנא מבשל דהוי בסממנים ונקט אופה ושיעורן של אלו כגרוגרת חוץ מחורש דבכל שהוא לקמן בפרק הבונה (דף קג.): הגוזז צמר. וכל שאר מלאכות שייכי בצמר של מלאכת המשכן: המלבנו. מכבסו בנהר: המנפצו. קרפי"ר בלע"ז: המיסך. אורדי"ר: בתי נירין. לי"ש שנותן שני חוטין בתוך הבית ניר ובגוה ובמלבן וכולהו אינך מפרש שיעורן לקמן בפרק האורג: הפוצע. מנתק פעמים שיש בשני חוטין יותר מדאי ומנתק מהן ומקלישן לאורך והני כולהו ממיסך ואילך עד קושר ומתיר שייכי ביריעות ולקמן מפרש מאי קושר ומאי מתיר איכא: ותופר וקורע. ביריעות הוא: על מנת לתפור. פעמים שהנקב עגול ואינו יכול לתופרו יפה אא"כ קורעו כדמפרש בגמרא אבל קורע שלא לתפור לא הוי במשכן: הצד את הצבי. וכל מלאכת עורו נוהגת בתחשים למשכן בעורותיהן: המולחו. לעור: ממחקו. מגרר שערו: מחתכו. מקצעו ומחתכו לרצועות וסנדלים: כותב ומוחק. לקמן (דף קג:) מפרש למאי מיבעיא למשכן שכן רושמין על קרשי המשכן לידע איזה בן זוגו וכותב אות בזו ואות בזו ומוחק פעמים שטעה: מכבה ומבעיר. באש שתחת הדוד של סממנין: מכה בפטיש. הוא גמר כל מלאכה שכן אומן מכה בקורנס על הסדן להחליקו בגמר מלאכה ומתניתין נמי לא מיחייב ליה אלא בגמר מלאכה: גמרא

תוספות

אלא לאו רישא בע"ז וסיפא בשאר מצות. תימה לר"י דלוקמא כולה בשאר מצות ומאי מה שאין כן בשאר מצות כגון שחט וזרק בחוץ דאינו חייב אלא אחת כדאמר אביי בפרק אחד דיני ממונות (סנהדרין לד:) שם תעשה עשאן הכתוב עשיה אחת ור' אבהו נמי דפליג מודה דלרבי ישמעאל בשחיטה וזריקה ולר' עקיבא בהעלאה וזריקה דאינו חייב אלא אחת דמחד קרא נפקי ושגג בלא מתכוין כגון שנתכוין לשחוט בהמת חולין והיה צריך לשל חולין ונמלאת (ד) של קדשים דכוותה בשבת נתכוין לחתוך תלוש ונמלא מחובר ולא היה צריך אלא לתלוש דפטור דמלאכת מחשבת בעינן וי"ל דלא מצינן לפרושי הכי דמשמע דפטור בשבת לפי ששגג בלא מתכוין דכה"ג אפילו נתכוין למחובר זה ונמלא מחובר אחר פטור דאין זה מלאכת מחשבת וליכא לאוקמי נמי דמיירי כשנעשה מחשבתו כגון שהיה צריך לחתוך מה שחתך אלא שהיה סבור שהוא תלוש ונמלא שהוא מחובר הא ליכא למימר דכה"ג אם פטור לענין שבת מאשר חטא בה פטור נמי לענין חוץ ומיהו עוד קשה דלוקמא כולה בשאר מצות כגון(ה) נרבע לזכר ורבע את הזכר והבא על הבהמה והביא בהמה עליו דבין לאביי ובין לר' אבהו לר' עקיבא אינו חייב אלא אחת והשתא שגג בלא מתכוין מיתוקם שפיר דמיפטר בשבת מאשר חטא בה וכגון שנעשית מחשבתו וגבי עריות לא מיפטר שכן נהנה:

העושה שני בתי נירין. צריך לפרש למה פירש כאן ובאורג* ובפוצע ובתופר ובכותב שיעור טפי מבשאר:

הקושר והמתיר. ל"ע אי מיחייב במתיר שלא על מנת לקשור אי לא ומדלא תני ליה כדתני מוחק ע"מ לכתוב אין לדקדק דהכי נמי לא קתני סותר ע"מ לבנות ובפ' במה מדליקין (לעיל לא:) אמרינן בהדיא דבעינן סותר ע"מ לבנות ולפי מה שפירש רש"י בגמרא (דף עד:) דאי מתרמי ליה תרי קיטרי בהדי הדדי בשני חוטין זה אצל זה שרי חד ומניח חד משמע דמיחייב בלא על מנת לקשור ולשון קטר לא משמע כפירושו אבל ר"ח פירש וכן משמע בירושלמי כשנפסק חוט בשני מקומות וקושר מתירין ב' הקשרים ומשליכין לחוץ האמצעי וחוזרין וקושרין שתי הראשים זה בזה ואין בו אלא קשר א' ולפי זה משמע דבעי מתיר ע"מ לקשור והא דלא תני ליה במתיר ובסותר פירשתי בפרק ב' (דף לא:) ד"ה וסותר:

עין משפט נר מצוה

כו א מיי' פ"ב מהלכות שגגות הלכה ז:

כז ב מיי' פ"א מהלכות שבת הלכה ח:

כח ג מיי' פ"ז מהלכות שבת הלכה א סמג לאוין סה:

רבינו חננאל

דאמר פטור מאי איכא למימר ואמרינן לא משכחת שגג בלא מתכוין לע"ז אלא באומר מותר. פי' כגון מי שנעלם ממנו עבודת אלהים אחרים ששכח הכל לגמרי שנמצא בידו העלם אלהים אחרים והעלם עבירות ואומר שמותר. וכי האי גוונא בע"ז (אחרינא) חייב בשבת פטור לגמרי ואקשי' ומי איכא למימר דפטור לגמרי דהא עד כאן לא בעא מיניה רבא מרב נחמן העלם זה וזה בידו. פי' העלם שבת והעלם מלאכות בידו מהו אלא לחיובי חדא או תרתי אבל למפטריה לגמרי לא וחזרנו לפרק פירוק אחר משום דקשיא דלא מיתוקמא סיפא דהא מתניתין בע"ז אוקמי הכי רישא בע"ז דקתני עשה שתים בהעלם א' בשבת חייב ב' משא"כ בע"ז שאם זיבח וקיטר וניסך בהעלם א' אינו חייב אלא אחת כר' אמי אבל סיפא דקתני בשאר מצות שגג בלא מתכוין חייב משא"כ בשבת דפטור. בשאר מצות דלאו ע"ז היא והיכי דמי כגון שהי' סבור שהוא שומן ואכלו ונמצא חלב. כגון זה בשאר מצות הוא דחייב. אבל בשבת כי האי גוונא נתכוון לחתוך בתלוש וחתכו ונמצא דמחובר לקרקע פטור ודחי אביי ואמר לא כי האי גוונא (לע"ז) לעולם אימא לך חייב והיכי דמי שגג בלא מתכוין דבשאר מצות חייב ובשבת פטור. כגון שנתכוין בבליעה דרוק ובלעה ונמצא חלב שאע"פ שלא נתכוין לאכילה דחייב בשאר מצות ובשבת כה"ג דנתכוין להגביה דבר תלוש והגביהו ונמצא שחתכו מן המחובר [פטור] אבל אם נתכוין לחתיכה בעלמא חייב. (כגון) [וכ"ש] בשאר מצות אם נתכוין לאכילה בעלמא [חייב] וכדר' נחמן דאמר המתעסק בחלבין ובעריות אע"פ שלא נתכוין חייב שכבר נהנה. והמתעסק בשבת פטור. מלאכת מחשבת אסרה תורה. ור' יוחנן התם בפרק ארבע מיתות כדתני תנא הדא מתניתין קמיה דהאה ואמר ליה פוק תני לברא. דכל מתניתין דלא מיתוקמא רישא וסיפא בחד טעמא לאו מתנית' תרצתא היא. ר' יוחנן לטעמיה דאמר בסוף פרק המפקיד מאן דמתרגם לי חבית אליבא דחד תנא מובילנא מאניה בתריה לבי מסותא: **נתכוון** לזרוק ב' חרק ד' אמות (רבא) [רבה] אמר (חייב) [פטור] אביי אמר (פטור) [חייב] פשוט' היא ומקשינן (לרבא) [לרבה] מתניתין' דקתני ארבעים חסר אחת ואמר ר' יוחנן עלה שאם עשאן כולם בהעלם אחד חייב על כל אחת ואחת ולא משכחת כהאי גוונא דחייב בכולן אלא בזדון שבת ושגגת מלאכות בשלמא לאביי דאמר כי האי גוונא חייב [כר] (וקא טעה) בשיעורין כגון זריקת ד' וכיוצא בהן אלא (לרבא) [לרבה] דאמר כל כה"ג פטור היכי משכחת [לה] בזדון [שבת] ושגגת מלאכה. הניחא אליבא דר' יוחנן דאמר כיון ששגג [illegible]

ראשי תיבות

אא"כ – אלא אם כן
אע"פ – אף על פי
ה"ד – היכי דמי
וי"ל – ויש לומר
דכה"ג – דכהאי גוונא
משא"כ – מה שאין כן
ע"מ – על מנת
צ"ע – צריך עיון
ר"ח – רבינו חננאל
דר"ע – דרבי עקיבא
רה"י – רשות היחיד
רה"ר – רשות הרבים
כרשב"ל – כרבי שמעון בן לקיש

מסורת הש"ס

[כ"ק כו: ע"ש]
[לעיל סט. ע:]
[לעיל ו: מט: סט. ע: לקמן עו: ב"ק ב. כריתות ג:]
[פי' מותח חוטי השתי]
[לקמן קה.]
[לעיל ב: שבועות ה:]

הגהות הב"ח

(א) גמ' רבא אמר פטור דהא לא קמיכוין: (ב) שם תרתי לא מיזדרקא ליה: (ג) שם משכחת לה דידע לאיסורא דשבת וידע לה לאיסור מלאכות: (ד) תוס' ד"ה אלא וכו' לשל חולין ונמלאת היא של קדשים וכו' זה ונמלא מחובר אחר: (ה) בא"ד בשאר מלות כגון הבא על הזכור והביא זכור והבא על הבהמה. נ"ב עי' פרק ד' מיתות דנ"ד:

גמ' מנינא למה לי *א"ר יוחנן שאם עשאן כולם בהעלם אחד חייב על כל אחת ואחת: הזורע והחורש: מכדי מכרב כרבי ברישא ליתני חורש והדר ליתני זורע *תנא בארץ ישראל קאי דזרעי ברישא והדר כרבי תנא הזורע והזומר והנוטע והמבריך והמרכיב כולן מלאכה אחת הן מאי קמ"ל *[הא קמ"ל] העושה מלאכות הרבה מעין מלאכה אחת אינו חייב אלא אחת א"ר *אחא א"ר חייא בר אשי א"ר אמי זומר חייב משום נוטע והנוטע והמבריך והמרכיב חייב משום זורע משום זורע אין משום נוטע לא אימא אף משום זורע אמר *רב כהנא זומר וצריך לעצים חייב שתים אחת משום קוצר ואחת משום נוטע א"ר יוסף האי מאן דקטל אספסתא חייב שתים אחת משום קוצר ואחת משום נוטע אמר אביי האי מאן דקניב סילקא חייב שתים אחת משום קוצר ואחת משום (א) זורע: והחורש: תנא החורש והחופר והחורץ כולן מלאכה אחת הן אמר רב ששת היתה לו גבשושית ונטלה בבית חייב משום בונה בשדה חייב משום חורש *אמר רבא היתה לו גומא וטממה בבית חייב משום בונה בשדה (ב) משום חורש *אמר רבי אבא החופר גומא בשבת ואינו צריך אלא לעפרה פטור עליה ואפילו לרבי יהודה דאמר *מלאכה שאינה צריכה לגופה חייב עליה ה"מ מתקן האי מקלקל הוא: והקוצר: תנא הקוצר הבוצר *והגודר והמסיק והאורה כולן מלאכה אחת אמר רב פפא האי מאן דשדא פיסא לדיקלא ואתר תמרי חייב שתים אחת משום תולש ואחת משום מפרק רב אשי אמר אין דרך תלישה בכך ואין דרך פריקה בכך: והמעמר: אמר *רבא האי מאן דכניף מילחא ממלחתא חייב משום מעמר אביי אמר אין עימור אלא בגידולי קרקע: והדש: תנא הדש והמנפץ *והמנפט כולן מלאכה אחת הן: הזורה הבורר והטוחן והמרקד: היינו זורה היינו בורר היינו מרקד אביי ורבא דאמרי תרוייהו כל מילתא דהויא במשכן אע"ג

גמ' מנינא למה לי. ליתני אבות מלאכות הזורע והחורש כו' ואנא חזינא אי ארבעין *נינהו: שאם עשאן כו'. ובא להודיעך שאם נתעלמו כל הלכות שבת ממנו (ג) חייב כמה חטאות עליו: מכרב כרבי. חורשין: בא"י. קשה היא ואין יכול לכסות בלא חרישה ואשמעינן דהא נמי חרישה היא: כולן מלאכה אחת הן. דזומר נמי לצמוחי אילנא הוא ונפקא מינה דאי עבד ליה כולן בהדי זורע לא מיחייב אלא חדא דהעושה מלאכות הרבה כו' זורע אב מלאכה ונוטע נמי אב מלאכה הוא דהיינו זורע אלא שזה בזרעים וזה באילנות וכן מבריך ומרכיב אבל זומר תולדה: זומר חייב. משום תולדת נוטע דלצמוחי עביד: ונוטע. גופיה וכן מבריך ומרכיב: חייב משום זורע. כלומר אינהו נמי זורע הן זה אב בזרעים וזה אב באילנות: משום נוטע לא. אמבריך ואמרכיב קאי: אימא אף משום זורע. דהך זריעה באילנות ואי עביד ליה בהדי זורע מיחייב חדא ותו לא: זומר. להצמיח הגפן: וצריך לעצים. להסקה משום דצריך להם הויא תולדה דקוצר דצריך נמי לקצור: דקטל אספסתא. שחת וקוצרין אותו ג' פעמים בחדש וחוזר וצומח: דקניב סילקא. חותך תרדין מן המחובר וחוזרין וגדלין: החורץ. עושה חריצין בקרקע: מלאכה אחת הן. אינו חייב אלא אחת דכולהו לרפויי ארעא עבידי: גבשושית. תל קטן: בבית. שייך בנין שמתכוין להשוות קרקעיתו: משום חורש. דמרפי ארעא: גומא וטממה. בעפר היינו חורש שהעפר שמילאה בו הוי רפוי וטוב לזריעה והשוה לקרקע להיות נזרע עם השדה: אלא לעפרה. לכסות צואה: פטור עליה. ואין כאן משום בנין בבית דקלקול הוא ולזריעה נמי לא חזיא אבל אם היה צריך לה חייב משום בונה: לרבי יהודה. בפרק המצניע (לקמן צג:) גבי מוציא את המת במטה: מתקן. כמו מוציא את המת לקוברו אינו צריך לגופה דהוצאה ולא למת אלא לפנות ביתו והוצאה הצריכה לגופה כגון שהוא צריך לחפץ זה במקום אחר: מקלקל הוא. את ביתו: גודר. בתמרים: ומוסק. בזיתים: אורה. בתאנים: דשדא פיסא לדיקלא. זרק פיסת רגבים לדקל: ואתר תמרי. השיר התמרים: תולש. תולדה דקוצר: מפרק. תולדה דדש שמפרק תבואה משבליה לשון פורק מן החמור דישקרגיי"ר בלע"ז רבינו לוי וגם בתשובת רבינו משולם הגאון מצאתי כן ואף זה מפרק התמרים מן המכבדות: אין דרך תלישה ופריקה בכך. על ידי זריקה אלא או ביד או בכלי ותולש כלאחר יד הוא ופטור: דכניף מלחא ממלחתא. שצבר מלח ממשרפות מים דמתרגמינן חרילי ימא (יהושע יא) שממשיך לתוכו מים מן הים והחמה שורפתן והן נעשין מלח ואותו חריץ קרי מילחתא: משום מעמר. שאף הוא כמאסף בשבלין הוא: המנפץ. פשתן בגבעולין: והמנפט. למר גפן בקשת כדרך האומנין ולמר גפן גידולי קרקע הוא להכי קרי ניפוט דיליה תולדה דדש שמפרק גרעינין ממנו ולא קרי ליה תולדת מנפץ דלמר: ה"ג היינו זורה היינו בורר היינו מרקד. היינו. כמו הי ניהו כלומר דמפליג להו תנא דמתניתין לתלת והלא כולן מלאכה אחת הן דמפריש אוכל מן הפסולת:

מכדי מכרב כרבי ברישא והדר כו'. לא שייך למידק הכי בהא דקתני המכבה ברישא והדר המבעיר דהכא כל סידורא דפת נקט כסדר לבד מחרישה: משום זורע. אין להוכיח מכאן דצריך להתרות אתולדה משום אב דהא לא קאמר שצריך להתרותו משום זורע אלא דאם התרה בו משום זורע דחייב אבל בריש פרק תולין (לקמן קלח.) משמע קצת דצריך להתרות אתולדה משום אב דקאמר משמר משום מאי מתרינן ביה (שיהא חייב) רבה אמר משום בורר רבי זירא אמר משום מרקד וגם זה יש לדחות דהכי פירושו משום מאי מתרינן ביה שיהא חייב רבה אמר משום בורר אבל אם התרו בו משום מרקד פטור כיון דמתרהו משום דבר שאינו דומה לו הוא סבר שהוא מלעיג בו ופטור אבל אם התרה בו סתם אל תשמר חייב ונראה שגם ר"ח רוצה לפרש כן ועוד ראיה דבריש בבא קמא (דף ב.) קאמר ולר' אליעזר דמחייב אתולדה במקום אב אמאי קרי ליה אב ואמאי קרי ליה תולדה ולא משני דלהכי קרי ליה אב דצריך להתרות אתולדה [משום] אב*: זומר וצריך לעצים חייב שתים. והא דאמר בפ' זה בורר (סנהדרין דף כו.) תוי חזיוה להוהו גברא דהוה קא כסח אמר להן כהן וחמיר אמרו ליה יכול לומר לעקל בית הבד אני צריך אף על גב דהכא אמר חייב משום נוטע התם מיירי בכה"ג שאין האילן מיתקן בכך אלא מתקלקל: וצריך לעצים. נראה דאפילו לר' יהודה דמחייב מלאכה שאינה צריכה לגופה בעינן צריך לעצים דלא מיקרי בעצים קוצר אלא בענין זה מידי דהוה אקורע על מנת לתפור ומוחק על מנת לכתוב וכדאמר רבי יוחנן לקמן בפ' חבית (דף קמה.) אחד כבשים ואחד שלקות שסחטן לגופן מותר למימיהן חייב חטאת ואמאי שרי לגופן ליהוי כמלאכה שאינה צריכה לגופה אלא טעמא לפי שאין דרך דישה בכך: ואחת משום מפרק. אין נראה לר"י כמו שמפרש רש"י שמפרק האילן ממשאו מן הפירות שעליו אלא כמו שפירש רבינו שמואל שיש על התמרים קליפה העליונה וכשהוא מכה בתמרים מפרק את הקליפה מן התמרים והוי כמו דש שמפרק את התבואה מן השבולת: מפרק. פירש"י דהוה תולדה דדש וקשה לר"ת דבשילהי המצניע (לקמן צה.) אמר דחולב חייב משום מפרק ואי הוה תולדה דדש הא אמר לקמן* גבי הפולע חלזון דלרבנן אין דישה אלא בגידולי קרקע ואין לומר דדוקא חלזון שהוא דג פטרי רבנן דלא הוי גידולי קרקע אבל בחולב מחייבי דבהמה חשיבא גידולי קרקע כדמוכח בריש בכל מערבין (עירובין דף כז:) דהא [ע"כ טעמא דרבנן משום] דילפינן להו מסממנין שבמשכן דאין דישה אלא בגידולי קרקע לגבי דבר הגדל ממש מן הקרקע לא חשיבא בהמה גידולי קרקע כדאמרינן בהשוכר את הפועלים (ב"מ פט.) מה דיש מיוחד שהוא גידולי קרקע ופועל אוכל בו אף כל כו' יצא החולב והמגבן כו' ודוחק לומר דברייתא דהמצניע אתיא כר"י דפליג לקמן אדרבנן ונראה לר"ת דמפרק חייב משום ממחק דכשחולב ממחק את הדד ומחליקו ואין נראה לר"י דבפרק חבית (לקמן קמד:) אמרינן חולב אדם לתוך הקדרה אבל לא לתוך הקערה ולר"ת מה לי לתוך הקדרה מה לי לתוך הקערה ולפירוש הקונטרס א"ש דמעיקרא כשהיה בדדין חשיב אוכל וכשחולב לתוך הקדרה (דהשתא) נמי הוי אוכל ולא דמי לדש שנשתנה ונראה דלפירוש הקונטרס הלכה כרבי יהודה דהא אמר בפרק אע"פ (כתובות ס.) *)אמר רבי מרינוס גונח יונק חלב בשבת מ"ט מפרק כלאחר יד הוא ובמקום צער לא גזרו רבנן ופסיק התם רב יוסף הלכתא כרבי מרינוס ואין נראה לומר דאף לרבנן אסור מדרבנן דמיחזי כמפרק ואף על גב דלא אסירא אלא מדרבנן לא שרי אלא משום דאיכא תרתי כלאחר יד ובמקום צער: [ועי' תוס' כתובות ס. ד"ה מפרק ותוס' יבמות קיד. ד"ה וקסבר]

*) נ"ל תני

[ועי' תוס' לקמן צו: ד"ה ולר"א דמחייב ובב"ק ב. ד"ה ולר"א]

רבינו חננאל

למה לי למיתנא מנינא [מ'] חסר אחת אטו עד האידנא מי לא ידעינן מניני ומשני ר' יוחנן שאם עשאן כולם בהעלם אחד חייב על כל אחת ואחת. (ת"ש) [תנא] הזורע והזומר והנוטע והמבריך והמרכיב כולן מלאכה אחת הן (קס"ד) [קמ"ל] כי העושה מלאכות הרבה מעין מלאכה אחת אינו חייב אלא חטאת אחת שמע' מינה שאלו השנויים במשנתנו חשובין אבות והשאר הן תולדות וכל העושה אב ותולדתו אינו חייב אלא אחת. והעושה ב' אבות או ב' תולדות דלאו אב אחד [חייב] שתים. ומפרשא בגמ' דהזורק דר' אלעזר מחייב בגמ' דכריתות אתולדה במקום אב דידיה תרתי ולית הלכתא כוותיה. ואסיק' מדוקיא דמתני' דמאן דעביד כל מלאכות שבעולם ואפילו אלף מלאכות אינו חייב יותר מארבעים חסר אחת חטאות שהכל נכללים בכלל אבות ובתולדותיהן הללו: ירושלמי כל דבר שהוא משביח הפרי חייב משום זורע. המבריך. המרכיב. והמקרסם. המזרד. המפסל. המזהם. המפרק. המעשן. המתלע. הקוסם. הסך. המשקה. המנקב. והעושה בתים. חייב משום זורע: אמרינן משמיה דרב הזומר חייב משום נוטע והנוטע והמבריך והמרכיב חייב משום זורע. שמעינן מינה מדמוקים המבריך והמרכיב משום נוטע ואף משום זורע דיש תולדה לתולדה. וכולן נכללין בכלל אב אחד. הנוטע וולד הוא של זורע. כי הנוטע נועץ יחור של אילן בארץ ומתגדל כגון המפיל הזרע לארץ וצומח והזומר המקום שזומר באילן מתגדל המקום ההוא ומוסיף פירות ונמצא כנוטע לפיכך אמרינן בזומר חייב (שתים) משום נוטע ואם הוא זומר וצריך לעצים ונמצא כשזומר חייב משום נוטע כמו שאמרנו ובנטילתו העצים נמצא כקוצר. לפיכך בזומר וצריך לעצים חייב שתים. משום נוטע ומשום קוצר וכן מאן דקטיל אספסתא ומאן דקניב סילקא כולן דרך אחת הן וחייב שתים. בזמן שיש שיעור קצירה ושיעור זריעה. פי' המבריך החופר בארץ ומבריך הייחור וטומנו לעפר ומוציא ראש הייחור במקום רחוק. החורש. החורץ. החופר כולן מלאכה אחת הן. אסיקנא כל אלו משום חרישה. כל שהוא ליפות הקרקע בשדה חייב משום חורש וכל שהן בבית להשוות חייב משום בונה. אבל להשוות קרקע השדה חייב משום חורש. כדכתיב הלא אם שוה פניה. והוא כגון המדייר והמעדר והמכבד שהוא משוה גומות והמפעפע גושים. המסקל. הממלא בקעים שתחת הזיתים. העושה עוגיות לגפנים. המברה בחרשים. המצית אור. בחישת הקנים ובאגם תמרים. ואמת המים המכשרת צדדים לזריעה. וכל דבר שהוא להנאת קרקע חייב משום חורש. כך הוא מפורש בירושלמי וכן הא דאמר רבה היתה לו גומא וטממה אף זה משוה פני אדמתו בבית

ראשי תיבות

בא"י – בארץ ישראל
א"ר – אמר רבי
א"ש – אתי שפיר
אע"ג – אף על גב
אע"פ – אף על פי
ה"ג – הכי גרסינן
ה"מ – הני מילי
בכה"ג – בכהאי גוונא
מ"ט – מאי טעמא
ע"כ – על כרחך
קמ"ל – קא משמע לן
ולר"ת – ולרבינו תם
לר"ת – לרבינו תם

עין משפט נר מצוה

מסורת הש"ס

הגהות הב"ח

(א) גמ' דקניב סילקא וכו' ואחת משום נוטע והחורש. (ב) שם בשדה חייב משום חורש: (ג) רש"י ד"ה שאם עשאן וכו' שבת ממנו כמה חטאות חייב עליו:

גליון הש"ס

... לר"י דמשמע פשיטא דניחא ק"ל הא פשיטא דניחא ליה בעצים להשתמש בהם אלא דעתה אינו עושה כן בשבילו מ"מ מיקרי צריכה לגופה כההיא דלקמן דף קג בתולש עולשין בארעא דלאו דיליה: תוס' ד"ה מפרק וכו' לגבי דבר הגדל ממש. עי' ברא"ש בפרשת וישלח בפסוק ויהי לי שור וחמור:

רב נסים גאון ואפילו לר' יהודה דאמר מלאכה שאינה צריכה לגופה חייב עליה הני מילי מתקן והאי מקלקל הוא כבר פירשנו בפרק א' עיקר דבריו של ר' יהודה אבל מקלקל הוא והוא ששנינו במשנה בפרק ר' אליעזר אומר האורג (לקמן דף קה) וכל המקלקלין פטורין:

אע"ג דאיכא דדמיא לה חשיב לה וליחשב נמי כותש אמר אביי שכן עני אוכל פתו בלא כתישה רבא אמר הא מני רבי היא דאמר אבות מלאכות ארבעים חסר אחת ואי חשיב כותש הויא ליה ארבעים וליפוק חדא מהנך ולעייל כותש אלא מחוורתא כדאביי: ת"ר היו לפניו מיני אוכלין בורר ואוכל בורר ומניח ולא יברור ואם בירר חייב חטאת מאי קאמר אמר עולא הכי קאמר בורר ואוכל לבו ביום ובורר ומניח לבו ביום ולמחר לא יברור ואם בירר חייב חטאת מתקיף לה רב חסדא וכי מותר לאפות לבו ביום וכי מותר לבשל לבו ביום אלא אמר רב חסדא בורר ואוכל פחות מכשיעור בורר ומניח פחות מכשיעור וכשיעור לא יברור ואם בירר חייב חטאת מתקיף לה רב יוסף וכי מותר לאפות פחות מכשיעור אלא אמר רב יוסף [א]בורר ואוכל ביד בורר ומניח ביד בקנון ובתמחוי לא יברור ואם בירר פטור אבל אסור ובנפה ובכברה לא יברור ואם בירר חייב חטאת מתקיף לה רב המנונא מידי קנון ותמחוי קתני אלא אמר רב המנונא [ב]בורר ואוכל אוכל מתוך הפסולת בורר ומניח אוכל מתוך הפסולת [ג]פסולת מתוך אוכל לא יברור ואם בירר חייב חטאת מתקיף לה אביי מידי אוכל מתוך פסולת קתני אלא אמר אביי [ד]בורר ואוכל לאלתר ובורר ומניח לאלתר ולבו ביום לא יברור ואם בירר נעשה כבורר לאוצר וחייב חטאת אמרוה רבנן קמיה דרבא אמר להו *שפיר אמר נחמני [ה]היו לפניו שני מיני אוכלין ובירר ואכל ובירר והניח רב אשי מתני פטור רבי ירמיה מדיפתי מתני חייב רב אשי מתני פטור והא תני חייב לא קשיא הא בקנון ותמחוי הא בנפה וכברה כי אתא רב דימי אמר שבתא דרב ביבי הואי ואיקלעו רבי אמי ור' אסי שדא קמייהו כלכלה דפירי ולא ידענא אי משום דסבר אוכל מתוך פסולת אסור אי משום עין יפה הוא דמכוין חזקיה אמר [ו]הבורר תורמוסים מתוך פסולת שלהן חייב לימא קסבר חזקיה אוכל מתוך פסולת אסור שאני תורמוסים דשלקי

רש"י

אע"ג דאיכא. אחריתי בהדה דדמיא לה חשבינהו לתרווייהו כאבות ואע"ג דחדא נינהו: **וליחשב נמי כותש.** חטין במכתשת להסיר קליפתן דהואי במקדש בסממנין אלא לאו משום דדמיא לדש לא חשיב לה דהא נמי מיפרקה מלבוש היא: **שכן עני אוכל פתו בלא כתישה.** לכך אע"ג דהואי במקדש ואב מלאכה היא כיון דתנא ליה דש לא תנא לה וזורה ובורר ומרקד סידורא דפת נינהו וכיון דהוו במקדש והכא אתחיל בסידורא דפת תנינהו כדאמרינן גבי אופה דה"ל למתני מבשל ולא אופה דלא הוה במקדש אלא משום סדורא דפת נקט ואתא הואיל ואופה בפת כמבשל בסממנין אבל כתישה עשירים הוא דלתתי וכתשי לעשות סלת נקיה אבל עניים לא טרחי הלכך לא תנא לה ומיהו ודאי אב מלאכה היא ובכלל דש היא: **רבי היא.** דיליף לקמן בפרק הזורק (דף נג:) דברים הדברים אלה הדברים למניינא: **וליפוק חדא מהנך.** או זורה או בורר או מרקד דהוו חדא ליפוק מינייהו חדא וליתני הך דהכי עדיף למיתני תרתי מהא ותרתי מהא מלמיתני ולמיכפל תלתא זימני בחדא ואיכא חדא דלא כפיל ביה מידי: היו לפניו מיני אוכלין גרסינן ול"ג שני: **ולא יברור.** לקמיה פריך מאי קאמר ברישא תנא בורר והדר תנא לא יברור: **ולמחר.** לצורך מחר: **וכי מותר לאפות ולבשל לבו ביום.** וה"נ אב מלאכה היא כיון דאמרת ולמחר חייב חטאת: **פחות מכשיעור.** פחות מכגרוגרת: **וכי מותר לאפות פחות מכשיעור.** נהי דחיוב חטאת ליכא איסורא מיהא איכא דקיימא לן חצי שיעור אסור מן התורה בפרק בתרא דיומא (דף עד.) והיכי קתני בורר לכתחלה: **בקנון.** כלי עץ שעושין כעין ליזור רחב מלאחריו וקצר מלפניו ובעלי מטבע עושים אותו והבורר בו קטנית נותן קטנית במקום הרחב ומנענעו והקטנית מפני שהוא סגלגל מתגלגל ויורד דרך פיו הקצר והפסולת נשאר בכלי: **פטור אבל אסור.** מותר לכתחלה לא הוי דדמי לברירה וחייב חטאת לא הוי דכלאחר יד הוא דעיקר ברירה בנפה וכברה אבל ביד לא דמי לבורר כלל: **מידי קנון ותמחוי קתני.** ה"ה נמי דפריך מידי נפה וכברה קתני אלא חדא מינייהו נקט: **אוכל מתוך הפסולת.** לא דרך ברירה היא: **ובורר ומניח לאלתר.** לאכול לאלתר שאין זה דרך בוררין: **לאוצר.** להצניע: **נחמני.** אביי: **והתניא.** לעיל חייב ואי בבורר ומניח לאלתר מותר לכתחלה הויא ופטור אבל אסור ליכא: **שבתא דרב ביבי הואי.** הגיע יומו להיות עומד ומשמש על התלמידים: **ושדא קמייהו.** ולא רצה לברור האוכל מתוך העלין ולתת לפני כל אחד ואחד אלא שטחן והם נוטלים ואוכלים ובשטוח זה נפרש האוכל מאליו: **הבורר תורמוסין.** לאחר שבשלן הוא בורר אוכל מתוך הקליפה: דשלקי

תוספות

אע"ג דאיכא דדמיא לה חשיב(א). והא דלא חשיב שובט ומדקדק לפי שהם לגמרי בכלל מיסך ואורג ולא חשיב נמי מנפץ אע"ג שבמשכן היו מנפצין פשתן לעשות יריעות ושאר דברים משום דהיינו דש ממש אלא שזה בתבואה וזה בפשתן אבל זורה ובורר ומרקד הם שלשה דברים: **שכן עני אוכל פתו בלא כתישה.** וא"ת מ"מ ליחשיב כתישת סממנין דהוה במשכן וא"ג דעני אוכל פתו בלא כתישה לענין סממנים מלאכה חשובה היא ואומר ר"י דלאו דוקא אוכל פתו אלא ה"ה דעני צובע בסממנים בלא כתישה וא"ת מרקד נמי לא ליתני שכן עני אוכל פתו בעיסה בלוסה כדאמר בסוף פרקין ויש לומר דרוב עניים אין אוכלין בלא הרקדה אלא שלענין חלה מצטרפין הסובין דקרינן ביה מלחם הארץ כיון דיש עניים שאוכלים בעיסה בלוסה ור"ת פירש בע"א ולא נתיישב לר"י: **היו לפניו שני מיני אוכלין גרסי'.** וכן פירש ר"ח דבאוכל מתוך אוכל שייכא ברירה שבורר אותו שאינו חפץ לאכול מתוך אותו שרוצה לאכול דאותו שאינו חפץ בו חשיב פסולת לגבי אותו שחפץ לאכול וכן משמע בירושלמי דגרס הבורר אוכלים מתוך אוכלים חזקיה אמר כו': **בורר ומניח.** פי' לצורך אחרים: **וכי מותר לאפות פחות מכשיעור.** והמתרץ ס"ד דפחות מכשיעור הוי דרך אכילה: **מתקיף לה רב המנונא מידי קנון ותמחוי קתני.** פי' הקונט' דה"נ הוה מצי למיפרך מידי נפה וכברה קתני וקשה לר"י מאי קמשני רב המנונא לדידיה נמי תקשה מידי [אוכל] מתוך פסולת קתני ועוד בסמוך פירש הקונטרס והתניא חייב דהיינו הך דהכא ומשני דבנפה וכברה מיירי והיכי משני הכא מידי נפה וכברה קתני ונראה לרבינו יצחק דדוקא מקנון ותמחוי פריך וה"פ מידי קנון ותמחוי קתני כיון דנחת לפרושי דיני ברירה דביד מותר ובנפה וכברה חייב חטאת לא היה לו להניח מלשנות קנון ותמחוי דפטור אבל אסור: **בורר ואוכל אוכל מתוך פסולת.** משמע דאוכל מתוך פסולת אין דרך ברירה בכך וקשה דבריש פרק תולין (לקמן קלח.) אמרי' מה דרכו(ג) של בורר בורר אוכל מתוך פסולת וי"ל דהתם בפסולת מרובה על האוכל הוי אוכל מתוך פסולת דרך ברירה דהתם במשמר איירי וקשה לרשב"א דתנן בפ"ק דביצה (דף יד:) הבורר קטניות בי"ט ב"ש אומרים בורר אוכל ואוכל וב"ה אומרים בורר כדרכו ואמר בגמרא בד"א כשהאוכל מרובה על הפסולת אבל פסולת מרובה על האוכל ד"ה נוטל את האוכל ומניח את הפסולת ואי בפסולת מרובה על האוכל הוי אוכל מתוך פסולת דרך ברירה היכי שרי לב"ש הא אינהו אסרי לברר כדרכו ול"ע שם: **והתניא חייב.** פי' בקונטרס דהיינו ברייתא דלעיל וקשה לר"י דלמאי דמוקמינן לה בנפה וכברה משמע דוקא לבו ביום אסור אבל לאלתר אפי' בנפה וכברה שרי ובפ"ק דביצה (גם זה שם.) משמע דבנפה וכברה אסור בכל ענין דתנן ב"ה אומרים בורר כדרכו בקנון ובתמחוי אבל לא בנפה ובכברה ולא מפליג בין לאלתר לבו ביום ועוד לכאורה לעולא דלעיל הוי בורר לבו ביום כמו לאלתר לאביי וא"כ שרי לעולא בנפה וכברה אפי' לבו ביום ובמתני' דביצה אסר לכל הפחות לבו ביום ונראה לר"י דברייתא דלעיל איירי בבורר ביד והכא דמוקי לה בנפה וכברה ברייתא אחריתי היא ואפי' לאלתר חייב חטאת וכן משמע מתוך פירוש ר"ח דפירש שיש ג' דינין בבורר לאלתר דביד מותר לכתחלה בקנון ובתמחוי פטור אבל אסור בנפה וכברה חייב חטאת: **ולא ידענא אי משום דקסבר אוכל מתוך פסולת אסור.** פי' לא ידענא מה שלא בירכם תחלה קודם שהביאם לפניהן אבל אין לפרש מה שלא בירכם בשעה שהניח לפניהם דא"כ מאי קאמר אי משום דקסבר אוכל מתוך פסולת אסור דהא לכ"ע שרינן אוכל מתוך פסולת לאלתר:

האי

עין משפט נר מצוה

לט א ב מיי' פ"ח מהל' שבת הלכה יב סמג לאוין סה טוש"ע או"ח סימן שיט סעיף א:
מ ג מיי' שם הלכה יג טוש"ע שם סעיף ד:
מא ד מיי' שם הלכה יב טוש"ע שם סעיף א ב:
מב ה מיי' שם הלכה יג טוש"ע שם סעיף ג:
מג ו מיי' שם טוש"ע שם סעיף ה:

רבינו חננאל

חייב משום בונה ובשדה משום חורש וקיי"ל בהני כולה כרבה. (א"ר אבא החופר גומא ואין צריך). פי' גבשושית תל של עפר שהיתה לו ונטלה בבית חייב משום בונה כו'. [אמר ר' אבא החופר גומא ואין צריך] לחפור חפירה אלא לעפר בעלמא בלבד הוא צריך. נטילת העפר אינה מלאכה משום חפירה אינו חייב שהרי לא נתכוין לחפירה. ואפילו לר' יהודה דאמר מלאכה שאינה צריכה לגופה חייב עליה ה"מ במתקן אבל האי דחפר מקלקל הוא בין בבית א) בין בשדה. וכי האי מילתא אמרו בהכל חייבין בראיה (חגיגה י') שהן כהררי' התלויין בשערה. מקרא מעט והלכות מרובות: ת"ר הקוצר הבוצר הגודר האורה כולן מלאכה אחת הן. פי' פיסה צרור של אדמה ולענין הלכה מאן דשרא פיסא לדיקלא ואתר תמרי קיי"ל כרב אשי דאמר אין דרך תלישה ולא דרך פריקה בכך. הא דאמר רבה מאן דכניף מילחא ממלחתא חייב משום מעמר קי"ל כאביי דאמר אין עימור אלא בגידולי קרקע ואינו חייב אלא (כשמעמר) [כשמעביר] ד' אמות ברה"ר. הדש (תנא) [הוא] המפרק הפסולת המחוברת באוכל ומכינתן לברירה או כברה [בורייה] או בהרקדה. המנפץ נופץ עפרורית מן האוכל וכן המנפט מולל שבלים נמצא זורה והבורר והמרקד כולן מעבירין פסולת המעורבות באוכל ואינה מחוברת (ואינה) כגון קליפה שצריכה פירוק או כגון עפרורית שצריך ניפוץ אלא מעורבת בלבד. וכן אם נטל בידו אדם תבוא' בתיבנא ובפסולת שיש בה וניפח בה ברוח פיו ובירר חשוב הוא כזורה. פי' בורר נוטל פסולת מבין האוכל ומשליכ' או נוטל האוכל ומניח הפסולת. מרקד שמטיל את האוכל והפסולת בכברה ונשארת האוכל ואם האוכל דק והפסולת עבה כמין תבן יוצא האוכל ונשארת הפסולת בכברה. וכיון דאסיק' כי הזורה והבורר והמרקד כולן מעין מלאכה אחת הן מפריש הפסולת מן האוכל ומשום דהוו במשכן הוו להו תלתא וחייב על כל אחת ואחת. ואקשינן ונחשוב נמי כותש שהוא מסיר קליפת החיטין מעליהן לטחון אותם להוציא סולת כגון כותש לעשות דייסא או טיסני והנה גם זה מפריש פסולת מן האוכל הוא ומשני אביי שכן עני אוכל פתו בלא כתישה כלומר כל בני אדם טוחנין בחיטין שלהן סלת הנה דרך העניים לברור ולטחון ולעשות עיסה בלוסה ואין אוכלין סלת לפיכך אין צריכין כתישה. ואע"פ דכתישה מלאכה היא דהא לגבי יו"ט גרסי' (ביצה יד.) אין כותשין במכתשת אע"פ שמותר ביו"ט אוכל נפש וכ"ש בשבת. אמר אביי האי דלא חשיב לה בהדי אבות משום דלא חשיבא שלא כל אדם אוכל בכתישה כמו שאמרנו. לפיכך אינה אלא כתולדות דמיא. רבא אמר אמאי לא חשיב לכותש בהדייהו משום דמתניתין ר' (חייא) [היא] דאמר קבלה היא בידינו אבות מלאכות [ארבעים] חסר אחת כנגד ב) עבודת המשכן ור' מ' חסר אחת שנה וכבר פירשנו להא דר' בבמה טומנין (מט:) כי המלאכות הללו מן המשכן למדתן. ואי חשיב כותש בהדייהו הוי להו מ' שלמות ור' מ' חסר אחת שנה לפי' לא תנא כותש בהדייהו ואקשינן וליפוק חדא מינייהו וניעול כותש ואסיק' אלא מחורתא כדאביי: ת"ר היו לפניו ב' מיני אוכלין בורר ואוכל בורר ומניח ולא יברר ואם בירר חייב חטאת. ומת' מאי קאמר [א'] עולא הכי קאמר בורר ואוכל בו ביום כו' ודחאה רב חסדא ואמר וכי מותר לאפות ולבשל בו ביום כו' ופרשה אביי בורר ואוכל לאלתר בורר ומניח לאלתר. ג) שלא לאלתר לא יברור. ואם בירר נעשה כבירר לאוצר וחייב חטאת. וקיי"ל כוותיה דאמר רבה שפיר אמר נחמני ולאלתר. דאמר אביי כל זמן שיושב על השולחן ואוכל דגרסינן בתלמוד דא"י ברר אוכלין מתוך אוכלין חזקיה אמר חייב ר' יוחנן אמר פטור מתניתא פליגא על חזקיה דאמר בורר ואוכל בורר ומניח על השלחן רבין בר חייא אמר תפתר כשהיו אורחין אוכלין ראשונה ראשונה. היו לפניו ב' מיני אוכלין בורר ואוכל בורר ומנית. רב אשי [מתני פטור רי"מ] מתני חייב ואוקימנא להא דרב אשי כבורר בנפה או בכברה חייב חטאת בקנון ובתמחוי פטור וכל פטורי דשבת פטור אבל אסור נינהו. וקיי"ל כרב אשי דבתראה הוא והא דאמר חזקיה הבורר תורמוסין מתוך פסולת שלהן חייב. הלכתא היא דהא

מקשינן

א) עי' תוס' פסחים מ"ז ע"ב ד"ה כתישה. ב) עי' בגמ' כאן ולעיל מ"ט ע"ב בתוס' ול"ע. ג) מכאן ועד סוף הענין הובא בא"ז בשם רבינו.

מסורת הש"ס

[נדרים נד: ועי' בר"ן טעם דקרי לאביי נחמני ועי' פירש"י בגיטין לד:]

הגהות הב"ח

(א) תוס' ד"ה אע"ג וכו' חשיב לה והא דלא חשיב. נ"ב עיין לקמן בפ' הזורק דף צו ומבואר לעיל. (ב) ד"ה בורר וכו' דרכו של בורר נוטל אוכל מתוך פסולת:

גליון הש"ס

תוס' ד"ה אע"ג וכו' לפי שהם לגמרי בכלל מיסך. עי' לקמן דף עה ע"ב ברש"י ד"ה שובט:

ראשי תיבות

דא"כ – דאם כן
וא"כ – ואם כן
וא"ת – ואם תאמר
אע"ג – אף על גב
ב"ה – בית הלל
וב"ה – ובית הלל
ב"ש – בית שמאי
בד"א – במה דברים אמורים
ד"ה – דברי הכל
ה"ה – הוא הדין
דה"נ – דהכי נמי
וה"נ – והכי נמי
וה"פ – והכי פירושו
בי"ט – ביום טוב
וי"ל – ויש לומר
לכ"ע – לכולי עלמא
ול"ג – ולא גרסינן
מ"מ – מכל מקום
ס"ד – סלקא דעתך
בע"א – בענין אחר
בפ"ק – בפרק קמא
ובפ"ק – ובפרק קמא
וצ"ע – וצריך עיון
ר"ח – רבינו חננאל
ור"ת – ורבינו תם
ת"ר – תנו רבנן

דשלקי ליה שבעא זימני ואי לא שקלי(א) ליה מסרח וכפסולת מתוך אוכל דמי: והטוחן: א"ר פפא האי מאן דפרים סילקא חייב משום טוחן אמר רב מנשה האי מאן דסלית סילתי חייב משום טוחן אמר רב אשי אי קפיד אמשחתא חייב משום מחתך: והלש והאופה: אמר רב פפא שבק תנא דידן בישול סממנין דהוה במשכן ונקט אופה תנא דידן סידורא דפת נקט אמר רב אחא בר רב עוירא *האי מאן דשדא סיכתא לאתונא חייב משום מבשל פשיטא מהו דתימא לשרורי מנא קא מיכוין קמ"ל דמירפא רפי והדר קמיט אמר רבה בר רב הונא האי מאן דארתח כופרא חייב משום מבשל פשיטא מהו דתימא כיון דהדר ואיקושא אימא לא קמ"ל אמר רבא האי מאן דעבד חביתא חייב משום שבע חטאות תנורא חייב משום שמונה חטאות אמר אביי האי מאן דעבד *חלתא חייב אחת עשרה חטאות ואי חייטיה לפומיה חייב שלש עשרה חטאות: הגוזז את הצמר והמלבנו: אמר רבה בר בר חנה א"ר יוחנן הטווה צמר שעל גבי בהמה בשבת חייב שלש חטאות אחת משום גוזז ואחת משום מנפץ ואחת משום טווה רב כהנא אמר אין דרך גזיזה בכך ואין דרך מנפץ בכך ואין דרך טווי בכך ולא והתניא משמיה דרבי נחמיה *שטוף בעזים וטוו בעזים אלמא טוויה על גבי בהמה שמה טוויה חכמה יתירה שאני תנו רבנן *התולש את הכנף והקוטמו והמורטו חייב שלש חטאות (*וא"ר) שמעון בן לקיש תולש חייב משום גוזז קוטם חייב משום מחתך ממרט חייב משום ממחק: הקושר והמתיר: קשירה במשכן היכא הואי אמר רבא (ג) שכן קושרין ביתדות אהלים *(קושרים) ההוא קושר על מנת להתיר הוא אלא אמר אביי שכן אורגי יריעות שנפסקה להן נימא קושרים אותה א"ל רבא תרצת קושר מתיר מאי איכא למימר וכי תימא דאי מתרמי ליה תרי(ג) חוטי קיטרי בהדי הדדי שרי חד וקטר חד *השתא לפני מלך בשר ודם אין עושין כן לפני ממ"ה הקב"ה עושין אלא אמר רבא ואיתימא רבי עילאי שכן צדי חלזון קושרין ומתירין: והתופר שתי תפירות: והא לא קיימא אמר רבה בר בר חנה א"ר יוחנן והוא שקשרן: הקורע על מנת לתפור: קריעה במשכן מי הוה רבה ורבי זירא דאמרי תרווייהו

שכן

רש"י

דשלקי ליה שבעא זימנין. למתקן: ואי לא שקלי ליה לאוכל מתוך הפסולת מתוך שהוא רך ונימוק ע"י שנשלק הרבה: מסרח. והלכך אוכל נמי כל זמן שמעורב בו הוי כפסולת ומיהו אוכל הוא ומחמירין עליה למיהוי הוא דשקיל כפסולת מתוך אוכל ול"נ הבורר תורמוסין מתוך פסולת שלהן משמשלקן פעם אחת ממרקין ומערין אותן המים ובורר המתולעות שלהן כמו שעושין לפולין וכן בכל פעם ופעם וזה בורר האוכל ומניח הפסולת ואי לא שלקי ליה מסרח גרסינן הלכך משמשלקום פעמים ושלש חשיב ליה פסולת הואיל ואי שביק להו הכי דלא הדר שליק להו מסרחי וכשהוא נוטלן מתוך שאר מינין גרועין המעורבין בהן כפסולת מתוך אוכל דמי דהנהו שאר מינין לא מסרחי דגמר להו בישולייהו פעם ראשונה ושניה ורבינו הלוי גרים ואי שקלי ליה מסרח כשנוטלו נימוח בין אצבעותיו ונמאס הלכך ההוא דשקיל הוי כפסולת והנשאר הוי אוכל עד שחוזר ונוטלו: דפרים סילקא. במ"ס גרסינן ולא בסמ"ך כדפירש בהעור והרוטב (חולין דף קכ.) מאי קיפה פירמא מינציי"ר בלע"ז מחתכו הדק: דסלית סילתי. עלים דקים להבעיר אש: ואי קפיד אמשחתא. לחותכן במדה: מחתך. העור מקצצו במדה: ונקט אופה. דלא שייך במלאכת המשכן כלל: סדורא דפת. שהתחיל בו נקט ואופה במקום בשול דסממנין הוא דהוא בישול דפת: דשדא סיכתא. שהשליך יתד לח לתנור חם ליבשו שיתקשה: לשרורי. לחזק ואין כאן בישול: דמרפי רפי. ע"י חום האור והמים שבתוכו יוצאין ולאחר שיצאו מימיו קמיט מתקשה וכי רפי ברישא הוי בישולו: דארתח כופרא. שהתיך זפת: דהדר אקושי. חוזר ומתקשה: חביתא. של חרס: שבע חטאות. טוחן הרגבים ושוחקן הדק הוי טוחן ובורר הצרורות הגסות מתוכן הרי שתים ומרקידן בנפה ומגבל הטיט דהיינו לש וממרח הטיט כשעושה הגולם שיהא חלק הרי ממחק ומבעיר את האור בכבשן ומצרפו בתוכו הרי מבשל חיובא דאופה ליכא דהיינו צריך אלא לעפרה: תנור חייב שמנה. דלאחר שצרפו בכבשן הוא טח עליו טפילה שיהא עב וחומו מתקיים והוא גמר מלאכתו ואמרינן לקמן (דף עה:) כל מידי דהוי גמר מלאכה חייב משום מכה בפטיש אבל גבי חבית ליכא משום מכה בפטיש דמהליך נגמרה מלאכתו בתנור: חלתא. כוורת של קנים: חייב י"א. זומר הקנים והוא צריך להם חייב משום קוצר ומשום נוטע אספס יחד הרי זה מעמר בירר יפות הרי זה בורר האליקן הרי זה ממחק עשאן דקות מאחת שתים או שלש הרי זה טוחן חתכן במדה הרי זה מחתך הסיך השתי הרי זה מיסך ארג אחת למעלה ואחת למטה כדי להעמידו הרי עושה שתי בתי נירין (ד) ארג הרי זה אורג חתך לאחר אריגתה כדי להשוותם הרי זה מכה בפטיש כדאמרינן לקמן [עה:] האי מאן דשקיל אקופי מגלימי חייב משום מכה בפטיש הרי י"א: ואי חייטיה לפומיה. לעשות לה שפה הוסיף כאן תופר וקושר שצריך לקשור לאחר התפירה ומשום בונה ליכא לחיוביה לא בחבית ולא בתנור ולא בכוורת דאין בנין בכלים מפשיט ליכא למימר בקנים דאין הפשטה אלא בעור וי"מ שקודח נקבים בעץ שתוחבין בו ראשי הקנים של שתי ומחייב ליה משום טוחן ולא נהירא לי דההיא טחינה מלאכה שאינה צריכה לגופה היא וטוב לי לפרש שעושה אותן דקות והוי כמאן דסלית סילתי: שטוף בעזים וטוו בעזים. קרא קדריש טוו את העזים (שמות לה) בגופן של עזים משמע: חכמה יתירה. כדכתיב וכל אשה חכמת לב אבל להדיוט אין דרכו בכך והוי כלאחר יד: התולש את הכנף. נוצה גדולה מן כנף העוף: והקוטמו. לאחר שתלשו חותך ראשו שהוא דק וראוי להניחו בכר וכסת: והמורטו. לצד זנבו שהוא קשה מורט שערו מכאן ומכאן ומשליך הקנה ונותן השיער בכר וכסת: משום מחתך. דקפיד לחתוך עד מקום שהוא ראוי וגם מן הקנה הורג כובעים ועושה כובעים מכנפי עוף בלא שיער: משום ממחק. דתנן גבי עור הממחקו: ביתדות אהלים. כותלים יתידות בקרקע כדכתיב יתדות המשכן וקושרין היריעות בהן במיתריהם: קושר ע"מ להתיר הוא. וכי האי גוונא פטרינן ליה לקמן דתנן כל קשר שאינו של קיימא אין חייבין עליו: בהדי הדדי. בשני חוטין זה אצל זה: שרי חד. לאחר אריגתן מתיר האחד מפני שבולטין ונראין: וקטר חד. כלומר מניח כמו שהוא: השתא כו' (ה) אין עושין. שכשמתירו נראה הנקב ביריעה שחוטיה היו כפולין שם והיו גסין ומתחלה היו זריזין בכך וכי מתרמו להו תרי קיטרי קושרין האחד ונותקין החוט השני מלמטה ולמעלה ומספקן בחוט ארוך וקושרין למעלה ולמטה ואין שם שנים קשרים סמוכין: צדי חלזון. לצבוע התכלת בדמו והוא כמין דג קטן ועולה אחת לשבעים שנה: קושרין ומתירין. שכל רשתות עשויות קשרים קשרים והן קשרי קיימא ופעמים שצריך ליטול חוטין מרשת זו ולהוסיף על זו מתיר מכאן וקושר מכאן: והא לא קיימא. הכי וכיון דלא קיימא לאו מלאכה היא: שקשרן. שקשר שני ראשי החוט:

דרכא

תוספות

האי מאן דפרים סילקא. דוקא בסילקא שייך טחינה אבל שאר אוכלין שרי*: מהו דתימא לשרורי מנא קא מכוין. ה"פ ואין בו בשול כלל קמ"ל דהכי דלשרורי מנא קא מכוין בשול מיהא יש בו דמירפא רפי והדר קמיט וחייב אבל אין לפרש קמ"ל דלא אמרי' לשרורי מנא קא מכוין דבפרק אין מעמידין (ע"ז לח.) אמרי' גבי האי נכרי דשדא סיכתא לאתונא אי קבר בה ישראל קרא מעיקרא שפיר דמי ופריך פשיטא ומשני מהו דתימא לבשולי מנא קא מכוין קמ"ל לשרורי מנא קא מכוין: חביתא ותנורא וחלתא. פי' רש"י דמשום בונה לא מיחייב דאין בנין בכלים ואין נראה דדוקא במחזיר מטה ומנורה של חוליות אמרי' *דאין בנין בכלים אבל כשעושה לגמרי כל הכלי מיחייב משום בונה דאמרינן בריש הבונה (לקמן ד' קב:) האי מאן דעייל שופתא בקופינא דמרא חייב משום בונה ול"ע דלא ליקשי ממנפח בכלי זכוכית דסוף פרקין*: חכמה יתירה שאני. והעושים אותם בטלה דעתם אצל כל אדם כדאמרינן בהמצניע (לקמן ד' צב:) גבי אנשי הוצל: שכן צדי חלזון כו'. בריש אלו קשרים (לקמן קיא:) פירש בקונט' קושרין ומתירין פעמים קושרין את המכמורת ופעמים מתירין אותם:

שכן

עין משפט נר מצוה

[ועי' בתוס' לקמן קיד: ד"ה אלא לקינת ירק כו' ע"ש]

מד א מיי' פ"ז מהלכות שבת הלכה ה ופ"ח הלכה טו ופכ"א הלכה יח סמג לאוין סה טוש"ע או"ח סי' שכא סעיף יב:

מה ב מיי' שם פ"ח הלכה טו:

מו ג ד מיי' פ"ט מהל' שבת הלכה ו סמג שם:

מז ה מיי' פ"י מהלכות שבת הלכה יג:

מח ו ז מיי' פ"ט מהל' שבת הלכה ז:

[לעיל מו. עי' תוס' שם ד"ה דמוליות]

מט ח מיי' פי"א מהל' שבת הלכה ז:

נ ט שם הלכה ו:

נא י מיי' פ"י שם הל' א סמג שם טוש"ע או"ח סימן שיז סעיף א:

נב כ מיי' שם הל"ט:

נג ל מיי' שם הלכה י:

[פי' הערוך ע"ז באריכות ממלא בערך חלתא ע"ש דקשיב חייב משום בונה ולא קשיב זה של' רש"י הכא בד"ה חייב משום ממחק עיי"ש ובזה תבין דעת וסברת תוס' ד"ה חביתא]

ראשי תיבות

א"ל – אמר ליה

א"ר – אמר רבי

וא"ר – ואמר רבי

ה"פ – הכי פירושו

וי"מ – ויש מפרשים

ול"נ – ולי נראה

ממ"ה – מלך מלכי המלכים

ע"י – על ידי

ע"מ – על מנת

וצ"ע – וצריך עיון

הקב"ה – הקדוש ברוך הוא

קמ"ל – קא משמע לן

מסורת הש"ס

ע"ז לח.

לקמן לט.

בכורות כה. [תוספתא פי"ו] [נ"ל אמר]

א"ל אביי כצ"ל

[פסחים עה: יומא מז.]

הגהות הב"ח

(א) גמ' שבעה זמני ואי לא שקלי) תא"מ ונ"ב ס"א לא שקלי וס"א ואי שקלי: (ב) שם אמר רבה שכן קושרים ביתד' אהלים הוא כצ"ל ותיבת קושרין נמחק: (ג) שם דאי מיתרמו ליה תרי קיטרי כצ"ל ותיבת חוטי נמחק: (ד) רש"י ד"ה חייב וכו' עושה שתי בתי נירין. נ"ב ולקמן ר"פ האורג פי' רש"י דהנך לאו נירין ממש כו' ע"ש בדף קה ע"א: (ה) ד"ה השתא כו' שכשמתירו נראה כצ"ל ותיבות אין עושין נמחק:

רבינו חננאל

מקשינן ופרקינן לפרושי שמעתיה דאמרינן לימא קסבר חזקיה אוכל מתוך פסולת אסור. ושנינן שאני תורמסין דשלק להו ז' זמני כו'. שמעינן מינה דאוכל מתוך הפסולת זולתי תורמסין שרי וכדאביי דשרי לאלתר כי היכי דלא תקשי חדא אחברתה וכבר פירשנוהו השמועה סלקא כאביי וכרב אשי וכחזקיה שמעינן מדברי שלשתן כי בורר ואוכל ביד בורר ומניח ביד שרי ולא כל היכא דבעי שרי אלא ברירת אוכל מתוך פסולת אבל פסולת מתוך אוכל לא. והאוכל מתוך פסול' דשרי [היינו] לברור ולאכול או לברור ולהניח כדי לאוכלו לאלתר על השולחן כמו שפירשנו אבל להניח שלא לאלתר לא וזה שאמרנו כי מותר לברור ולאכול ולברור ולהניח ולאוכלו לאלתר שרי ה"מ ביד אבל בקנון ובתמחוי לא ואם בירר פטור אבל אסור ובנפה ובכברה דברי הכל אסור ואם בירר נעשה כמי שבירר לאוצר בשוגג חייב חטאת ואע"פ דגרסינן (גיטין כז כח) לענין מי שאבד לו גט אם מצאו לאלתר כשר ואמרינן היכי דמי לאלתר י"א כל שלא עבר [אדם] שם ואחרים אומרים כל שלא שהה אדם שם הכא כיון דאשכחינן מפורש בתלמוד א"י כוותיה עבדינן ומסקינן לשמעתיה שיעור מה שמיסב על השולחן באותה סעודה בלבד וכענין הזה גרסינן בגמרא ביו"ט פרק א' (ביצה יג:) תנן התם המקלף שעורין מקלף אחת אחת על יד ואוכל. ואם קילף ונתן לתוך חיקו חייב. א"ר אלעזר וכן לשבת. והא רב מקלפי ליה כסי כסי ור' חייא מקלפי ליה כסי כסי אלא אי אתמר אסיפא איתמר המולל מלילות של חיטין (למחר) מנפח על יד על יד ואוכל ואם נפח ונתן לתוך ידו חייב. א"ר אלעזר וכן לשבת. מ"ט דמלאכת מחשבת אסרה תורה והאי לאו מלאכת מחשבת היא. דלא קא מכוון במלאכה אלא לאכילה בלבד ולפי' א' כיצד מנפח ואסיק' א"ר אלעזר מנפח בידו אחת ובכל כחו. הטוחן אמר רב פפא האי מאן דפרים סילקא. פי' כעין כתישה ולא כעין חיתוך חייב משום טוחן וכן מאן דסלית סילתי פי' עצי הדקלים שעומדין שיבי שיבי כעין נימין וכשמפרק הנימין הללו יוצא בינית כמין קמח דק לפי' (המנפץ) חייב משום טוחן ואי קפיד אמשחתא כלומר אם מתכוין לחתוך אלו סילתי זרת זרת אורך כל אחד ואחד חייב משום מחתך. הלש והאופה אמר רב פפא שבק בישול סממנים ונקט אפיה ולא מפרש בהדיא האי מלתא*) ואשכחן בירושלמי דאמר הכי את חמי אפיה תולדת בישול הוא ואת אמרת הכן אלא כיון דתני סדר עיסה תניתא בהדייהו: ההוא דשחק [מלח] חסף (מלא) [פלפלין] חייב משום טוחן. האי מאן דגבל גירגבסין עפר קילורין מלוגמא סממנין חייב משום לש. מאן דשדא סיכתא לאתונא חייב משום מבשל פי' הנותן יתידות לחים בכבשן כדי לייבשן לנעצם בספינות וכיוצא בהן. פי' לשרורי לחזק ויש מי שאומרים סיכתא הן גלל בהמה דקיקין אם הטילם לכבשן מה שחייב משום מבעיר הרי חייב. ועוד חייב משום מבשל. וזה שנצרך לומר כן דלא תימא אין המפחר כלי חרס מבשל מפני שמחזיק הכלי. אשמעי' דמירפה

*) לפנינו בגמ' מפרש בהדיא הטעם משום לסידורא דפת נקיט וכמש"כ בירושלמי ואולי דלפני רבינו לא היה זה בנוסחת הגמ'.

רב נסים גאון

שכן צדי חלזון קושרין ומתירין. וזה חלזון היו צובעין בדמו תכלת ומשכחת לה במנחות בפרק התכלת (דף מד) תנו רבנן חלזון זה גופו דומה לים ברייתו דומה לדג ועולה פעם אחת לע' שנה ובדמו צובעין תכלת לפיכך דמיו יקרים ואמרו עוד (שם מג) אמר ליה אביי לרב שמואל בר יהודה הא תכלתא היכא צבעיתו אמר ליה מייתינן דם חלזון וסמנין כו':

גליון הש"ס גמ' האי מאן דפריס סילקא חייב. עי' לקמן דף קכח ע"א ברש"י ד"ה שלא יקטוס: שם תולש חייב משום גוזז. עי' לקמן דף קז ע"ב ובחידושי רשב"א שם: שם דאי מתרמי ליה תרי חוטי. עי' לעיל דף עג ע"א תוס' ד"ה הקושר: שם השתא לפני מלך וכו'. פסחים דף עה ע"ב יומא דף מז ע"א:

שכן יריעה שנפל בה דרנא קורעין בה ותופרין אותה אמר רב זוטרא בר טוביה אמר רב ^א^המותח חוט של תפירה בשבת חייב חטאת ^ב^והלומד דבר אחד מן המגוש חייב מיתה והיודע לחשב תקופות ומזלות ואינו חושב אסור לספר הימנו *מגושתא רב ושמואל חד אמר חרשי וחד אמר גדופי תסתיים דרב דאמר גדופי דאמר רב זוטרא בר טוביה אמר רב הלומד דבר אחד מן המגוש חייב מיתה דאי ס"ד חרשי הכתיב *°לא תלמד לעשות (דברים יח) אבל אתה למד להבין ולהורות תסתיים אר"ש בן פזי א"ר יהושע בן לוי משום בר קפרא כל היודע לחשב בתקופות ומזלות ואינו חושב עליו הכתוב אומר °ואת פועל ה' (ישעיה ה) לא יביטו ומעשה ידיו לא ראו א"ר שמואל בר נחמני א"ר *יוחנן ^ג^מנין שמצוה על האדם לחשב תקופות ומזלות שנאמר °ושמרתם (דברים ד) ועשיתם כי היא חכמתכם ובינתכם לעיני העמים איזו חכמה ובינה שהיא לעיני העמים הוי אומר זה חישוב תקופות ומזלות: ^ד^הצד צבי וכו': ת"ר *הצד חלזון והפוצעו אינו חייב אלא אחת רבי יהודה אומר חייב שתים שהיה ר' יהודה אומר ^ה^פציעה בכלל דישה אמרו לו אין פציעה בכלל דישה אמר רבא מ"ט דרבנן קסברי ^ו^אין דישה אלא לגדולי קרקע וליחייב נמי משום נטילת נשמה אמר רבי יוחנן שפצעו מת רבא אמר אפילו תימא שפצעו חי מתעסק הוא אצל נטילת נשמה והא אביי ורבא דאמרי תרווייהו ^ז^מודה *ר"ש בפסיק רישא ולא ימות (א) שאני הכא דכמה דאית ביה נשמה טפי ניחא ליה כי היכי *)דליציל ציבעיה: ^ח^והשוחטו: שוחט משום מאי חייב רב אמר משום צובע ושמואל אמר משום ^ט^נטילת נשמה משום

רש"י

דרנא. תולעת ומנקב בו נקב קטן ועגול וצריך לקרוע למטה ולמעלה את הנקב שלא תהא התפירה עשויה קמטין קמטין: **המותח חוט של תפירה.** בגד התפור ועומד והניח החוט ארוך ונתפרדו שתי חתיכות הבגד זו מזו במקצת וחוטי התפירות נמשכין ומותח את ראשי החוט להדק ולחבר זו היא תפירתו וחייב: **והלומד דבר אחד מן המגוש.** מין המושכו לע"ז אפי' דבר תורה אסור ללמוד ממנו: **והיודע כו'.** הני תלת שמעתתא שמעינהו (*מר) זוטרא מרב כי הדדי וגרסינהו: **אמגושא.** דאמרינן בכל דוכתא רב ושמואל פליגי ביה: **חד אמר חרשי.** מכשף: **וחד אמר גדופי.** מין האדוק בע"ז ומגדף תמיד את השם ומסית אנשים לע"ז: **דאי סלקא דעתך חרשי.** וטעמא משום דכתיב לא ימצא בך וגו' וקא חשיב מכשף: **והא כתיב.** לעיל מיניה לא תלמד לעשות כדי שתעשה: **להבין.** שתוכל לעמוד בהן ואם יעשה נביא שקר לפניך שתבין שהוא מכשף: **תסתיים דגדופי הוא.** הלכך כל דבריו דברי ע"ז והסתלק מעליו שלא ישיאך: **לעיני העמים.** שחכמה הניכרת היא שמראה להם סימן לדבריו בהילוך החמה והמזלו' שמעידין כדבריו שאומר שנה זו גשומה והיא כן שנה זו שחונה והיא כן שהכל העיתים לפי מהלך החמה במזלותיה ומולדותיה במזל תלוי הכל לפי השעה המתחלת לשמש בכניסת החמה למזל: **הפוצעו.** דוחקו בידיו שיצא דמו: **אינו חייב אלא אחת.** משום צידה אבל אפליעה ליכא חיוב: **בכלל דישה.** שמפרק דמו הימנו כמפרק תבואה מקשין שלה: **מתעסק הוא אצל נטילת נשמה.** כלומר לגבי נטילת נשמה הוי מתעסק בדבר אחר ולא הויא מלאכת מחשבת שאינו מתכוין שימות: **טפי ניחא ליה.** שהדם החי טוב מדם המת וכיון דכל עצמו מתכוין וטורח לשומרו שלא ימות בידו אפי' מת אין כאן אלא מתעסק וכי מודה ר' שמעון במידי דלא איכפת ליה אי מיתרמי ומיהו איכווני לא מיכוין: **דליציל ציבעיה גרסינן.** שתהא מראית צבעו צלולה: **שוחט משום מאי מיחייב.** שחיטה במלאכת המשכן היכא ומאי עבידתי': אי מעורות אילים מאדמים למה לי בהו שחיטה בחניקה נמי סגי:

תוספות

שכן יריעה שנפל בה דרנא כו'. תימה לר"י דבריש האורג אמרי' קורע על מנת לתפור שתי תפירות היכי משכחת לה ומשני דעבידא ככיסתא ואומר ר"י דבמשכן היו אומנים ביותר והיו נזהרים שלא היו עושים ככיסתא והתם לא קאמר שנפל בה דרנא דנקט דשכיח טפי ועוד דהתם בעי לאשכוחי קורע על מנת לתפור שתי תפירות ותו לא ויריעה שנפל בה דרנא צריך לקורעה מתחלתה ועד סופה ויש בה כמה תפירות ואע"ג דהשתא לא משכח' במשכן על מנת לתפור שתי תפירות ותו לא סברא הוא דבשתי תפירות הוי דבר חשוב: **אמגושא.** פי' בערוך דפליגי בהא דאמר רב פפא באלו מגלחין (מו"ק יח.) פרעה אמגושי היה דכתיב הנה יוצא המימה חד אמר לעשות כשפים היה יוצא וחד אמר גדופי שהיה עושה עצמו ע"ז שהיה אומר לי יאורי ואני עשיתני ואין נראה לר"י דפליגי רב ושמואל במאי דאמר רב פפא אלא פליגי באמגושא שנזכר בשום מקום במשנה או בברייתא: **הצד חלזון.** למאן דמוקי לה בשפלטו חי אתי שפיר הא דנקט הצד חלזון דדרך לפולטו מיד אחר צידה כל זמן שהוא חי וקמ"ל דאע"פ שפלטו חי לא מיחייב משום נטילת נשמה ואפילו למאן דמוקי לה כשפלטו מת קמ"ל דלא מיחייב בצידה שלו משום נטילת נשמה דאף על גב דאמרי' בפרק שמונה שרצים (לקמן דף קז:) השולה דג מן הים כיון שיבש בו כסלע כו' הכא שאני חלזון דרכו לפרכס ולקרב מיתתו ול"ע דבירושלמי משמע דצד חלזון לא מיחייב משום צידה: **וליחייב נמי משום נטילת נשמה.** ואפי' לרבי יהודה דאמר מקלקל בחבורה פטור פריך שפיר דהיכא דאיכא תיקון קצת חייב כדאמרי' בפסחים (דף עג.) בסוף אלו דברים והכא נמי במה שממיתו יש תיקון קצת שאינו מפרכס לכאן ולכאן ונוח ליטול ממנו הדם ולמאי דמסיק דכמה דאית ביה נשמה טפי ניחא ליה אתי שפיר נמי לרבי יהודה דהשתא ליכא תיקון כלל ומיהו שמעתין אתיא אפי' לר"ש דמחייב מקלקל בחבורה מדמשני מתעסק הוא אצל נטילת נשמה ולא קאמר מקלקל הוא: **מתעסק הוא אצל נטילת נשמה.** האי מתעסק לאו דוקא דהא מתעסק בחבורה חייב לר"ש דאמר בס"פ ספק אכל (כריתות יט:) הנח לתינוקות הואיל ומקלקל בחבורה חייב מתעסק נמי חייב וטעמא כדיליף בהורג (לקמן קו.) מדאיצטריך למישרי מילה מכלל דמקלקל בחבורה חייב ולא חיישינן למלאכת מחשבת דמקלקל דעלמא לא מיפטר אלא משום מלאכת מחשבת כדאמר בספ"ק דחגיגה (דף י:) ומתעסק דהכא היינו דבר שאין מתכוין כיון דאין מתכוין כלל למלאכה מותר אפי' בחבורה אע"פ דלא בעי מלאכת מחשבת כמו כל איסורים שבתורה דלא שייך בהו מלאכת מחשבת ושרו אין מתכוין כדאמר מוכרי כסות מוכרין כדרכן ובלבד שלא יתכוין בחמה מפני החמה כו' (כלאים פ"ט משנה ה) וכן מוכח בפ"ק דכתובות (ד' ה:) דאמר את"ל דם חבורי מיחבר לדם הוא צריך או להנאת עצמו הוא צריך ואת"ל להנאת עצמו הוא צריך הלכה כרבי יהודה או הלכה כר"ש פירוש בדבר שאין מתכוין ואת"ל הלכה כר' יהודה בדבר שאין מתכוין במקלקל הלכה כמאן משמע דאי הלכה כר"ש בדבר שאין מתכוין תו ליכא לספוקי במקלקל דאפי' מקלקל בחבורה חייב כיון דאין מתכוין מותר: **טפי ניחא ליה כי היכי דליציל ציבעי'.** פי' אע"ג דהוי פסיק רישיה דמודה ר"ש הכא מיפטר משום דהוי מלאכה שאינה צריכה לגופה דאפי' במקלקל פטר ר"ש במלאכה שאינה צריכה לגופה כדאמר בפרק הנחנקין (סנהדרין פד:) מאן שמעת ליה דאמר מקלקל בחבורה חייב ר"ש הא אמר מלאכה שאינה צריכה לגופה פטור עליה וכי מודה ר"ש בפסיק רישיה ה"מ במידי דניחא ליה אי מתרמי דהוי צריכה לגופה אבל במידי דלא איכפת ליה לא מודה ורש"י פי' דהא דמודה ר"ש בפסיק רישיה היינו במאי דלא איכפת ליה אי מתרמי וליתא דהא מזרד זרדין בארעא דחבריה פטר ר"ש בפ' הבונה (לקמן קג.) והתם לא איכפת ליה אי מתרמי אלא כדפי' ותימה דבספ"ק דחגיגה (דף י:) משמע דהא דפטר ר"ש מלאכה שאינה צריכה לגופה היינו משום דבעי מלאכת מחשבת וא"כ בחבורה דלא בעי מלאכת מחשבת ליחייב בה מלאכה שאינה צריכה לגופה: **כי היכי דליציל ציבעיה.** קשה לר"י דמ"מ על נטילת הדם ליחייב משום נטילת נשמה ונראה כלשון אחר שפי' בקונט' בריש שמונה שרצים (לקמן קז.) דחובל בהן חייב משום דהוי תולדה דשוחט וחייב משום נטילת נשמה ונטילת הדם היינו נטילת נשמה כדכתיב כי הדם הוא הנפש ולכך ח' שרצים שיש להם עור חייב בנצרר הדם אע"פ שלא יצא דכיון שנצרר סופו לצאת אלא שעתה העור מעכבו ושאר שרצים שאין להם עור אינו חייב עד שיצא מהם דם אבל בנצרר הדם ולא יצא לא מיחייב דכיון שלא יצא סופו לחזור דאם היה סופו לצאת היה יוצא מיד שאין העור מעכבו והשיב לו ר"ת דדם חלזון הראוי לצביעה מיפקד פקיד ולא מיחייב על אותו הדם משום נטילת נשמה ועל דם אחר היוצא עמו נמי לא מיחייב דלא ניחא ליה כי היכי דליליל ליבעיה אבל אין לפרש דנטילת נשמה היינו שמחליש אותו דבר שחובל בו דגבי דם בתולים מה צריך לחלישות האשה וגבי מילה מה צריך לחלישות התינוק אלא לנטילת הדם קרי נטילת נשמה כדפי': **שוחט משום מאי מיחייב.** לאו אשוחט דמתני' קאי דהכוא פשיטא דלא הוי אלא משום נטילת נשמה דלוקע תנן בהדיא במתני' אלא אשוחט דעלמא קאי:

*) [נ"ל דליצלה פי' דלא ניחא ליה דתיפוק נשמה דלכל כמה דאית ביה נשמה טפי מללא לצביעה שלבעו מתעלה יפה ויהא לבעו יפה ובריא כי אז תלליה. ערוך]

אין

עין משפט נר מצוה

נד א מיי' שם הלכה ט סמג שם טור שו"ע או"ח סימן ש"ח סעיף ו:
נה ב שו"ע יו"ד סימן קעט סעיף יט:
נו ג סמג עשין מז:
נז ד מיי' פ"י מהלכות שבת הלכה יט סמג לאוין סה טוש"ע או"ח סימן שטז סעיף ה:
נח ה מיי' פ"ח מהלכות שבת הלכה ז ופכ"א הלכה יב:
נט ו מיי' שם פ"ח הלכה ז:
ס ז מיי' פ"א מהלכות שבת הלכה ו טוש"ע או"ח סימן שלז סעיף א:
סא ח ט מיי' פי"א מהל' שבת הלכה א:

רבינו חננאל

רפה כשהן טיט ומתבשלין ואחר כך מתחזקין כשיצטרפו (מתחפרו) [ויתפחרו]. וכן מאן דארתח כופרא. אף על גב דהדר אקיש מבשל הוא. אמר רבה מאן דעבד חביתא חייב ז' חטאות פי' כגון שהיתה לו גבשושית ונטלה וייפה הקרקע חייב משום חורש. שחק חייב משום טוחן ניקהו מן הצרורות חייב משום בורר וכשמחתך (ממנו) [היינו] מחתך. ועיקר מלאכה א) (בנין מלאכה) וגמר מלאכה והשואתה חייב משום מכה בפטיש הרי שבע ב) בתנור עוד מוסיף אחד שצריך להחליק את תוכו ולשוף אותו גחלים וחייב משום ממחק. מאן דעבד חלתא חייב י"א חטאות. חתך קנה נעשה זומר וצריך לעצים חייב משום קוצר ומשום נוטע כינס הקנים חייב משום מעמר דקדק הקנים חייב משום טוחן. חתכם כשיעור כגון אמה אמה חייב משום מחתך. קילפם חייב משום רש. השליך קליפהן וקצין שאין ראויין למלאכה חייב משום בורר. הטיל שתיו חייב משום מיסך וכשמטיל הערב עושה שתי בתי נירין וכשמכה אותן כדי לקרבן זה לזה (ולהדחיק אריג) ג) זה כל זמן שעושה (ארבעת) [ארעי'] הכוורת וכשכופף הקנים למעלה לאריגה [והן] קורותיה בונה הוא וגמר מלאכה שיש בקרומיות היוצאת משום מכה בפטיש הרי אלו י"א מלאכות ואם כפף פיה למטה ותפרה (כשיבינו החיט) [כשמותח החוט] חייב משום טווה. כרב דאמר המותח חוט של תפירה בשבת חייב (משום) חטאת וכשתופר חייב משום תופר הרי אלו י"ג חטאות: **ירושלמי** ההיא איתתא כד משתייא בקיבה משום מיסכת כד יהבה קירומה משום עושה בתין. כד מקימה לון משום בונה. כד מחיי' משום אורגת כד מקטעא בנימא משום מחתכת. כד גמרה מלאכתה משום מכה בפטיש. אזנים של דיסקיא [קושר ומתיר] נעשה כנועל ופותח וכן חותלות של תמרים קושר ומתיר. א"ר יוחנן המווה צמר מעל גבי בהמה בשבת חייב ג' חטאות משום גוזז ומנפץ וטווה. ודחה רב כהנא ואמר אין דרך גוזז ולא דרך ניפוץ ולא דרך טוויה בכך. ואקשינן על רב כהנא והתניא משום נחמיה שטוף בעזים. אלמא שטפוהו בעזים וטוות מעליהן בלא גזיזה ופריק' חכמה יתירה שאני דכתיב וכל הנשים אשר נשא לבן אותנה בחכמה טוו את העזים. ואע"ג דרב כהנא לגבי רב תלמיד הוה כיון (ריש) ראשכחן בתלמוד א"י דקיימי כוותיה תרגימנן התולש כנף מן העוף חייב משום גוזז המורטו חייב משום מוחק הקוטמה חייב משום מכה בפטיש ודחינן לא דמיא תולש כנף עוף לתולש שער בהמה דעוף שאין לו גזיזה תלישתה היא גזיזתה ברם בהמה אינו חייב עד שיגוז הרע שהוא כן דתני תלש מן המתה חייב תלישתה זו היא גזיזתה מן החיה פטור ותו מדתנן (לקמן נד:) הנוטל צפרניו זו בזו או בשיניו וכן שערו וכן שפמו וכן זקנו ר' אליעזר מחייב חטאת וחכמים אומרים משום שבות כלומר אין דרך נטילת שער בשיניים וכיון דקיימי חכמים כרב כהנא קי"ל כוותיה: **אמגושתא.** פי' בלשון ערבי זמזמה. מגוש בלשון יון מכשף. גידופי כופר בעיקר: **הצד** צבי השוחטו כו'. ת"ר הצד חלזון והפוצעו אינו חייב אלא אחת ר' יהודה אומר חייב שתים שפציעה בכלל דישה ורבנן סברי אין דישה אלא בגידולי קרקע ואקשינן לרבנן ליחייב משום צידה ומשום נטילת נשמה ופריק ר' יוחנן שפצעו מת. רבא אמר אפילו תימא שפצעו חי. מתעסק אצל נטילת נשמה וקיי"ל המתעסק [בחלבים ובעריות] חייב משום דנהנה המתעסק בשבת פטור מלאכת מחשבת אסרה תורה דלא קא ניחא לנטילת נשמה דניחא

א) אולי צ"ל ועל עיקר מלאכת התכית חייב משום בונה וגמר מלאכה וכו'. ב) לפי מה דמשיג רבינו אין כאן רק שש חטאות ואולי דחסר בדברי רבינו וצ"ל וכשמצרף אח"כ בכבשן חייב משום מבשל וכ"ה ברש"י. ג) אולי צ"ל חייב משום אורג וזה כל זמן וכו'.

מסורת הש"ס

[נ"ל רב]
ס"א אמגושא
[ר"ה כד: ע"ז מג. סנהד' סח.]
[נ"ל יונתן]
[תוספתא פ"ט ע"ש]
לקמן קג. קיא: קז. קכ: קנג. קמג. [בילה לו. כתובות ו: בכורות כה. סוכה לג:]

הגהות הב"ח

(א) גמ' שאני הכא. נ"ב עמ"ש דף קג:

ראשי תיבות

וא"כ – ואם כן
א"ר – אמר רבי
א"תל – אם תמצי לומר
אע"ג – אף על גב
ואע"ג – ואף על גב
אע"פ – אף על פי
דאע"פ – דאף על פי
ואת"ל – ואם תמצי לומר
דמ"מ – דמכל מקום
ס"ד – סלקא דעתך
בס"פ – בסוף פרק
בספ"ק – בסוף פרק קמא
דבספ"ק – דבסוף פרק קמא
ע"ז – עבודה זרה
בע"ז – בעבודה זרה
לע"ז – לעבודה זרה
בפ"ק – בפרק קמא
וצ"ע – וצריך עיון
קמ"ל – קא משמע לן
וקמ"ל – וקא משמע לן
ר"ש – רבי שמעון
אר"ש – אמר רבי שמעון
לר"ש – לרבי שמעון
ר"ת – רבינו תם
ת"ר – תנו רבנן

רב נסים גאון

שכן קרע שנפל בו דרנא. פי' דרנא תולעת ובסוף פרק אלו טריפות (חולין דף סז) משכחת ואת נבלתם תשקצו לרבות את הדרנין של בהמה: **רבא** אמר אפילו תימא שפצעו חי מתעסק הוא אצל נטילת

משום צובע אין משום נטילת נשמה לא אימא אף משום צובע אמר רב מילתא דאמרי אימא בה מילתא דלא ליתו דרי בתראי וליחכו עלי צובע במאי ניחא ליה ניחא דליתוום בית השחיטה דמא כי היכי דליחזוה אינשי וליתו ליזבנו מיניה: והמולחו והמעבדו: היינו מולח והיינו מעבד ר' יוחנן ור"ל דאמרי תרוייהו אפיק חד מינייהו ועייל [א] שירטוט אמר רבה בר רב הונא האי מאן דמלח בישרא חייב משום מעבד רבא אמר אין עיבוד באוכלין אמר רב אשי ואפילו רבה בר רב הונא לא אמר אלא דקא בעי ליה לאורחא אבל לביתא לא משוי איניש מיכליה עץ: והממחקו והמחתכו: אמר רבי אחא בר חנינא [ג] השף בין העמודים בשבת חייב משום ממחק אמר רבי חייא בר אבא ג' דברים סח לי רב *אשי משמיה דרבי יהושע בן לוי המגרר ראשי כלונסות בשבת חייב משום מחתך הממרח רטיה בשבת חייב משום ממחק והמסתת את האבן בשבת חייב משום מכה בפטיש אמר ר' שמעון (א) בן קיסמא אמר רבי שמעון בן לקיש הצר צורה בכלי והמנפח בכלי זכוכית חייב משום מכה בפטיש א"ר יהודה האי מאן דשקיל אקופי מגלימי חייב משום מכה בפטיש והני מילי דקפיד עלייהו: והכותב שתי אותיות: ת"ר *כתב אות אחת גדולה ויש במקומה לכתוב שתים פטור מחק אות גדולה ויש במקומה לכתוב שתים חייב אמר רבי מנחם בר' יוסי וזה חומר במוחק מבכותב: הבונה והסותר המכבה והמבעיר והמכה בפטיש: רבה ור' זירא דאמרי תרוייהו כל מידי דאית ביה גמר מלאכה חייב משום מכה בפטיש: אלו אבות מלאכות: *אלו לאפוקי מדר"א דמחייב על תולדה במקום אב: חסר אחת: לאפוקי מדר' יהודה *דתניא ר' יהודה מוסיף את השובט והמדקדק אמרו לו [ל] שובט הרי הוא בכלל מיסך מדקדק הרי הוא בכלל אורג: **מתני'** ועוד כלל אחר אמרו כל הכשר להצניע ומצניעין כמוהו והוציאו בשבת חייב חטאת עליו וכל שאינו כשר להצניע ואין מצניעין כמוהו והוציאו בשבת אינו חייב אלא המצניעו: **גמ'** כל הכשר להצניע לאפוקי מאי רב פפא אמר לאפוקי דם נדה מר עוקבא אמר לאפוקי עצי אשרה מאן דאמר דם נדה כ"ש עצי אשרה מאן דאמר עצי אשרה אבל דם נדה מצנע ליה לשונרא ואידך כיון דחלשא לא מצנע ליה אמר רבי יוסי בר חנינא האי דלא כר"ש דאי כר"ש האמר *לא אמרו כל השיעורין הללו אלא למצניעיהן: וכל שאינו כשר להצניע: אמר

רש"י

משום צובע. שצובע את הבשר של בית השחיטה ולקמן מפרש אמאי מיכוין לצובעו וצביעה הואי במשכן אב מלאכה: משום נטילת נשמה. דנטילת נשמה הואי במשכן באילים מאדמים ותחש וחלזון*: אף משום צביעה. ונפקא מינה לחיוביה תרתי: מילתא דאמרי אימא כו'. דבר תימה אמרתי להזכיר צביעה בשחיטה צריך אני לומר בו דבר טעם דלא ליתו דרי בתראי השומעים וליחכו עלי: צובע בשר במאי ניחא ליה. להאי שוחט בצביעת הבשר היינו אוכל ואני אומר בו טעם: ניחא ליה דליתוום בית השחיטה בדמא. שיהא צבוע בדם: כי היכי דניחזייה אינשי. שנשחטה היום וניתו וניזבנו: היינו מולח היינו מעבד. אטו מליחה לאו צורך עיבוד הוא: ועייל שירטוט. לפי שדרך הרצענין כשהוא בא לחתכו משרטטו תחלה כפי מה שהוא רוצה להאריך ולהרחיב ולקצר החיתוך ואחר כך מעביר הסכין דרך השירטוט וכן בעורות המשכן כשחתכום: דקבעי ליה לאורחא. שמולחה הרבה: השף בין העמודים. כגון עמודי אכסדראות שעשוים חלוקות חלוקות ונסמכין בחלוקות בין עמוד לעמוד והשף שם בקרקעית הבנין שמשפעין עליו כדי שיהא חלק חייב משום ממחק: המגרר ראשי כלונסות. שיהו ראשיהן שוין וחדין: ממרח רטיה. מחליק תחבושת על המכה: מסתת את האבן. לאחר שנעקרה מן ההר ונחצבה מחליקה: משום מכה בפטיש. שהוא גמר מלאכה: הצר (ב) בכלי צורה. בכלי שעומד לכך לנאותו: מנפח בכלי זכוכית. כשהותך נעשה על ידי נפוח: דשקיל אקופי. ראשי חוטין התלויין ביריעה במקום קשורין כשניתק בה חוט וקשרוהו וכן קשין וקסמים דקין שנארגו בה בלא מתכוין ונוטלין אותם ממנה לאחר אריגה גמר מלאכה הוא וחייב משום מכה בפטיש: כתב אות אחת גדולה כו' פטור. שבקרשי המשכן שתים היו כותבים אחת בזו ואחת בזו כדי לזווגן כשסותרים אותן: מחק אות אחת כו' חייב. שאין מלאכת מחיקה חשובה אלא ע"מ לכתוב והרי יש מקום לשתי אותיות: אמר רבי מנחם ברבי יוסי. הא קמ"ל מאן תנא קמא ר' מנחם ברבי יוסי: לאפוקי מדרבי אליעזר. דהא אמרן דלא נמנו כאן אלא להודיענו מנין חטאות של העלם אחד ותנא הרי אלו למעוטי שאם עשה תולדותיהם עמהן דאינו מביא עליהן חטאת ודלא כרבי אליעזר דמחייב אתולדה עם האב בכריתות: שובט. משוה השתי בכרכר שקורין ריו"ל: מדקדק. כשמותח חוט הערב מכה בכרכר עליו במקומות מקומות ליישבו שלא יהא מתוח יותר מדאי שהמתיחה מעכבתו מהתחבר יפה עם הארג: שובט הרי הוא בכלל מיסך. דהיינו מיסך ממש שמסדר חוטי השתי: הרי הוא אורג. דהיינו אורג ממש ולא דמי לזורה ובורר ומרקד דזה בקשין וזה בצרורות וזה בקמח: **מתני'** כל הכשר להצניע. שהוא מין העשוי לצורך האדם: ומצניעין כמוהו. כמות זה כלומר שיש בו שיעור הראוי להצניעו: אין חייב אלא המצניעו. אם נעשה חשוב לאדם א' והצניעו חייב על הוצאתו אם חזר והוציאו אבל אדם אחר אינו חייב עליו דלגביה לאו מלאכה הוא: **גמ'** מ"ד דם נדה. אינו כשר להצניע כ"ש עצי אשרה דאיסורי הנאה נינהו ומאיסי וצריך לאבדן: כיון דחלשא. המאכיל דם האדם לחתול נעשה חלש אותו אדם: הא. דתנא כל הכשר להצניע ויש בו שיעור שרוב ב"א עשוין להצניע כשיעור הזה חייב כל אדם על הוצאתו ואפילו אדם עשיר שאין שיעור זה חשוב לו: דלא כר' שמעון. לקמן בהמוציא: אמר

תוספות

אין עיבוד באוכלין. אין להתיר מכאן מליחת אוכלין דאסור מדרבנן מליחה בפרק שמונה שרצים (לקמן דף קח:) ואפילו בי"ט אסור בפ"ק דביצה (דף יא.): השף בין העמודים בשבת חייב. פירש ר"ח *דשף העור על העמוד כדי להחליקו וכן משמע בירושלמי ורש"י פירש ששף קרקעית שבין עמודי חלונות ולא נהירא: והמסתת את האבן כו' חייב משום מכה בפטיש. אבל משום מחתך וממחק לא מיחייב דמיירי שכבר היא מרובעת ומתוקנת אלא שמייפה אותה ועושה בה שירטוטין ויפוי כעין שעושין עכשיו מסתתי האבנים. ר"י וכן ריב"א: הרי אלו לאפוקי מדרבי אליעזר דמחייב אתולדה במקום אב. וא"ת מרישא שמעינן לה דתנן העושה מלאכות הרבה מעין מלאכה אחת אינו חייב אלא אחת וי"מ דה"ק מעין מלאכה אחת היינו שתי תולדות מאב א' אבל האב ותולדה דידיה מיחייב תרתי קמ"ל: חסר אחת לאפוקי מדר' יהודה. תימה דממילא דרישא שמעינן לה וליכא למימר תנא ושייר *דהא אלו קתני ומיהו הא ליכא לאקשויי דהא מאלו דרישא שמעינן לאפוקי מדר' אליעזר דאיכא למימר דנקט ברישא אלו אבות משום דקאי אדקתני לעיל חייב על כל אב מלאכה וי"ל דממילא דרישא לא שמעינן לאפוקי מדרבי יהודה דאיכא למימר דלא חשיב אלא מלאכות חשובות אבל שובט ומדקדק אע"ג דמלאכות הן לא קתני להו משום דאינם מבוררות כל כך וכה"ג משני בפ"ק דקדושין (דף טז:) גבי אלו מעניקין להן דבר שיש לו קצבה קתני דבר שאין לו קצבה לא קתני*: לאפוקי עצי אשרה. דלא כרבי יהודה דאמר בפרק רבי עקיבא (לקמן דף צ.) אף המוציא משמשי ע"ז כל שהוא חייב אלא כת"ק דפליג עליה כן פירש בקונט' התם וקשה לרשב"א הא דקאמר הכא מ"ד דם נדה כ"ש עצי אשרה מנא ליה דילמא סבר כרבי יהודה ומחייב בעצי אשרה שמצניעין אותן לשריפה: הא דלא כר' שמעון. פירש בקונטרס הא דתנן כל הכשר כו' שרוב בני אדם עשויים להצניע כשיעור הזה חייב כל אדם על הוצאתו אפילו אדם עשיר שאין שיעור זה חשוב לו משמע מדבריו דלא מחייב ר' שמעון אלא בסתם בני אדם שרגילין להצניעו שאותו שיעור חשוב להן ואפילו לא הצניעו הוא ולקמן פי' לא נאמרו שיעורים שבמשנה אלא למצניעין אותו קודם לכן וחזר המצניע והוציאו משמע דוקא בהצניעו חייב ואומר ר"י דיש ליישב פירושו דמה שמצריך

[ועי' תוס' יבמות פד: ד"ה אלא]

עין משפט נר מצוה

סב א ב ג מיי' פי"א מהלכות שבת הלכה ה סמג לאוין סה טוש"ע או"ח סימן שכא סעיף ה:
[עי' בערוך ערך שף]
סב [א] [מיי' פי"ז מהל' שבת הלכה א ופי"א הלכה יח]:
סב [ג] [מיי' פי"א שם הלכה ו]:
סג ד מיי' שם הלכה ז:
סד ה מיי' שם הלכה ו ופכ"ג הלכה יא טור שו"ע או"ח סימן שכח סעיף כו:
סה ו מיי' פ"י מהלכות שבת הלכה יח:
סו ז שם הלכה טז:
סז ח מיי' שם הלכה יח טוש"ע או"ח סימן שב סעיף ג:
סח ט י מיי' פי"א מהל' שבת הלכה ט סמג שם טוש"ע או"ח סימן שמ סעיף ג:
סט כ מיי' פ"י שם הלכה טז ופכ"ג הלכה ד סמג שם:
ע ל מיי' פ"ז שם הל"ז וח ופ"ז מהל' שגגות הלכה ה:
ע [ל] [מיי' שם פ"ט הלכה יח ויט]:
עא מ נ מיי' פי"ח מהל' שבת הלכה כב:

רבינו חננאל

ליה דנהוי חי כי היכי דלצלח צביעה דכל כמה דהוא חי מצלח ציבעיה. שוחט משום מאי מחייב רב אמר משום צובע אסיק' ניחא ליה כי היכי דנתוום בית שחיטה דידיה דמא. כי היכי דידעי אינשי דחי הוה וכי היכי (דניחה) [דנחזיה] אינשי דנשחט הוא וקאתי למזבן מיניה ולא ימרו של נבילה הוא. והא דאמר רב משום צובע הכי קאמר חדא משום נטילת נשמה דהא בהדיא תנן באבות מלאכות השוחט. וסבר רב השוחט בשבת חייב שתים אחת משום נטילת נשמה ואחת משום צובע והוא אב (אחד) [אחר]. והמולחו והמעבדו. אקשינן דמולח היינו מעבד כדאמרינן (לקמן עט:) לענין חיפה מליח וקמיח שנמצאת מליחתו עבודו ופרקן ר' יוחנן ור"ל דהמולח והמעבד תרווייהו מלאכת עיבוד נינהו ותני חדא והוא הדין לאחרינא. אי הכי בצרי להו עייל שירטוט ושני במתני' המולחו והמשרטטו: ירושלמי מה עיבוד היה במשכן שהיו משרטטין בעורות מהו משרטטין מסרגלין. מליחת בשר חי בשבת. אם כוונתו לצאת בו לדרך או לאוכלו אחר כמה ימים חייב משום מעבד אבל לאוכלו ביומו לא ולית הלכתא כרבה בר רב הונא (דרבה בר רב הונא) [דרבא] דחי לה ואמר אין עיבוד באוכלין: השף בין העמודים. פי' מחליק חייב משום מוחק והוא כמו ממרח את הרטיה: ירושלמי הממחק. מה מחיקה היתה במשכן (פי') שהיו שפין העורות ע"ג העמוד. השף את העור ע"ג העמוד חייב משום (מוחק) [ממחק].

הממרח איספלנית חייב משום מוחק. הגורר ראשי כלונסות חייב משום מחתך. הממרח רטיה חייב משום מוחק. וכן הצר בכלי צורה כל שהוא חייב משום מכה בפטיש. ואע"ג דפליג ר' ישמעאל (לקמן קג:) ואמר עד שיצור כל הצורה יחידאה היא ואי ההיא צורה אית בה אותיות דמיקרו חייב משום כותב ואי לאו חייב משום מכה בפטיש וכן המנפח בכלי זכוכית הוא גמר מלאכתו שמלאכת זכוכית בניפוח הוא. פי' אקופי כגון נימין הניתקין מן האריגה דנתלין בבגד או חתיכות עצים קטנים המסבכין בצמרן של בגדים חדשים וכשמשלים האומן מלאכתו כל ראשי נימין התלויים בין קיסם וקליפה שנסתבכו בבגד נוטלן. ונקראין אקופי.

ראשי תיבות

א"ר – אמר רבי
וא"ת – ואם תאמר
אע"ג – אף על גב
ב"א – בני אדם
דה"ק – דהכי קאמר
בי"ט – ביום טוב
וי"ל – ויש לומר
וי"מ – ויש מפרשים
כ"ש – כל שכן
מ"ד – מאן דאמר
בפ"ק – בפרק קמא
קמ"ל – קא משמע לן
מדר"א – מדרבי אליעזר
ר"ח – רבינו חננאל
כר"ש – כרבי שמעון
ת"ר – תנו רבנן

מסורת הש"ס

ע"כ שייך לעיל
[נ"ל אסי]
[תוספ' פי"ב]
לקמן לו: ב"ק ב. כריתות טו:
לקמן לז:
לקמן עו:

הגהות הב"ח

(א) גמ' אמר ר"ש בר ביסנא אמר ר"ש בן לקיש הצר: (ב) רש"י ד"ה הצר צורה כצ"ל ותיבת בכלי נמחק:

גליון הש"ס

תום' ד"ה חסר אחת וכו' דהא אלו קתני. כדאי' בקדושין דף טז ע"ב:

רב נסים גאון

נטילת נשמה קיי"ל שהמתעסק לענין שבת פטור. ומשכחת עיקר דילה במסכת כריתות בפרק ספק אכל חלב (דף יט) אמר רב נחמן אמר שמואל [המתעסק] בחלבים ובעריות (בחלבים פטור ובעריות) חייב שכבר נהנה מתעסק בשבת פטור מלאכת מחשבת אסרה תורה ומשכחת לה בסנהדרין בפ' ד' מיתות (דף סב) ובגמרא דהזורק דבני מערבא (הלכה ו) גרסי הזורק בשבת פטור האיך עבידא אמר הריני קוצר חצי גרוגרת וקצר כגרוגרת פטור בגמ' דכל שעה בפסחים (דף לג) גרסי לה אם אמרת בשאר מצות שכן לא חייב בהן שאין מתעסק במתעסק שאם נתכוון להגביה את התלוש וחתך המחובר פטור וכגון זה כל מלאכה שהוא באה חילוף מה שנתכוון העושה אותה מתעסק מיקרי שהרי לא נעשית מחשבתו:

אלו לאפוקי מדר' אליעזר דמחייב על תולדה במקום אב. ואשכחנן דברי ר' אליעזר בכריתות בפרק אמרו לו אכלת חלב (דף טז) אמר ר' עקיבא שאלתי את ר' אליעזר העושה מלאכות הרבה בשבתות הרבה מעין מלאכה אחת בהעלם אחד מהו חייב על כל אחת ואחת או אינו חייב על כולן אלא אחת אמר לו חייב על כל אחת ואחת מקל וחומר ואמרו בתלמוד בעי מיניה ולדי מלאכות כמלאכות דמיין או לא ופשט ליה הוי דולדי מלאכות כמלאכות דמיין. דאי ר' שמעון הא אמר לא נאמרו כל השיעורין האלו אלא למצניעיהן. בפירקא דלקמן המוציא יין (דף עו) משכחת לה דלאו דר' שמעון:

סליק פרק כלל גדול

גמרא

א"ר אלעזר הא דלא כר"ש בן אלעזר *דתניא כלל אמר ר' שמעון בן אלעזר כל שאינו כשר להצניע ואין מצניעין כמוהו והוכשר לזה והצניעו ובא אחר והוציאו נתחייב זה במחשבה של זה: **מתני'** [א]המוציא תבן כמלא פי פרה עצה כמלא פי גמל עמיר כמלא פי טלה עשבים כמלא פי גדי עלי שום ועלי בצלים לחים כגרוגרת יבשים כמלא פי גדי ואין מצטרפין זה עם זה מפני שלא שוו בשיעוריהן: **גמ'** מאי עצה אמר רב יהודה תבן של מיני קטנית כי אתא רב דימי אמר המוציא תבן כמלא פי פרה לגמל ר' יוחנן אמר חייב ר"ש בן לקיש אמר פטור באורתא א"ר יוחנן הכי לצפרא הדר ביה אמר רב יוסף שפיר עבד דהדר דהא לא חזי לגמל א"ל אביי אדרבה כדמעיקרא מסתברא דהא חזי לפרה אלא כי אתא רבין אמר המוציא תבן כמלא פי פרה לגמל דכולי עלמא לא פליגי דחייב כי פליגי במוציא עצה כמלא פי פרה לפרה [ב]ואיפכא איתמר ר' יוחנן אמר פטור [ג]ריש לקיש אמר חייב ר' יוחנן אמר פטור אכילה על ידי הדחק לא שמה אכילה *ריש לקיש אמר [ב]חייב אכילה *ע"י הדחק שמה אכילה: עמיר כמלא פי טלה: והתניא כגרוגרת אידי ואידי חד שיעורא הוא: עלי שום ועלי בצלים לחים כגרוגרת ויבשים כמלא פי הגדי ואין מצטרפין זה עם זה מפני שלא שוו בשיעוריהן: אמר ר' יוסי בר חנינא [ג] אין מצטרפין לחמור שבהן אבל מצטרפין לקל שבהן וכל דלא שוו בשיעורייהו מי מצטרפין והתנן *הבגד ג' על ג' והשק ד' על ד' והעור ה' על ה' מפץ ו' על ו' *ותני עלה הבגד והשק השק והעור העור והמפץ מצטרפין זה עם זה ואמר ר"ש מה טעם מפני שראויין ליטמא מושב טעמא דראויין ליטמא מושב אבל אין ראוי ליטמא מושב לא אמר רבא הכא

הכא

רש"י

א"ר אלעזר הא. דקתני מתניתין דאינו כשר להצניע והצניעו *אחר הוא מתחייב על הוצאתו וכל אדם פטורין דלא כר' שמעון בן אלעזר: **מתני'** עצה. מפרש בגמרא: **כמלא פי גמל.** נפיש שיעורא מפי פרה אבל כמלא פי פרה לא מיחייב דהא לא חזו לפרה: **עמיר.** קשין של שבלין: **פי טלה.** נפיש מפי גדי הלכך עמיר דלא חזי לגדי לא מיחייב כמלא פי גדי עד דאיכא מלא פי טלה אבל עשבים הואיל וחזו בין לטלה בין לגדי מיחייב אפי' כמלא פי גדי: **לחין.** הראויין לאדם כגרוגרת דזה שיעור לכל מאכל אדם לשבת אבל כמלא פי גדי לא דלחים לא חזו לגדי: **גמ' המוציא תבן כמלא פי פרה.** והוליאו להאכילו לגמל שפי גמל גדול מפי פרה: **דהא חזי לפי פרה.** הלכך שיעור חשוב הוא ולכל מי שיוליאנו לא פקע שיעוריה בהכי: **דחייב.** דהאיכא שיעורא דחזי לפרה הלכך כשר להצניע הוא ומצניעין כמוהו: **עצה.** לא חזיא לפרה אלא ע"י הדחק אלא לגמל הוא דחזי וזה הוליאו לפרה: **רבי יוחנן אמר פטור.** דהא לגמל דחזי ליה ליכא שיעורא ואי משום דלצורך פרה הוליאו ולגבה איכא שיעור אכילה ע"י הדחק לאו אכילה היא הלכך לא משערי' ליה בפרה: **אין מצטרפין לחמור שבהם.** מי שבשיעורו גדול הוי קל ואינו מצטרף להשלים שיעורו של חמור דהא לא חשיב כי ההוא אבל החשוב משלים את הקל לכשיעור תבן מצטרף עם עצה להשלי' פי גמל ועצה אין מצטרף עם התבן להשלים מלא פי פרה: **מי מצטרפין.** אפילו להשלים חמור את הקל: **ג' על ג'.** לטומאת מדרס הזב ליעשות אב הטומאה: **הבגד והשק מצטרפין.** שהבגד משלים שיעור השק שק עשוי מנוצה של עזים: **ואמר ר' שמעון מה טעם.** מצטרפין: **הואיל וראויין ליטמא מושב.** אם צירף משניהם יחד לטלאי מרדעת של חמור כשיעורו לענין מושב הזב אם קצע משניהם מהן ותקן טפח על טפח לישב עליו מיטמא ליה אב הטומאה במושב הזב דתניא(א) המקצע מכוון טפח על טפח טמא מושב ואמרינן טעמא בפ"ק דסוכה הואיל וראוי לטלות על גבי חמור שאינו מקפיד אם הוא משני מינין:

הכא

תוספות

שמצריך לקמן הצנעה היינו לאדם עשיר שאין דרכו להצניע ומכל מקום פירוש מילתיה דר"ש צריך לפרש כמו שפירש כאן דאי מיירי במצניעין אותו דבר עצמו שמפורש במשנה כמו שפירש התם אם כן כולהו הוה מצי למימר בכל שהוא בכדי שיפת קילור כדתנן בפ' המצניע (לקמן צ:) דלרפואה בכל שהוא ואתיא כר"ש מדלא קאמר התם בגמ' הא דלא כר"ש כי היכי דקאמר (דף נח.) הא דלא כר"ש בן אלעזר ומהתם נמי יש לדקדק דלר' שמעון סתם בני אדם שרגילין להצניעו מיחייבי אפי' לא הצניעו מדקתני המצניע לזרע כו' וכל אדם אין חייבין עליו אלא כשיעורו משמע בלא הצנעה וכר"ש נמי אתיא כדפי' ואין לפרש דבעשיר שאין דרכו להצניע לא מיחייב לר"ש אפי' בהצניעו דהא אמר בהמוציא יין בד"א במוציא אבל במצניע כל שהוא ר"ש אומר בד"א במצניע כו' ומפרש מצניע דרבנן בתלמיד שאמר לו כו' דבר שאינו חשוב לכל אי אצנעיה רביה אין אי לא לא ודומיא דהכי נראה דהוי מצניע דר"ש דתליא מילתא באותו שהצניעו היינו בעשיר קשה לרשב"א דמהאי טעמא דקאמר הכא מתני' דלא כר"ש משום דמתני' סתמא קתני דחייב משמע שכל בני אדם חייבין עליו אפי' אותן שאין חשוב להן שיעור זה מהאי טעמא נמי הוה ליה למימר בההיא דבפרק המצניע דהויא דלא כר"ש ושמא י"ל דהכא דנקט לפרושי הוה ליה לפרושי טפי: **אכילה ע"י הדחק לא שמה אכילה.** והא דאמר בפ' כיצד הרגל (ב"ק דף יט.) אכילה ע"י הדחק שמה אכילה ה"מ לענין נזקין דלא חשבינן ליה משונה אבל לאחשובה לענין שבת לא חשיבא אכילה: **אידי ואידי חד שיעורא הוא.** והא דנקט במתני' כמלא פי טלה ולא נקט כגרוגרת לאשמעי' דמשום אכילת טלה נתנו בו חכמים שיעור זה דאי נקט כגרוגרת לא הוה ידעינן למה נתנו בו חכמים שיעור זה: **מפני שלא שוו בשיעוריהם.** אבל אותם ששוו כגון עמיר ועלי שום ועלי בצלים לחים מצטרפין וכן חמור לקל כגון תבן לעצה למלא פי גמל ואפי' לא יהא תבן ראוי לגמל שמא אגב העצה הוא ראוי: **הבגד והשק והעור כו'.** דווקא בכה"ג הבגד והשק השק והעור והעור והמפץ אבל הבגד והעור והשק והמפץ אין מצטרפין שאין ראויין להתחבר יחד והמחברן בטלה דעתו ואין טמאים מדרס. ר"י: **ואמר ר"ש מה טעם כו'.** תימה לר"י דמה צריך להאי טעמא דהא כיון דמצטרפין זה עם זה א"כ ראוי לחברן וחזו למדרס וכיון דחזו למדרס פשיטא דמצטרפין לטומאת מדרס דהא אפי' כופת שאור שייחדה לישיבה טמאה מדרס כדאמרינן בהעור והרוטב (חולין קכט.) והכא בטומאת מדרס איירי מדקאמר הבגד שלשה על שלשה דלענין טומאת מת אפי' ג' על ג' כדפרישית לעיל ואור"י דודאי הא דקתני הבגד שלשה על שלשה לא מיירי אלא למדרס אבל סיפא דשק ועור ומפץ מיירי נמי בטומאת מת והכי איתא במס' כלים בפכ"ז הבגד שלשה על שלשה [למדרס ומשום ג' על ג'] לטומאת מת השק ד' על ד' העור ה' על ה' המפץ ו' על ו' שוו בין למדרס בין לטמא מת אלא שהש"ס מביאה בקוצר כמו שרגיל בכמה מקומות ועל טומאת מת קאמר מה טעם מצטרפין בשלא יחדו למדרס ולא צריך האי טעמא אלא לצירוף דעור ומפץ [ד]דמפץ לא מטמא במת אלא כשטמא בזב דהיינו כשיחדו למדרס ומק"ו דפכין קטנים כדאמרינן בפ' ר' עקיבא (לקמן פד:): **הואיל וראויין ליטמא מושב.** פי' בקונטרס אם קיצע משניהם וצירף יחד לטלאי מרדעת החמור והביא דהמקצע מכוון טפח על טפח דמעילה היינו שבין כולם יש טפח ואין נראה לר"י דמה צריך להביא ראיה שראויין להצטרף בלאו טעמא דמושב נמי שמעינן ממתני' דהכא שראויין להצטרף יחד באותו סדר כמו ששנויים בגד לשק ושק לעור ועור למפץ דדווקא נקט לפי שאלו ראויין להצטרף יחד ונראה לר"י כמו שפי' ריב"א דהואיל וראויין ליטמא מושב היינו הואיל ושוו שיעוריהן לענין מושב וכמו שפירש בקונטרס בפ"ק דסוכה (דף יז:) דהמקצע מכוון היינו מאיזה מהן שיקצע יהא טמא ולעו"ג שכאן אין שיעורן שוה מצטרפין הואיל ולענין מושב שיעורן שוה והא דקאמר ה"נ חזו לדוגמא היינו נמי דשיעורן שוה לדוגמא כדתנן בפרק המצניע דלדוגמא כל שהוא הלכך מצטרפין אפי' לענין דבר דלא שוו שיעורייהו וה"ה דהוי מצי למינקט הכא ולזרע ולרפואה דהוו נמי בכל שהוא אלא דלא כל דברים שייך בהו זרע ורפואה אבל דוגמא שייכא בכל דבר והא דקאמר בסוכה המקצע מכוון כו' הואיל וראוי לטלות על גבי חמורו לשון הואיל וראוי לאו דווקא דדווקא אם עשה מהן טלאי ויחדן לכך טמא בטפח על טפח וכן מצינו לקמן בפ' ר"ע (דף צ.) הואיל וראויין למתק הקדרה דהוה ליה למימר הואיל וממתקין דהא מיירי שנפלו לתוך הקדרה. ר"י: **תוספתא*** המקצע למשכב אין פחות משלשה על שלשה למושב טפח ולמעמד כל שהוא:

חמשת

עין משפט נר מצוה

עב א ב מיי' פי"ח מהל' שבת הל' ג:
[עב] [ב] [מיי' שם]:

רבינו חננאל

ומנקה הבגד ודומה למנקב דתנינן בכמה מקומות ואם נשארו כגון אלו בבגד ובעל הבגד קפיד עלייהו ושקיל להו בשבת חייב משום מכה בפטיש. פי' כל דבר שהוא גמר מלאכה נקרא מכה בפטיש: **המוחק** אות אחת גדולה שיש במקומה שיעור לכתוב ב' אותיות חייב והכותב אות אחת גדולה שיש במקומה שיעור לכתוב ב' אותיות פטור. זה חומר במוחק מבכותב. אלו אבות מלאכות לאפוקי מדר' אלעזר דמחייב אתולדה במקום אב כמו שכבר פרשנוהו למעלה (דף עג:) דמאן דעבד ב' אבות או ב' תולדות משני אבות או אב ותולדה דאב (אחר) [אחר] בהעלם אחד חייב בזה אחד ובזה אחד. ואי עביד אב ותולדתו לא מיחייב אלא חדא. ועוד חזר ושנה מ' חסר אחת לאפוקי מר' יהודה דאמר שובט ומדקדק מאבות מלאכות הן. אמרו לו שובט הרי הוא בכלל מיסך. מדקדק בכלל אורג. *) פי' יש לארוגין עץ או עצם שראשו חד ונקרא כדבר ודומה למחט של סקאין. וכך שמו בלשון יון כדבר. מעבירו על השתי כשהוא מותח לפניו לארינה ושובט בו החוטין ומקרב המבדילין בין ב' החוטין העליונים והתחתונים ומרנחים להתפרק העליונים מן התחתונים ונפתח נפש המסכת לידות בתוכם חוט הערב ואין לה אב אלא הרי הוא בכלל מיסך והמדקדק הוא המדקדק על חוט הערב כדי להדחק ולהלחץ עם חבירו וזהו בכלל ארינה: **ועוד** כלל אחר אמרו כל הכשר להצניע ומצניעין כמוהו והוציאו בשבת חייב עליו חטאת. כל הכשר להצניע רב מתנה אמר למעוטי דם נדה שאין חייבין בהוצאתו. וכ"ש איסורי הנאה. ועצי אשרה שאין חייבין בהוצאתו. מר עוקבא אמר לאפוקי עצי אשרה אבל דם נדה חייב כו' וזה ששנינו ומצניעין כמוהו א"ר יוסי ב"ר חנינא דלא כר' שמעון דאי ר' שמעון האמר דברים הללו לא נאמרו אלא למצניעיהן. והכין סבירא ליה לר' שמעון לענין המוציא יין כדי מזיגת הכוס חלב כדי גמיעה כו' דכולן שיעורן ברביעית ושיעורין הללו כדי גמיעה וכדי ליתן על הכתית כו'. לא נאמרו אלא למצניעיהן כלומר אם הצניע בחול [פחות] משיעורין הללו אע"פ שהוציאו בשבת פטור ורבנן סבירא להו אם הצניעו אדם בחול כל שהוא אע"פ שאין כשר להצניע והוציאו בשבת חייב דהא (אשביה) [אחשביה] בהצנעתו. וזה ששנינו כל שאין כשר להצניע ואין מצניעין כמוהו והוציאו בשבת אין חייב אלא המצניעו אבל מי לא שהצניע בחול אם הוציאו בשיעורין הללו חייב. ואם לא פטור. וזהו כמו דתנן המצניע לזרע לדוגמא ולרפואה והוציאו בשבת חייב עליו כל שהוא. ושאר כל אדם אין חייבין עליו אלא כשיעורו נמצא ר' שמעון מיקל מדברי חכמים ור' שמעון בן אלעזר מחמיר מדבריהם. דקאמר כל שאינו כשר להצניע ואין מצניעין כמוהו והוכשר לזה והצניעו ובא אחד והוציאו נתחייב המוציאו ממחשבת המצניעו ואע"פ שאינו כשר להצניעו ואין מצניעין כמוהו חייב עליו. ורבנן אמרי אינו חייב בפחות מכשיעור אלא המצניעו. תמו הכללות. ובאנו לפרש שיעורי ההוצאה: **המוציא** תבן כמלוא פי פרה. עצה תבן הקטנית וקשה ממנו שיעורו כמלוא פי גמל. עמיר כמלוא פי טלה. עשבים כמלוא פי גדי ולענין המוציא תבן כמלוא פי פרה לגמל (הלכה) כו"ע לא פליגי דחייב שזה הוא שיעור הוצאתו ולא אכפת לן [אין] לגמל נתכוין להוציאו או לפרה אלא כי פליגי ר' יוחנן ור' אושעי' במוציא עצה כמלוא פי פרה לפרה. ועיקר הדבר שאין העצה מאכל פרה ואין שיעור כמלוא פי פרה אלא כמלוא פי גמל שהוא יותר ממלוא פי פרה. ועכשיו שנתכוון לפרה איפליגו ר' אושעי' סבר אכילה ע"י הדחק שמה אכילה אע"פ שאין פרה אוכלת אותו כדרכה אלא כיון שאוכלת אותו ע"י הדחק וישנו מלא פיה והוציאו לה חייב עליו. (ור') [ור"י] סבר אכילה שע"י הדחק לאו שמה אכילה (וזה) ופטור: לענין הא דתנן אין מצטרפין זה עם זה מפני שלא שוו בשיעוריהן א"ר יוסי ב"ר חנינא אין מצטרפין לחמור שבהן אבל מצטרפין לקל שבהן אם הוציא עמיר ועשבים אם יש בין שניהם כמלוא פי טלה מצטרפין כי החמור משלים לקל וחייב אבל אם אין בהם כמלוא פי הגדי פטור שאין מצטרפין כי אין הקל משלים לחמור וכן עשבים משלימין לתבן ואין התבן משלים לעשבים ומקשינן היאך תאמר בהני דלא שוו בשיעוריהן להדדי דמצטרפין והלא הבגד והשק והעור לענין טומאה שלא שוו בשיעוריהן אע"ג דתנן הבגד והשק מצטרפין והשק והעור מצטרפין והעור והמפץ מצטרפין דקתני סיפא. א"ר שמעון מה טעם הואיל וראויין ליטמא מושב דייקת מינה טעמא דראויין ליטמא מושב הא אי לא הוו ראויין ליטמא מושב לא הוו מצטרפין משום שלא שוו בשיעוריהן להדדי. וא"כ היכי קאמר ר' יוסי בר' חנינא מצטרפין לקל שבהן והכין הוה ראוי שלא יצטרפו כל עיקר. ופריק רבא לר' יוסי ב"ר חנינא ואמר הכי נמי ראויין לדוגמא כשם שהבגד והשק אף על פי שאין בזה כשיעור ולא בזה כשיעור כיון שאלו מצטרפין יש בעיניהם כשיעור השק שהוא הקל ואפשר לחברן זה בזה ולישב עליהן וראויין ליטמא מושב. כן התבן והעצה אפשר להוציא מזה כמעט ומזה כמעט להראותן דוגמא לקונה לומר מאלו אני מוכר ולהבין חשובין בחיבורין ויש צורך להוציאו כסדר הזה משום כן מצטרפין לקל שבהן אבל אוכלין שיעורן כולן כגרוגרת לפיכך מצטרפין זע"ז אבל קליפיהן ועוקציהן וסובן ומורסנן אין מצטרפין עמהן.

ר'

*) עי' ערוך ערך שבט א' וע' דוך:

מסורת הש"ס

נ"ל אחד

לקמן נח. זבחים מז.

[הכסף משנה העתיק רבי אושעיא אמר חייב וכו' ופסק הרמב"ם כרבי אושעיא שהלכ' כמותו לגבי ר' יוחנן עכ"ל]

לקמן עט. מעילה יח. סוכה יז: כלים פכ"ז מ"ב

כלים כ"ב פ"ג

הגהות הב"ח

(א) רש"י ד"ה הואיל וכו' דתניא. נ"ב במעילה ס"פ קדשי המזבח דף יח:

גליון הש"ס

גמ' ואיפכא איתמר. כעין זה דף לד ע"א שם ר"ל אמר חייב. בכסף משנה פי"ח הלכה ג מהלכות שבת הגירסא ר' אושעיא: תוס' ד"ה ואמר ר"ש וכו' דמפץ לא מטמא במת. עי' פכ"ד מ"ו דכלים וברע"ש שם:

ראשי תיבות

א"כ אם כן
א"ל אמר ליה
א"ר אמר רבי
ואע"ג ואף על גב
בפכ"ז בפרק כ"ז
וה"ה והוא הדין
ה"מ הני מילי
ה"נ הכי נמי
י"ל יש לומר
ע"י על ידי
בפ"ק בפרק קמא
ומק"ו ומקל וחומר
ר"ש רבי שמעון
דר"ש דרבי שמעון
וכר"ש וכרבי שמעון
כר"ש כרבי שמעון
לר"ש לרבי שמעון

NOTES

The Jewish Learning Multiplex

Brought to you by the Rohr Jewish Learning Institute

In fulfillment of the mandate of the Lubavitcher Rebbe, of blessed memory, whose leadership guides every step of our work, the mission of the Rohr Jewish Learning Institute is to transform Jewish life and the greater community through the study of Torah, connecting each Jew to our shared heritage of Jewish learning.

While our flagship program remains the cornerstone of our organization, JLI is proud to feature additional divisions catering to specific populations, in order to meet a wide array of educational needs.

THE ROHR JEWISH LEARNING INSTITUTE
is the adult education arm of Chabad Lubavitch,
a branch of *Merkos L'Inyonei Chinuch*, Lubavitch World Headquarters.

Torah Studies

Torah Studies provides a rich and nuanced encounter with the weekly Torah reading. See how our primary Jewish text continues to speak with a message that is timely and fresh.

MyShiur
TALMUD LEARNING INITIATIVE

My Shiur's innovative and user-friendly format introduces students to the world of Talmudic debate and provides them with the skills to engage in independent Torah study.

Sinai Scholars Society
IN PARTNERSHIP WITH CHABAD ON CAMPUS

This exclusive fellowship program invites a limited number of students at member campuses to participate in a rigorous eight-week course of study and special follow-up learning opportunities.

JLI Teens
YOUNG SMART JEWISH

IN PARTNERSHIP WITH CTEEN: CHABAD TEEN NETWORK

Our interactive courses invite teens to eight weeks of relaxed social interaction, self-exploration, and serious fun as they examine their values and forge their Jewish identities.

JLI On Campus
JEWISH LEARNING INSTITUTE

Our campus foundational course, *Jewish Essentials*, introduces the basics of Judaism to students in eight self-contained lessons designed for maximum flexibility.

TorahCafé™

TorahCafé allows students to enjoy the excellence of JLI teaching at a convenient time and location as they listen to syndicated lectures from top-rated instructors.

National Jewish Retreat
BRILLIANT LEARNING. NATURALLY.

The National Jewish Retreat is in a class of its own, providing rejuvenation of mind, body, and spirit and a powerful synthesis of Jewish learning and community.

Rosh Chodesh Society

Founded in memory of Rebbetzin Rivkah Holtzberg, this program invites women to join together once a month for intensive textual study that is both engaging and practical.

JLI Training Academy
THE ROHR JEWISH LEARNING INSTITUTE — Pedagogy · Curriculum · Marketing

This exclusive fellowship program invites top JLI instructors to partner with their peers and noted professionals as leaders of innovation and the commitment to excellence.

The Land & the Spirit
Mission to Israel

This mission brings participants to the Holy Land for an educational adventure, delving into our nation's rich past, while exploring its modern-day relevance and meaning.

Made in the USA
Middletown, DE
28 February 2025

71780472R00127